Fire Hall Revisited

Fire Hall Revisited

William Oehlke

2006

Fire Hall Revisited

OUTLINE

ACKNOWLEDGEMENTS

These days, "twenty-four/seven" seems a commonly used term, but for me it was a way of life for even longer than the 28 years I served as fire chief of the volunteers of the City of Devils Lake. Remembering the significant events that impacted my life during those years has culminated in the fulfillment of a promise made long ago to a dying fireman . . . to keep alive the history of this special department and the wonderful group of firemen who willingly give their 'blood, sweat, and tears' to ensure the safety of their fellow citizens.

I was diagnosed with a rare neuromuscular disease in 1993. My condition significantly limited the physical activity I was capable of doing, and brought a definite change in my attitude. I truly began to understand what camaraderie really meant. As walking became more difficult, a simple word—'Hand'—was all that was required before I was besieged by countless offers of help to maintain my balance. My retirement at the end of 2003 gave me the time necessary to follow a new career path.

The process of writing a book seemed overwhelming, but the possibility of doing so became more of a reality when I joined the Lake Region Writers group in the fall of 2004. With their encouragement, as well as that of my wife Mary, I began seriously researching the documents that would accurately support my memory of past events. Since many of the old written records had been destroyed, I relied on the memories of those men I had worked with for so long. While no two people ever recall the same incident in exactly the same way, it was gratifying to hear the stories from some of the old timers, and realize they were very similar to my recollections. In some cases it was the only way to identify individuals who had been involved in particular situations.

I have attempted to make certain that all the names, dates and events are as accurate as possible. However, please accept my apologies for any errors that may have occurred. Chief Jim Moe, my successor, and members of the department have been more than generous in supporting my endeavor. A special thanks to Alvin Schroeder for assembling the photographs used in this book, and to Tim 'Bear' Kurtz for the afternoon teas and for putting me on the right track.

I still go to the fire hall each week for coffee with the guys, and the same cordial atmosphere is provided to me as well as to my fellow retirees. Not long ago I noticed a wheelchair in the corner of the weight room. Chief Moe informed me that it would be there if and when I ever needed it. Retirement from the fire service isn't the end of a career, it's just the beginning of a time to reflect and graciously pass on the things you've learned.

So, a heartfelt thanks to the members of the Devils Lake Fire Department—paid personnel and volunteers—who have always been there for me, and to my wife Mary, for your assistance and advice in editing, I want to say from the bottom of my heart - Writing this book was a Great Experience. I love you all."

CHAPTER I

MY FIRST FIRE—

THE GAMBLE ROBINSON WAREHOUSE

Standing in the driving rain watching fire and smoke roll out of the three story warehouse, I could think of nothing more exciting than being part of the group of firemen attempting to extinguish the blaze. I was nine years old, dressed in a rain poncho, standing next to Fire Chief Clarence Christianson on that Sunday morning in July 1947. No youngster could have been more proud than I, listening to this Abe Lincoln look-alike direct firemen in their various duties.

Earlier that summer, I had gone with my dad, Herman, across the street to purchase carpet for installation in some rooms of the Mayer Hotel, a family owned business. From the back of the store came a tall, raw-boned balding man known as 'Christie.' After greeting one another, Dad said, "Christie, I'd like you to meet my son, Bill."

A heavy knuckled hand covered mine, and in a friendly voice Christie said, "You'll have to come over to the hall someday and we'll go for a ride on a fire truck."

For a boy of nine who had only seen fire trucks in books, the chance to see the inside of a fire hall, let alone ride on a fire truck was not hard to take. "Thank you," I mumbled.

That invite was all I needed and from that day on, when my parents would allow, I would ride my bike the two-and-a-half blocks to the fire hall, go inside and make, what I realize now, a pest of myself.

The great part of being at the fire hall was the people I got to meet. Although I never did get to ride in a fire truck, I was thrilled when on occasion 'Sarge' would say, "I had a hard time seeing the gauges the other day on the way to Johnson's fire; must be dirty." This would be the only incentive I would need. I would dust all the fire equipment using a clean towel from the pile by the sink, and when I had completed my chores would be given a bottle of pop. Sometimes I sat on the tailboard of a fire truck and waited for Christie to come by and give me a ride. Although that never happened, I never became disillusioned. Sometimes policemen, who had their office on the apparatus floor, would offer me a cookie from their stash under the counter. I remember two big Doberman Pinchers belonging to Russell Clark chained to the wall outside the back door to the Police Department Office. I never had any problems with them if they were loose in the fire hall, maybe it was because I would sneak them a cookie. Sarge hated having them run free in the fire hall, and he and Russell Clark would have words: "Russell, if those dogs shit on my floor, they're going to end up in somebody's stew."

"You wouldn't dare," Russell would say. If Russell didn't move fast enough, Sarge would start a fire truck making all kinds of exhaust smoke. This would be upsetting to any prisoners in the jail cells next to the office, and they would soon begin shouting. It wouldn't be long before the dogs themselves were at the back door barking to be let outside.

At the Gamble Robinson Building, hoses were spraying water into the front and back of the building, the men doing their best to stop the fire from spreading upwards. Jack Voiles told Christie that the bulk of the fire was in the basement, and when they tried to enter through the front door the flames drove them back. Twice they were denied access. The third time I watched them slide along the wall and dive through the door on their stomachs. "WOW," I mumbled to myself.

I don't think anything had a more profound effect on me than seeing the fire belching from that doorway and wondering what happened to the firemen inside. I looked up at Christie, and noticing the serious look in his eyes as he looked down I remember thinking, *he looks like dad when I'm in line for a spanking.*

Not more than five minutes went by and the firemen came crawling back out of the building. "Damn," Christie said. All four had retreated from inside the warehouse and were now sitting or leaning against the outside wall. Christie waved and the one called Jack pushed himself up and came to where we were standing. "How bad is it, Jack?" Christie asked.

"It's hot," replied Jack. "I agree with Harold; it's one Son of a Bitch."

As I listened to Jack, I looked toward the firemen and saw Harold sitting on the sidewalk with his back against the wall. I remembered seeing him at Mann's Department Store when I was buying a Hardy Boys book. He wasn't very big, and now dressed in fire gear looked real little. He's not much bigger than me, I thought. Comparing him to Christie and Jack, I concluded that not all firemen are big.

"Could you get in there with masks?" Christie asked.

"I don't know," Jack said. "I guess we could try it, but nobody likes them."

"Put on the masks, and turn your helmets around; you'll make it," Christie ordered.

Jack gave in. "Might as well give it a try. Maybe crawling and wearing gas masks will give us the edge we need. If the filters don't plug we might make it."

"Whatever you do, be careful," Christie said. With a wave Jack hurried back to his comrades.

We were standing about 50 feet away from the burning warehouse and unable to hear what Jack was telling the firemen. Through the rain I could see the firemen occasionally glance in our direction as Jack talked to them. Years later, remembering that day in the rain, I imagined what Jack had told the firemen: "Christie wants us to try wearing the masks."

"He's crazy; we can't see a damn thing with them on."

"Nevertheless, he's the boss, let's give it a try."

Jack waved toward the big engine getting the attention of Gus Kirchoffner, the pump operator. Jack indicated to Gus by using hand signals that he needed some masks. After a few moments of hand signals, Jerome Markel came jogging across the street carrying the masks. As I watched what was going on I felt sorry for the firemen. They were going back into that burning building on their stomachs, dragging a hose, with a rope tied to their boots. No wonder they looked concerned. Putting on the masks and turning their helmets so the brim was to the front, they reached toward their boots and checked the knot on their rope tether. With smoke and flame making its way out to just over their heads, they began crawling through the doorway. Just as Jack got to the doorway he turned and waved in our direction, receiving a thumbs-up sign of encouragement from Christie. It sure was something, watching them crawl through that doorway, black helmets and coats shining in the rain. They looked fearless, and the filters on the masks looked like Uncle Ed's snuff box lid. As the last fireman entered the burning building, I noticed two men with ropes in their hands moving into position just outside the entrance. "What are they doing?" I asked.

"They've got the ropes that lead to the firemen. Shut down your hose lines," Christie shouted to the firemen spraying into the front of the building.

There were no more flames, and the smoke had lightened in color when I noticed the outside firemen gathering up the slack and pulling on the rope tethers. "What now?" Christie exclaimed.

As the tethers were gathered, two firemen scrambled through the doorway, ripped off their masks and sat down on the curb. Jack appeared in the doorway, ripped off his mask, and threw up. Christie moved toward the firemen who were gasping for air. "Where's Harold?" he shouted.

"He's still inside. I tried to get him to come out, but he just said, 'Bull Shit'," Jack replied.

"I hope Harold is okay," I said to myself. As if in answer to my prayer, Harold appeared in the doorway, pulled himself erect, and came through the opening.

"Look," Vince Seward hollered. "It's Harold."

Before anyone could move, Jack jumped up, hollered, "Holy shit," and ran over to Harold, picking him off the ground and hugging and kissing him on the cheek. "Thank you, Lord, thank you!" he shouted. The others clapped Harold on the back and for the first time that day, Christie appeared to be smiling through tear-filled eyes.

I snuck in a little closer to hear Harold's account. "All of a sudden the smoke ventilated and I was able to knock down most of the fire. It looks like it started in the crates by the furnace and worked its way up the elevator shaft to the top floor."

"You're damn lucky you made it," Christie said. "You could have died in that basement." Christie grabbed Harold by the shoulders, and shook him so hard I thought his bobbing helmet would fly off. "Don't ever stay in there alone!" he ordered. Turning to Jack and the other firemen, Christie continued, "Don't ever leave your partner."

The rain was just a drizzle now and I could see respect in their eyes as they looked at the Fire Chief. Jack was the first to apologize to Christie, echoed by the others.

4

Firemen are a different breed. One moment they are gruff or heroic, the next humble or sad. I learned early on that the gruffest of the bunch could also be the most caring. All firemen do their best to avoid displaying their feelings, but sooner or later their emotions get the best of them, and the mask they tried to create fails.

Years later when I became Fire Chief, the mask was an important part of my make up. I loved my men and served my community with dedication and pride. Joys and sorrows of the firemen's families were a part of my everyday life. The worry lines on my forehead became more prominent. Often my wife would sit and listen as I recited the emergency of the day. Never interrupting, she was always ready with a Kleenex; I shed my share of tears.

Harold finished retying his tether and the other firemen pulled hard on their ropes making sure they were secure. "Let's go," he said. *I bet they hope this is the last time*, I thought to myself.

The attack crew and some of the other firemen had been inside for a while, and I was getting itchy wondering what was going on. Christie finally said, "Let's go see what they are doing." Motioning for me to halt just outside the entry door, he went inside to the head of the steps.

I heard talk coming from the basement, but couldn't make out what was being said. Suddenly Christie exclaimed, "What did you find?"

I'm not sure if my hearing got better, or it was because the rain had suddenly stopped, but someone said, "He's got a damn spider!" That got my attention.

"We've got another one!"

"Run that by me again," Christie said.

"We've got two dead scorpion spiders that must have come in with a load of bananas."

"Finish putting out the fire," said Christie, "and bring them out when you're done. Check the coal pile, that's probably the source of the fire. Pitch the coal outside. Jack, you're in charge, I'm going around to the back."

I followed Christie along the outside of the building to the rear of the warehouse where the aerial truck had raised its ladder to the roof over the loading ramp. On top of the roof were four firemen and a heavy line they had been using to fight fire from the outside of the structure.

"How's it going?" Christie asked.

"We lost our pressure," Iver shouted.

"I'll see what's going on. Where's the rest of the crew?"

Tom Goulding emerged from beneath the loading platform. "Who shut off the water?" he asked.

"I did." From behind the ladder truck where he had been taking a pee, came Assistant Chief Floyd 'Sarge' Reardon.

"Good move," replied Christie, "It helped get to the seat of the fire."

"Roxy was drawing negative pressure. I told him to shut down a hose line. I guess he shut off the wrong line."

"That worked out okay," Christie replied, "the guys were able to get into the basement."

I didn't think firemen ever made mistakes, and then Christie said, "That's one of the few times a mistake has helped put out a fire. Plus, they were able to see the spiders before they got bitten."

"What?" asked Sarge.

"They found two dead Scorpions. I told them to bring them to the fire hall."

The Assistant Chief had all the respect in the world for his Chief and would follow Christie anywhere and carry out his orders without hesitation. But when Fire Chief Christianson said, "Spiders—Take them to the fire hall," that was enough. In a voice that could be heard out into the street, Sarge exclaimed, "You better be kidding about bringing those spiders into my fire hall!"

"Why not, Sarge?"

"Well . . . they could have a disease and we'd have to decontaminate the place," Sarge quickly replied.

"Let's get the pickup," Christie said. "We'll get the spiders and you can dump them in the garbage."

At the front of the warehouse, Christie motioned for me to wait while he walked through the building. Not long after he went inside, Jack's entry team came out. Drawing his hand across his throat Jack indicated to Gus to shut down his pumper. I stood out of the way while the hose was rolled and loaded onto the pickup for transport back to the fire hall. At the same time, coal was being shoveled out from its location in the basement into the parking lot they shared with Dakota Seed and Feed. (In 1951 this elevator burned when a fire in a boxcar on the railroad siding caught fire and spread to the elevator.)

Just as the last roll of hose was being thrown into the pickup, Sarge came around the corner and went into the building. Moments later he returned carrying a bag, "I've got them," he said.

Once everything was wrapped up out front, Gus and Jerry Markel went inside the warehouse to see what else had to be done. It wasn't long before everyone came out of the building and Christie said to Jerome, "Stay here for a while and keep and eye on the inside."

Christie handed me his white helmet. "Climb in the back, we'll drive over to the fire hall."

Dad was visiting with Highway Patrol Officer Bill Chapman at an intersection when Christie stopped next to Bill's patrol vehicle. "Looks like we've got it under control; Markel is going to be fire watch. Give us a few minutes and you can open up the intersection."

Dad looked up at me in the back of the pickup, and said, "Who's that young man holding your helmet?"

I'll never forget Christie's reply. "He's my helper."

Next we drove to the 5th Street and 2nd Avenue intersection where my friend Roxy had just climbed into the cab of his Seagraves pumper. I noticed rolls of used hose piled high on the rear platform of 202. Coming down the tracks from behind the elevator was the Mack Ladder Truck driven by Tom Goulding. It came to a stop just as it eased into the street.

"We're going back to hall," Christie shouted.

"I'll give your passenger a ride," Roxy said, pointing in my direction.

With a wave of his hand, Christie indicated for me to get into the pumper. I hesitated, not wanting to wrongly interpret his hand signal. "Go ahead," Christie said.

"How did Gus do?" Roxy asked.

"Reminds me of a young Roxy Caye," Christie replied.

Back at the fire hall, in the afternoon sun, a number of firemen were washing hose. As we backed into the fire hall, I noticed Harold, Jack, Kenny and Edgar sitting on the tailboard of 201 looking at the apparatus floor. The big Chemox units were lying in the middle of the floor, and next to them in a straight row, were the four masks with the shiny clean filters that reminded me of Uncle Ed's snuff box lid.

CHAPTER 2

FIREMAN—SAVE MY BABY

The Crazy Day celebration brought people from all over the region into the community of Devils Lake. Businesses would place merchandise for sale on tables in front of their stores and employees would dress in costumes and parade through the uptown area.

It was a sunny day in 1956 and I was visiting with Duane 'Bud' Johnson in front of Shark's Clothiers. Bud was dressed as a fireman, which was his secondary vocation. "Isn't it a little warm for fire gear this time of year?" I asked.

"If it gets any warmer I'm going to take it off," Bud said.

Watching costumed employees parading past the store, I noticed a broad, bare-chested individual pushing a wheelbarrow. "Who's the big guy in the hula skirt?"

"It's Tim Kurtz. He works for Del Howes at the furniture store."

"He is one big SOB."

"Yep, he'd make two of you."

Bud wasn't kidding, I thought. Tim must weigh all of 250 pounds, and I only weigh 145. Suddenly, I thought I heard a siren.

Bud said, "Go to the corner and listen."

KDLR was playing music through outside speakers, so I had to go to the bank corner to be sure I was hearing the donkey bray of the fire siren. Looking back I waved at Bud, pointed toward the fire hall, and started running. At the Arcade corner, I turned to make sure Bud was coming, and through the crowd I saw volunteer Iver Johnson visiting with Tim Kurtz. *Maybe Iver will get him involved,* I thought.

Bud ran by me and went to the back of the fire hall. I hadn't been there for a quite awhile and I knew I was in for an ass chewing, so instead of following Bud I went around to the front of the hall and through the door. Immediately inside the front entrance stood the short muscular Assistant Chief of the Devils Lake Fire Department, Sarge Reardon. "Where have you been? I haven't seen you for awhile," he said with a smile. *That's Sarge*, I thought to myself. But before I could respond, the front door opened and Iver came into the fire hall followed by Tim Kurtz.

"Get in the engine," Sarge said to Iver.

At age 17, I wasn't old enough to become an official volunteer. My duties were to support the different operations and not get myself into trouble. I would go to the blackboard and write the address of the emergency and names of the personnel riding out on the engine. Then I'd head to dispatch until LaVerne Gloger was available.

I was writing on the blackboard when a passing fireman rubbed me on the head and smiled at me on his way to the tailboard of the engine. It was my old friend Roxy Caye, and behind him stood Tim Kurtz where Iver had left him. "Get over here," shouted Iver, and Tim dutifully climbed into the cab. It reminded me of the comic strip Mutt and Jeff. Iver stood 5'5" tall and Tim was over 6' tall; it was almost comical! I tried to imagine him climbing through a window with breathing apparatus on. *He wouldn't need a window; he could just punch a hole in the wall*, I thought.

Roxy reached into a compartment at the rear of the engine and removed a gray sweatshirt. "Hey, ticket taker, put this on. You look like hell with your nipples sticking out," Roxy shouted. At the mention of ticket taker, Tim turned and looked at Roxy. *Oh shit*, I thought, but to my surprise, Tim waved at Roxy and reached for the sweatshirt. I was adding Tim Kurtz's name to the list on the blackboard when the back door opened and LaVerne Gloger shouted, "I've got dispatch."

The pumper engine starting was the signal to open the doors. I folded back the bay doors and checked the drain valves under the truck. Noting they were closed, I gave the thumbs up signal to Sarge. He released the clutch and the pumper eased out into the flow of Crazy Day traffic. *Will Sarge ever let anyone else drive?* I wondered. Once in the street, the siren started its howl. As quickly as it sounded, it died down. Too much traffic, I guessed.

Sometimes a siren sound can be detrimental. I recalled hearing some volunteers discuss a funny situation that happened when a truck was responding to the southwest side of town. Jerome stepped on the siren as the truck approached the railroad underpass. The driver of a car in front of the fire truck froze and blocked the underpass. Sarge told Jerome to get out and move the car. The driver turned out to be Sarge's sister-in-law. "Pretty funny," they said. Sarge was driving the fire truck. He didn't talk to Jerome for a month. I wonder who punched the siren this time?

The pumper finally cleared traffic and moved to the center of the street as the siren resumed its howl. Bud had told me they drive in the middle of the street because kids hear the siren and come running out to see what's going on. It gives the driver a little more time to react.

"I'm out of here," I shouted to Digger. He gave me a wave and I was out the door. I ran to my car behind Ramsey Drug. As I left the parking lot, I tried to catch up to the engine. Maneuvering in Crazy Days traffic was fruitless. I could have had red lights and a siren; it wouldn't have made any difference.

As I drove, I began recalling some of the things Roxy had told me go through his mind when responding to an emergency. Is everybody out of the house? How big is the house? Is the garage attached? What's in the garage? Where's the hydrant? Which way is the wind? What's the temperature? "The man in charge considers other things," Roxy said, "such as manpower, traffic control, vandalism, water, fuel, evidence, victims, etc." I wondered if all of these things would be addressed this day.

With all the traffic in the uptown district I decided not to follow 201 down 8th Avenue, but take 12th Avenue and go south to Walnut Street. Approaching the intersection, I saw the ambulance go through and quickly pulled in behind it. Nearing Walnut, I saw smoke coming from a home up the street.

Charlie Wittkop stepped from the ambulance and waved at me as I came to a stop, blocking the remaining portion of the intersection. "When did you start driving the ambulance?" I asked.

"I just got certified," said Charlie. "Sister Mary made arrangements with Sarge for my education. I don't care for the responsibility but it's part of the job."

"You'll do a fine job," I assured him. "Here's my car keys; move it if you have to."

"Thanks, I'll keep an eye on it," Charlie replied.

With a loud bang the smoke from the house turned from gray to dirty black.

"Sounds like a woman screaming," said Charlie. He opened the side door of the ambulance and retrieved the first aid bag and resuscitator.

As I ran toward 201 I was grabbed by a screaming woman. "Save my baby!" she said with tears streaming down her face. Looking around I located Bud, who was putting on a breathing apparatus. "Bud," I called. "She says her baby is inside."

"Where in the house?"

"He's in his crib, through that window," she said, pointing to a small window in the northwest corner of the house.

Tim overheard the exchange. "Did she say baby?"

"Yes. Bud's going to look for him."

From the front of the engine Sarge said in a calm voice, "Help string the hose."

"Come with me," Roxy said, grabbing Tim by the arm. Pointing at the hose load, he continued, "Grab the hose and drag it toward the garage."

Seeing the bewildered look on Tim's face as he climbed up on the tailboard, I offered, "Here let me help you."

"What's that on his back?" Tim asked.

"It's a breathing apparatus. He can go into smoke and breathe fresh air while he's inside."

Becoming impatient, Roxy shouted, "What the hell are you doing, cuffing your carrot?"

"Here Tim, grab this hose and drag it to the garage."

We off-loaded hose and dragged it to Harold Armentrout and Iver Johnson who were standing in front of the garage putting on their breathing apparatus. "Roxy's going to use tank water until we get hooked up to the hydrant," I told Harold.

Back at the truck, Tim was holding a female coupling in his hand. "Why are the threads so big?"

"They're easier to clean when they get crap in them, like ice or dirt," I replied.

I finished tightening the coupling on a discharge and shouted to Roxy, "Number three." I grabbed a hydrant wrench from its holder on the side of the pumper and handed it to Tim with instructions on attaching the suction hose to the hydrant. Suddenly a 'Bang' came from inside the garage.

"What was that?" Tim exclaimed.

"I think a tire on the car exploded."

"It sounded like a shotgun went off."

"Put your wrench on the top nut of the hydrant and open it slowly. It'll take about 21 turns to open it all the way. Don't open it too fast."

As the water began filling the suction line, I shouted "Water's coming!"

"When it's open all the way, come around to the other side of the pumper and Roxy will show you what he's doing."

I was watching fire ground activity and behind me Roxy was explaining the pump operation to Tim. "It's like turning on a water faucet," Roxy said. "We hook up to the hydrant and supply the hoses with water." I listened as Roxy continued to explain the pump operation, transferring from tank water to hydrant water.

Two inch-and-a-half lines were stretched into the garage and the smoke from the car fire had begun turning gray. Harold came out of the garage and headed down the street. *What's he up to now*, I wondered? At the opposite end of the house, Sarge stood near the window which the distraught mother had indicated led to the bedroom where her baby was sleeping. As I watched, glass from the window shattered and a bundle wrapped in a blue blanket was thrust through the opening into Sarge's waiting hands. Hugging the bundle, Sarge waved and Charlie came on the run with his medical kit and resuscitator.

When she realized what was happening, the mother let out a scream. "He'll be okay, just stay out of the way," Sarge said. Taking his fire coat off and laying it on the ground, Sarge placed the small bundle on top of the warm wool liner. "I'll handle the mask," he said to Charlie, "you take care of the oxygen." As Sarge and Charlie worked on the little guy I did something I would find myself doing many times in years to come: I prayed.

The smoke in the garage was diminishing as a Dodge Power Wagon pulled up in front of the structure. Harold climbed from the cab, grabbed a chain from the truck box and hooked it onto the bumper of the car. "Ain't going to work," the driver shouted. He jumped from the cab and with smoke swirling around him scurried under the car and reattached the chain to the chassis. Faster than you can say 'what the hell', he was back out and climbing into the truck. He eased the car out of the garage and down the driveway to the curb.

Most of the paint was burned off of the car, the windows were gone and there weren't any tires left on the driver's side. That explained the bangs and black smoke. With the car out of the way, firemen were working inside the garage raking debris and shoveling it outside for watering down.

Bud waved me over as he came out of the garage. Handing me the breathing apparatus, he said, "Here, take this and put it on the engine." I carried the breathing apparatus to the fire truck and laid it on the passenger's seat. I was about to go and examine the car when Roxy said, "Show Tim how to roll the extra hose; leave the soft suction until we're sure the fire's out."

Retrieving the used 150 feet of inch-and-a-half attack line, I began showing Tim the need for rolling the hose properly in order to protect the coupling threads. We were rolling hose when I heard a child cry. I looked over my shoulder and saw the mother holding the baby and at the same time trying to hug Sarge and Charlie. The three of them were only 50 feet away, and I heard her say, "Thank you, you saved my baby." It was hard to keep from smiling; Sarge's face was the color of the stop sign behind him.

"Looks like we'll need a fund-raiser for this family," Bud said.

Both the debris and car fire had been extinguished and I was watching Tim shut down the hydrant. It didn't take long for him to catch on. Moments later, he removed the soft suction and put the cap back on the hydrant. We tied the soft suction back onto the fire truck and laid the wet hose on the tailboard. Sarge loaded the mother and baby into Charlie's ambulance.

Roxy had been showing off his pumper to Tim, so I made it back to the fire hall ahead of them. Roxy backed the big pumper into its slot on the apparatus floor, and Tim climbed from the cab. Waving at Sarge, Tim said, "Thanks for letting me help."

"Where are you going?" asked Sarge. "You can't leave until everything is cleaned up."

I was watching Tim when Harold walked over and said, "Welcome aboard." Others gathered around welcoming Tim with a handshake or a pat on the back.

"You're so big, we'll have to order gear from Grand Forks Tent and Awning for you," Roxy said.

"Golly, I don't know what to say," Tim replied.

Roxy grabbed Tim by the forearm and said, "Let's go and load the truck. I'll start you out on the easy stuff first. Are you married?" he asked.

"Yep," Tim replied.

"Call home and tell your wife you won't be home for supper: you're eating at the fire hall tonight. The second and fourth Wednesdays are for the fire department. Set them aside and don't let anyone talk you out of it. Lucky you! Tonight Sarge is cooking roast beef."

"I have something to do, but I'll be right back," said Tim.

"Where are you going?" I asked as we walked out the back door.

Smiling, he said, "I have to go get my wheelbarrow."

"Sure glad you took off your grass skirt," I said with a smile.

CHAPTER 3

MAJESTIC CLEANERS—

ONLY ONE EXIT

It was a cold winter evening in December of 1966, and I was relieving the desk clerk for supper when Ruben Will, local banker, stopped for his evening paper and cigar. I enjoyed my visits with Ruben; they were always informative and didn't last more than five minutes. This evening was no different, but as he opened the front door of the hotel to head home, I heard the fire siren calling the volunteers.

Lavada 'Babe' Schwab, the desk clerk had just returned from supper when Dick Ratchke, a lineman for the local power company came in and announced, "They've got a fire at Majestic Cleaners."

"Oh no, they do our linens," Babe said.

"They did laundry, but won't be doing anything for a while," Dick responded.

I put on my parka and told Babe, "If anybody wants me, I've gone to find out what's happening to our laundry service."

It was a short walk to Majestic Cleaners where I joined a group of on-lookers gathered in front of the American Legion Building across the street from the burning structure. Majestic Cleaners was a 30x140 foot brick building containing washing and dry cleaning equipment in the basement; reception and sales occupied the first floor and the second story contained the living quarters of owners John and Mary Lou Kowalski. I couldn't see any fire through the front windows, but the flame reaching into the sky indicated a serious situation. It was almost like the whole building was on fire. To the west was an open lot used by Lake Supply for displaying farm equipment, and about 50' to the east was Leevers Super Valu grocery store.

As four firemen struggled to raise a Bangor ladder to the top of the parking lot wall, I felt a surge of wanting to help stir through me, but caution kept me from rushing headlong across the street. Not having been to the fire hall for more than ten years, I wasn't sure whether or not I would be accepted. I had been back in town for over three years, and the only contact I had with most of the volunteers was an occasional, "Hi," when they came into the Mayer Bar for a beer.

Stretching like snakes from pumper 201 were three hoses; two charged lines wiggled their way across the ice-covered parking lot toward aerial ladder 203 at the rear of the structure. The other hose line lay uncharged and coiled at the base of the Bangor ladder.

Within a few moments the Bangor ladder was positioned against the wall and Charlie Olson began climbing, carrying a rope in his hand. When he reached the top of the ladder he used the rope to pull the uncharged line up to him. At the bottom of the ladder Byron Nelson was just finishing securing his end of the hose when it stiffened and the surge caused Byron to stumble backwards and fall on his back. Before anyone could help, he rolled over and got to his knees. *Bet that rattled his bones,* I thought. In a moment he struggled to his feet and looked around to see if anybody was watching. Byron checked his lashings one last time and hurried toward the rear of the structure. I couldn't believe he had left Charlie alone: *That's taking a big chance on the ice covered lot.* I had heard through the grapevine that Byron had been hired by the fire department, and as I watched him leave Charlie by himself, I figured this must be his first big fire.

Another fireman I didn't recognize approached Chief Reardon. Following their conversation the Chief began speaking into his radio, and shortly thereafter the fire siren on top of the Memorial Building began sounding once again. *Damn,* I thought, *they need more help.*

Still keeping an eye on Charlie, I searched the crowd for the owners of Majestic Cleaners. At the far edge I spotted John and Mary Lou Kowalski. I moved through the crowd and hugging Mary Lou asked, "How are you doing?"

Mary Lou was a small lady, dark skinned and pretty, and quite a contrast to her husband John, who was big and husky. "What are we going to do?" she asked.

"I've never known you to give up before," I said, and turning toward John I extended my hand. Ignoring the motion he grabbed me in a bear hug. *Damn, he's strong!*

"Did anyone get hurt?" I asked.

"No," Mary Lou said, "but I nearly did."

"She was one lucky lady," said John putting his arm around her.

Mary Lou continued. "I was upstairs in the apartment looking through my purse when I heard a pop. I turned around and the Christmas tree was on fire! The wall started burning and fire came across the ceiling toward me."

Having previously been upstairs negotiating linen contracts with John and Mary Lou I had a pretty good idea how the apartment was laid out, but for curiosity's sake I had to ask, "How did you get out?"

"It was so damn hot. I pulled the hood up on my coat and ran through the flames and down the steps. I screamed at John, he grabbed an extinguisher and ran up the steps. He hollered at me to call the fire department." As she was relating her experience, I noticed the fur on her parka was singed, lending credence to her story.

"That soda acid extinguisher was like pissing into the wind!" John exclaimed.

I could feel bystanders crowding in around us as they tried to hear what we were discussing over the continued wailing of the fire siren on top of the Memorial Building. *Sure are nosey; makes you feel like you're a sardine in a can,* I thought. As the distinctive howl of the siren wound down I said to John, "They need help; let's go see where we can be of assistance."

"You go," John replied, "I won't be much help tonight."

I'm not dressed for this shit, I thought, as I made my way slipping and sliding across the street to the base of the Bangor ladder. Careful not to surprise Charlie I called, "Charlie; HEY, CHARLIE, I'm holding the ladder." Without turning he waved his mitten-covered hand in response.

Between keeping an eye on Charlie and looking around for something to anchor the ladder to the wall of the cleaners, I failed to notice someone approaching me from behind. "It's about time you came to see us," a voice said. The hood of my parka prevented me from turning all the way around; but nevertheless, I was able to glimpse the squat, silver-clothed figure of Fire Chief Sarge Reardon.

"It has been a long time, good to see you." I watched him walk away and realized it only took a few words from him to let me know where I stood.

At that very moment Sarge's greeting was overshadowed by the collapse of a portion of the wall, dropping Charlie and the top of the ladder toward the fire area. Shouts from bystanders brought men slipping and sliding across the parking lot to help me support the ladder while Charlie climbed to the ground. The 55' Bangor weighed 360 pounds, but with six people moving the weight we were able to reposition it to a more suitable location. Charlie had just put his foot on the bottom rung with intentions of going back up when Sarge said, "Stay off the ladder, let some of the young guys climb." Charlie reluctantly stepped to the side allowing two others to take his place. As the second fireman got to the base of the ladder, two men finished repositioning the tormentor poles and two others placed themselves on each side of the base of the ladder. It was good to see all the volunteers wearing mittens instead of gloves to keep their hands warm. Moments later the hose swished like a snake's tail as the nozzle was opened and water began flowing into the burning structure.

"Charlie," said Sarge, "the Assistant Chief's job is on the ground, not hanging from a ladder somewhere. That doesn't set much of an example for the new firemen. You're lucky someone was watching out for you."

We knew better than to respond to Sarge's criticism. It wouldn't prove anything, especially when Charlie was wrong and Sarge was right. So began three weeks of silence between of Sarge and Charlie. It was Sarge's way of teaching someone a lesson.

Sarge had been gone for a few minutes leaving Charlie and me standing with the two volunteers at the base of the ladder. Charlie said, "I guess Sarge was right; I'm not as young as I used to be." I smiled at Charlie's response. It had been a long time since I'd visited with him. *Sounds like he's getting a little mellow.*

"Who's operating the pumper at Keating's Corner?" I asked.

"Roxy," Charlie said with a smile. "According to Roxy there's only one pump operator in this department. Oh," he continued, "we're using real breathing apparatus now; I just wish we'd had more time to train with them before this fire."

"Does anyone know how to use them?" I asked.

"A couple of guys are in the basement checking drains, and they've got them on; nothing like on-the-job training," Charlie replied.

Charlie and I began walking around the structure and we observed an obviously inebriated individual staggering toward the entrance to the Cleaners with what looked like a bundle of clothes in his hand. "Hey," Charlie shouted, "you can't go in there."

The entryway was constructed in such a way that it did a pretty good job of preventing outside air from rushing through the doorway. There were eight steps leading up to the reception area, and steam from the cleaning operation in the basement had swollen the wooden casing making the doorway somewhat watertight. Under the street light it looked like the water level was up about 4 feet on the glass entrance door. Water was seeping out from under the door onto the sidewalk, where it froze in an ever widening puddle.

At Charlie's shout the subject hesitated, and turned at the very edge of the frozen puddle. "Says who?"

"I said," Charlie replied.

"Why are you dressed like that? It ain't Halloween."

I smiled, but Charlie didn't, he was visibly pissed; as Assistant Chief he wasn't usually questioned, especially on the fire ground.

"I'm a fireman," said Charlie, "and you aren't going in that door."

"Is there a fire someplace?" asked the subject.

"Yes," Charlie said, "right here."

"Really? Well, I still have to get my stuff cleaned," said the drunk and turning he slipped and slid as he reached for the door handle. Charlie couldn't take it any longer; he reached for the man, and they both fell to the ground. "Son of a bitch," Charlie hollered.

I checked my footing and helped them to their feet. "Put this guy in the slammer," Charlie said to Police Chief Russell Clark, who had come across the street when Charlie fell. Russell left with the subject of Charlie's misery in one muscular grip and the gentleman's clothes in the other.

I hadn't noticed the cold until Charlie fell; now I could feel it through my parka as we walked to the rear of the Cleaners. At the corner was a big man dressed in silver fire gear talking to some firemen. Above him stretched the aerial ladder some thirty feet to the top of the wall. As I rounded the corner two more firemen emerged from inside the building, and Tim Kurtz leaned to hear their report.

Looking up as we rounded the corner, Tim acknowledged my presence with a nod. Although I had just seen him at the Mayer Bar where he had been having a beer with Bob Mahanna, he extended his leather mitten and asked, "How you do'in?"

I had retuned to Devils Lake when my dad died, and almost every night I would visit with Tim and Bob in the bar when they came in for their daily beer. Not once had either of them included me in their conversation when they were talking about a fire, and occasionally they would stop talking altogether when I approached. Always amiable, they would never discuss other people's misfortunes with an outsider. Seeing that big guy dressed in silver helped me to understand the camaraderie among the fire department personnel. Although Tim had never spoken of his ongoing involvement in the fire department since I first met him in 1956, it was apparent he felt comfortable in his position.

"Not bad," I replied. "I see you've got your own gear."

"Yep, and this truck is my responsibility," he said, gesturing toward aerial ladder 203.

Not wanting to interfere with Tim and the firemen, I continued around the building and came upon an unoccupied ladder. Behind me Charlie said, "You want to take a look?"

"Yeah, that'd be great." I climbed to the top of the wall.

Bill Eisenzimmer stood at the top of the aerial ladder a few feet away operating a heavy straight stream nozzle. At the other end of the building Byron Nelson was working a heavy hose stream from the top of the repositioned Bangor ladder. Below me, partially visible among roof debris I could see what appeared to be the remains of the stairway leading to the upstairs living quarters. Seeing the damage up close, I could only imagine what Mary Lou had gone through sliding past the burning tree.

I had been at the top of the ladder a few moments when I heard tapping on the metal, and looked down to see Charlie waving me to the ground. As I stepped from the ladder he handed me a coat and helmet and said, "I should have gotten this for you earlier; if you're going to be moving around you had better put this on."

I recognized it as Charlie's spare coat and helmet. By itself the rubberized fire coat was too large for my frame. Putting it on over my Air Force parka solved the problem, but made it hard to maneuver.

We returned to the alley side of the fire, and I visited with Tim while Charlie and Sarge roamed around the exterior of the building watching progress and keeping an eye out for frostbite on the firemen.

A shout from Bill Eisenzimmer to Tim indicated it appeared safe to go into the building if he used the loading dock. "Let's give it a try," Tim said. Excited by the prospect of getting a firsthand look at the damage caused by the fire, I followed Tim past the smiling Jerome through the rear door of the cleaning establishment.

Once inside I could see water cascading from the collapsed roof structure and disappearing through various openings to the basement below. In front of us a couple of roof joists blocked our way. Tim shouted, "Bring me an axe." In moments Albert Janzen appeared and handed Tim an axe similar to a broad axe from the days of the Vikings. "Shine your light over here," Tim said. Albert adjusted the beam on his hand lantern and illuminated the area Tim had indicated. Once the light was positioned to Tim's satisfaction, a few swings of the big axe made short work of the 2x14 inch timbers, providing a place to crawl through.

Once we got through the opening Tim created, Albert's light exposed the remainder of the loading dock area and what was left of the stairway to the second floor. "Look out for the puddles," Tim said. On the floor at the edge of the hand lantern beam was a glistening black puddle. Albert continued sweeping with the light, exposing more pools of melted roof tar. Except for some collapsed roof sections, I could see very little fire damage to this end of the building. To the west the light illuminated the ruins of the stairway which led to the upstairs living area. Most of the bottom steps were undamaged. Looking upwards I could see more damage. *Looks like steps are missing,* I thought to myself.

"Turn off the water," Tim shouted.

Albert returned to the outside and shouted Tim's order to Bill Eisenzimmer. In moments the flow slowed and stopped. Now that all was quiet, I could hear Tim talking to Bill. Moments later Albert came through the doorway leading a two-man entry team carrying an extension ladder, and dragging a charged inch and half hose line. The group maneuvered cautiously, doing their best to avoid snagging the hose and ladder on the damaged roof sections. Eventually they got past the debris and were able to raise the extension ladder to the second floor. Slowly the nozzle man climbed the ladder and peered over the edge of the remaining wall. *Wonder what he's thinking,* I thought to myself. After a moment, followed by his backup, he continued climbing into the living area to observe the destruction caused by the Christmas tree fire.

Albert was the next team member up the ladder, followed by Tim. "Send up a hand lantern," Tim shouted. Recognizing my chance, I grabbed the lantern from an outstretched hand and climbed to the second floor. Looking around, I saw steam rising from baseboard radiators. "Have somebody disconnect the gas meter," Tim radioed to someone on the ground.

Usually when you see steam, it indicates the hose stream has reached the seat of the fire. In this case, the boiler was still operational and making steam. Unless the fuel was turned off, the burner could keep on firing until the tank ran dry and the heat split the tank. *I hope nobody sprays it with a stream of water,* I thought.

"There's where it started," said Albert motioning toward a corner of the living room.

"What do you mean?" I asked.

"I knew it had something to do with a Christmas tree standing in a corner; you can see the heat and burn lines over there."

"I was visiting with the Kowalski's," I offered. "Mary Lou said she heard a pop and turned to see the Christmas tree on fire. She dropped her purse and slid past the tree and down the stairway. John said he emptied a soda-acid extinguisher into the doorway, but it didn't do any good."

"Is that what they said?" Tim asked.

I hesitated, realizing I had offered information before I had been asked. Although Tim and I were good friends, I knew I was out of line and was there only because 'Sarge' allowed it.

"Sorry," I replied.

"You'll learn."

Byron was watching our activity from the top of the Bangor ladder. "Sarge told me to shut down the nozzle when you guys got upstairs. Do you need me anymore?"

"Wait a minute," Tim replied. I watched Tim disappear into the back of the apartment and when he returned, signal Byron to wrap it up. "We'll handle the rest with the small line," he said.

That was my first large fire since my experience with Christie when I was nine years old, and once again I had learned something. Keep your mouth shut unless you're the boss.

As I drove up to the barricade the next morning, I saw pieces of frozen hose lying in various locations in the street. Two firemen were dragging a section of hose down the street to the fire hall. A few minutes later they came back down the street and when they reached for another length of hose, I climbed from my pickup cab and asked, "What's up?"

"I didn't think about the hose freezing, and when I saw the nozzle flowing water down the storm drain, I turned it off," said the smaller of the two.

"Hi," said the other fireman putting out his hand, "I'm Jerome Hoffart."

Returning the hand shake, I looked around and said, "Looks like you've got some work ahead of you."

"Yeah," Jerome said, "we've got to drag each piece back to the fire hall to thaw them out."

"I really feel shitty about my screw up," said the smaller fireman.

This was my introduction to Don Erickson and Jerome Hoffart. Jerome was a paid fireman who eventually became my Assistant Chief. Don was a live-in, who died a few years later from diabetes complications.

It took almost two hours to drag each length of uncoupled hose one block through sightseeing traffic to the fire hall where it was placed on a drying rack. Each 50 foot length of hose weighed about 50 pounds dry, but with frozen water inside weighed over 250 pounds.

Only in the North Country can a fireman experience the recovery of frozen hose. It was the first of many lessons I would learn as I progressed up the ranks of the Devils Lake Fire Department.

CHAPTER 4

THE ELKS CLUB FIRE—
CLOSE DOESN'T ALWAYS COUNT

It was the 26th of December 1969 and I was repairing the dishwasher in the kitchen of the Mayer Café attached to the family hotel business when the siren sounded its donkey bray calling the volunteers to the fire hall.

Sliding my tools under the counter and hurrying out of the hotel, I ran to my pickup and drove three blocks to the parking lot next to the fire hall on 5th Street. As I rounded the corner of the fire hall, I saw the 55-foot aerial ladder positioned against the wall of the Elks Club about 75 feet to the east. Throwing open the front door of the fire hall with a slam against the Iron Lung, which had been used to treat patients with Polio, I startled Ray Eisenzimmer on his way out of the building. "What's going on?" I asked.

"There's a fire in the mechanical room on top of the Elks Building," Ray replied.

"I'll be right over as soon as I get my gear on."

"Hurry up," Ray said, "we're short of help."

The Elks was a brick building about 50x140 feet, located on the southwest corner of 5th Street and 5th Avenue. The construction of the building was split level, with a bowling alley six feet below grade. A few steps upward led into the lounge area, which contained two entrances to the lodge room. The lodge room was open construction with a 12 foot ceiling. It filled the remaining portion of the first floor for 80 feet as it stretched toward the south. Approximately 20 feet above the street on the roof above the lounge was a structure housing the heating and cooling systems. Access to this area was from a stairway inside the lounge office. Approximately 15 feet to the west of the Elks Building was the Gilbertson

Building containing 16 apartments, the Employment Office, Gilbertson Funeral Home, and Elroy's Upholstery Shop.

Since Clarence Christianson had retired in 1966, Floyd 'Sarge' Reardon was now the Chief of the Department, and as I stepped out the front door of the fire hall I could see him motioning toward the roof of the Elks Building as he talked to Bob Mahanna who was hanging over the wall. I hurried to the base of the aerial in time to hear the chief say to Bob, "They were doing some work on the heating unit yesterday and this morning the building was filled with smoke."

Although Jim Meyers and Joe Belford were standing next to Sarge, he ordered me to, "Get up the ladder and help."

I reached past Joe and grabbed a support bracket and pulled myself up onto the ladder base. As I climbed the aerial 20 feet to the roof, I could see smoke puffing out from different areas of the building. By the time I reached the top of the ladder, smoke and fire were rolling from inside the doorway to the maintenance room and a heavy line led to where Ray Eisenzimmer and Don Hall were spraying water into the room. Observing the activity was Bob Mahanna, who had been with the volunteers a long time, and was known to have the ear of the Chief of the department. Although Bob wasn't a paid fireman, he was respected for his fire fighting understanding and the fact he could 'talk back' to Sarge and get away with it. "What happened?" I asked.

"The manager noticed smoke coming through the vents and instead of calling the fire department, he tried to put it out himself. Someone finally called. Ray and Donnie were having coffee at the fire hall, and they came right over. I think the fire is in the lodge room now."

"How long have you been here?" I asked.

"Not long, about 15 minutes. They called some of us before they set off the Plectrons and the sirens," Bob replied. "Go over to the pumper and get a hundred feet of inch-and-a-half, and a nozzle." He looked around the roof and added, "Better bring a wye, too."

I climbed down the aerial ladder and as I started running toward the pumper someone shouted "What are you up to?" Without turning I pointed back toward the roof. It was only 100 feet to the pumper. When I was almost there, the pump operator turned and said, "Slow down, you'll live longer." By this time I was pretty excited and hadn't given much thought as to who might be operating the pumper. Surprised and pleased I recognized my long time friend, Roxy Caye.

"How can I help you, my boy?" Roxy asked with a smile.

"Hi, Roxy! Bob sent me after 100 feet of inch-and-a-half, a wye and a nozzle."

"I can provide you with the wye and the nozzle but all the light hose line is inside the Elks Building on the business end of a two-and-a-half inch line."

Still smiling, he reached into the storage compartment, produced a wye and went around to the rear of the pumper and quickly returned with a nozzle. I followed Roxy's gaze as he looked toward the Elks Building. "I don't think that little hose will do you any good," he said, "but there's plenty of light stuff on the rack at the fire hall."

As I turned and started toward the fire hall Roxy warned again, "Don't run." Waving back I slowed to a trot.

I hadn't been a volunteer long enough to realize that running was unacceptable. I had always wondered why I didn't see it happening; I'd guessed it was because many of the volunteers were older and maybe not in shape. Sarge looked at me curiously as I passed, and I said, "I've got to pick up some hose for Bob."

Jogging in fire gear wasn't easy, but I made it to the station and grabbed a couple of lengths of inch-and-a-half hose. Hurrying back to the aerial, I laid the two rolls on the ladder platform and passed my rescue rope through the center of each and tied them together. I climbed the ladder 20 feet to the roof and began pulling up the hose rolls.

From behind me Bob said, "Forget the hose! Help Ray and Don."

Ignoring Bob's instructions I finished dragging the hose onto the roof, laid down the wye and nozzle, and put the rescue rope back into my coat pocket. I grabbed the hose behind Ray, and Bob moved to the parapet wall and shouted over the side to Chief Reardon, "It doesn't look good, we'd better get off the roof! Send me a ladder."

Within moments I heard, "Give me a hand." I tapped Ray on the shoulder and receiving a nod of understanding, helped Bob pull up a 35-foot extension ladder. Climbing, and at the same time assisting lifting the big ladder, was Jim Meyers. He was just about to climb over the wall onto the roof when Bob warned, "Don't come up, the roof's going!"

Without looking behind him Jim started backing down the ladder and I heard, "What the hell," from Joe Belford.

"Get down! Bob said the roof is going to go," Jim shouted.

I looked around the roof trying to see what Bob had seen. Tar was bubbling by the furnace room doorway and hearing Bob shout to Jim, Donnie lifted his feet as if they were hot. Looking down, he quickly stepped to the side of the doorway and shut down the nozzle he was holding.

"What's going on?" asked Ray.

"Look at the roof," Donnie said as we went by them with the ladder.

The ladder was heavy and unwieldy for two individuals under normal conditions, but with stability of the roof a concern, Bob and I hurriedly positioned and raised it to the top of the Gilbertson Building wall in what had to be record time.

We had just completed the raise when Donnie brushed past us and with a shout of, "I'm out of here," began climbing the ladder to the safety of the roof of the Gilbertson Building.

Bob said, "You guys take the ladder up, I'll take the aerial down."

Don climbed over the wall and moments later dropped a rope end for tying onto the hose. Ray secured the rope around the hose nozzle and positioned the hose on the ladder. He looked up toward Donnie and shouted, "Where in hell did you get this piece of clothesline?"

"Get up here and help me hoist the hose," shouted Don. We haven't got time for bullshit."

As the rope tightened I could see it was definitely a piece of clothesline. *I hope it holds,* I thought to myself.

Ray climbed, one hand on the beam of the ladder and the other dragging the fire hose. In moments he and the nozzle disappeared over the top of the ladder 25 feet above, onto the roof of the Gilbertson Building. I began climbing and suddenly felt the ladder moving, and looked down to see it sinking into the roof tar.

I had to get out of there! Over my shoulder I could see the aerial had been removed from its position against the wall 30 feet away. *Too far for me to reach,* I thought. Looking up toward Ray and Don, I shouted, "Get me off the roof!"

I grasped the beams of the ladder and continued climbing. Below me I could see the roof giving away and exposing the fire raging below. *Oh, shit, it's really getting hot!* Now I wished I had straddled the wall and waited for the aerial ladder to take me down.

"Hold on," Ray shouted.

"We're not letting you go," hollered Don.

I climbed upwards rung after rung, all the time waiting for the ladder with me on it, to fall in to the fire below. *I can't believe they can hold me,* I thought. *Please Lord, I prayed, help Ray and Don, and if you've got a little left over, don't let me jar the ladder!*

I concentrated on the brick wall of the Gilbertson Building as I climbed to the top of the ladder. Finally I heard, "Over the top and your home free." I felt someone grabbing the collar of my fire coat and suddenly I was over the top of the wall landing on the roof. From my sprawled position I saw obvious relief on the faces of Don and Ray. Grateful to be safe for the moment I could only say, "Thanks." To this day, I don't know how Ray and Don managed. The 50 foot length of hose resting on the ladder weighed about 250 pounds full of water, and if it had slipped over the side of the ladder to the side of the Gilbertson Building, my rescue might have had a different ending.

We needed more hose in order to maneuver the nozzle, so the three of us began pulling on the hose to get the excess off the Elks Building roof. Suddenly the charged line swung free from where it had been on the ladder, and began dragging the three of us toward the parapet wall. I heard "I should have tied it!"

"Oh shit!" I shouted as I began sliding across the roof of the Gilbertson Building.

Ray fell against the parapet wall, and Don and I slid to a stop next to him. "Don't let go!" Ray hollered.

"Wowee, that was a pisser!" Don exclaimed.

Reaching into Ray's coat pocket and retrieving his rescue rope, I tied it to mine and to the nozzle. I tried three or four times unsuccessfully to throw the rope around a cast iron sewer stack about six feet away and maintain my grasp on the hose at the same time. Ray finally said, "Gimme the rope; you hold the hose and I'll play cowboy." I grasped the rough canvas material with both hands and held on.

I was lying across one of Ray's legs, leaving him in an awkward position. But after a few tries and some cussing he called, "I got it." Twisting toward him, I could see he had managed to snag the sewer vent, and was tying a half hitch on the nozzle. The rope began tightening as soon as I relaxed my grip on the hose. I carefully pulled my leg from under the fire hose and away from Ray's leg, all the time watching for movement from the hose. Ray was watching too, and when it didn't stretch any further he peered over the wall and shouted, "Add another hundred feet of hose."

Moments later the hose went limp as Ray's directions were conveyed to Roxy. When the couplings were separated between the pumper and ladder truck we pulled up as much hose line as we could and tied it off to a couple of sewer stacks further to the south. Before Roxy charged the line once again, we went back to the edge of the roof and peered down to where the extension ladder had once rested firmly on the roof of the Elks Building. The ladder had dropped just out of our reach and was now resting on the remains of a burning floor joist. "Damn, that was close," I said to no one in particular.

To the south, fire was coming through the roof of the lodge room. Portions of the roof on our side of the building had given way and were burning out of control in an area untouched by streams of water from the east. Roof sections further to the east were beginning to give way exposing uncontrolled fire burning in the lodge room below. *Heat duct must have carried the fire throughout the ceiling,* I thought. Occasionally the smoke changed color as a stream of water was able to penetrate the burning debris. On occasion the sound of rushing water could be heard tearing into the fallen debris. *Must have the monitor nozzle set up.* More of the roof gave way, and now we could see a water stream coming from the east entrance of the lounge into what remained of the Lodge Room. "They're trying to save the bar; hope the ceiling doesn't fall in on them," Don said.

There was a crash and when the smoke cleared we could see where more of the lodge room ceiling had collapsed. "Help me drag the hose before they charge it," Don said.

Water began filling the hose once again, but this time we had anchored it to a couple of sewer stacks. Between two of the stacks we had looped 20 feet of hose leaving us an excess that could be advanced if needed. No matter how well we had anchored the hose, it still took two of us to maneuver it to do the most good. Once it was full, we sprayed water into the lodge room to keep the roaring blaze from radiating into the apartments of the Gilbertson Building.

Don and I were directing our stream of water into the lodge room, and Ray was peering over the wall and giving us directions, when he said, "They're trying to close the window shutters." Don shut down the nozzle, and we looked over the edge of the roof to where Ray was pointing. Almost directly below us was a puny stream of water coming through the window of an apartment.

"Who's squirting water out the window?" Don shouted. The water kept spraying out through the opening and no answer was forthcoming. Once again Don shouted, "Who's shooting water out the apartment building onto the fire?" The water began losing it force and came to a halt.

"It's me, Walt Poissant." Sticking his head out through the opening and at the same time shielding it with an upturned collar, the diminutive resident of the building looked up to where we were peering down at him. "Get back inside," Ray ordered. A fireman on the ground was looking up to where we were talking to Walt and shouted, "We'll close the shutters if you guys give us some protection from the heat."

In order to protect the men closing the fire shutters over the windows of the Gilbertson Building, the three of us maneuvered the hose to the edge of the wall and sprayed water down between the two buildings. *It even looks like the bricks are hot on the Elks Building,* I thought. We kept a careful eye on the activity below and did our best to prevent the water stream from striking the firemen working below us. Until they finally reached Walt's position, he had kept that little stream peeing out the window opening. *Quite a guy,* I thought to myself.

Not being able to move around when operating a heavy line, it doesn't take long before you become cramped. Rotating manpower on a heavy stream is important. When relieved, you stand up and walk around to relieve cramps and restore circulation in your legs. Sometimes bystanders would question each other as to what firemen were doing just walking around. I was fortunate to belong to a department that was well respected in the community and questions such as this weren't part of an everyday discussion. In some communities, the fire department was considered to be a social club. Coffee drinkers would discuss the department's activities on a daily basis. Occasionally these discussions would lead to unfounded and vicious rumors.

During the next hour we had rotated the nozzle operation a number of times, from hose man, to nozzle man, and finally the person resting. Depending on the situation, the above process is taught and used to this day, along with the one person sitting on a circled hose line operating a heavy hose stream nozzle. There just are some places heavy hose streams are needed and operate efficiently.

About an hour had gone by and I had been relieved by Don on the nozzle. I went to the alley side of the Gilbertson Building and saw the volunteers that had been closing the fire shutters come out of the back door of the mortuary. "What's happening?" I shouted.

Startled by my shout he looked around and finally glanced up to where I was leaning over the parapet wall. Recognizing the helmeted fireman as Harold Armentrout, I repeated my inquiry. "How's it going in the building?"

"It was close, but with the custodian's help we put the fire out. There was some serious damage in one apartment, but Walt stopped it before it got too far inside," Harold replied.

My legs felt better and I went back to where Ray and Don were now directing the hose stream into areas of the lodge room that the other hose lines couldn't reach. I told them what had happened and Ray told me to work the nozzle while he checked out the roof hatches for access to the interior of the building.

With a good portion of the roof gone, I could see where two attack teams were moving into the lodge room. Jim Nelson, with his helmet on backwards, was leading one entry team, and Jerome Hoffart was working the opposite side of the room with his crew. Major damage had been done to the lodge room before the monitor was put into operation. When the roof fell, salvage was no longer an option and the entry teams waded through the piles of debris throwing things around as they worked hard to complete extinguishing the fires before dark.

I heard shouting from the opposite end of the roof and noticed Ray looking over the parapet wall to the ground below. "I thought he was going to find a way down?" I questioned Don.

"He's asking them to send up something to eat," Don replied.

It was my first big fire as a volunteer and because of the excitement I hadn't considered food until Don had mentioned sandwich. Glancing at my watch, I saw it read 3 o'clock. "Holy shit!" I exclaimed.

"Time flies when you're having fun," Don said.

Moments later Ray approached and said, "They had lunch down below and no way to get it up to us."

"Why couldn't they set up the aerial ladder?" Don asked.

"Damned if I know," Ray replied.

"I've got something to ease the pain if we split it three ways," Don said. Reaching into his coat pocket he brought out a cigar and bit off a piece. Ray took the remainder from Don's outstretched hand and after taking a bite handed it to me. I looked it over and decided what the hell, and put the remainder in my mouth and started chewing. I was pleasantly surprised; the more I chewed, the better it tasted.

Ray left Don and me to check roof hatches for a way to get off the roof, and we continued directing the water stream into various portions of the lodge room. To the east I could just make out the recognizable figure of Jim Nelson directing his entry team. Since the monitor nozzle had been silenced, two firemen were working along the north wall of the lodge room scattering debris as they attempted to extinguish hidden fires.

"How's it look?" Don asked. "Can we shut her down?" I appreciated Don's trust in my judgment, but I wasn't about to take a chance on the welfare of the entry teams.

"They're still working in from the east end. I think we should leave it here in case we need it," I replied. I closed the nozzle and Don looped a rope around the hose and tied it off to a television antenna anchor.

I continued watching the extinguishing activity in the lodge room while Ray and Don resumed searching for a way down to ground level. A few minutes went by and hearing a noise, I looked to see Ray pounding on a roof hatch. Don moved to another hatch about 20 feet away and began pounding. After a few minutes Ray quit pounding and lifted the top open. Out through the opening popped Walt's smiling face. Don came across the roof and just as he got to where Walt and Ray were visiting, he spit out the remains of his cigar and began puking all over the roof deck. I had my fill of the cigar an hour before and spit it over the wall when I was working the nozzle. I wasn't about to admit I hadn't swallowed it. Shortly after Don's upset stomach, Walt indicated he wanted them to follow him and with a wave toward me they climbed down the ladder into the Gilbertson Building.

Although there were fires illuminating various places inside the lodge room, the sun was setting and hand lights were now being used. I could see a third entry team coming my way down the center of the lodge room. *Pretty soon it'll be dark,* I thought.

I had been alone with my thoughts for about a half hour when a hatch opened behind me and two volunteers I didn't recognize at first made their way onto the roof. Just as the first fireman was offering his hand to introduce himself, I noticed the hose losing its pressure. "I'm George Roehm; they call me Buck. This is Joe Dunn. We uncoupled the hose and we'll help get it down to the ground."

I shook Buck's big hand and although it was getting dark, I recognized the smiling face of Joe Dunn, a beer salesman for Jerome Candy Company. "Sorry I wasn't at the meeting when you were introduced," he said, "I was on the road."

"Have a seat," Buck said. "We'll take care of the hose."

After opening the nozzle and allowing air to release its hold on the water remaining inside the hose, they lashed an end of rope to the nozzle and dragged it back toward the north end of the building where Joe made a loop around a sewer pipe before they began lowering the hose to the ground. In moments they were finished and Buck retrieved the rope and returned my way. "Let's get out of here."

We climbed through the hatch to the third floor where we were met by Walt. "I'll take you down in the elevator," he said.

"I'd like to look at the room you were in," I said. The four of us strode down the hall to the open door of Apartment 303. Walt reached inside the entry door and turned on the light switch. "Wow!" I said. The damage on the Elks side of the room proved without a doubt that we could have been fighting a fire in the Gilbertson Building also, if it hadn't been for a diligent Walt Poissant. Joe placed his hand on Walt's shoulder and said, "You did a great job, Walt."

"No," Walt said with a smile. "You guys did all the work. Ain't nothin' to holdin' that little bitty standpipe hose."

We returned to the end of the corridor and rode the freight elevator to ground level. As we stepped into the alley and looked back, you could see the smile on Walt's face as we thanked him for his help. "Anytime," he replied. In the background I could hear his wife Flossie calling from somewhere down the hall: "Walt, get in here, it's time for supper."

"Quite a little guy," Buck proclaimed as we walked down the alley.

"I'll check the wall," Joe said as he turned left down the corridor between the buildings. Above us I could see a reflection from the glowing fire, and smoke trailing into the sky. The pungent odor of melting tar was overwhelming. As Buck and I reached the end of the alley and headed north, I asked, "Wonder how Joe's doing?"

"Don't worry about that boy," Buck replied. "He's been around for a lot of years and can handle himself." At that time Joe Dunn had been on the department for 37 years.

In front of us a portion of the Lodge Room wall had fallen to the sidewalk and I heard "We need a little help over here." At first I was concerned that it had fallen on a fireman, and then I remembered seeing bystanders on the street behind the monitor nozzle and thought maybe some of them had gotten close and were under the pile. *That's all we need*, I thought.

I frantically began throwing bricks into the street when Buck shouted, "Stop! We don't even know what's going on."

Once again I had rushed into something without thinking, and I had an ass-chewing coming, but all Buck said was, "Let's find out what's going on." He waved down the sidewalk toward the digging firemen and asked, "What are we looking for?"

Someone shouted back, "We've got some hose pinched under the pile over here."

Buck said, "You never want to hurry in this business. You might hurt yourself, or worse, someone else. You're in this for the long haul - THINK."

Thanks to Buck, when I began teaching classes in the early seventies I encouraged the participants to take a moment and THINK through a situation. Eventually it became a household word in the fire service, and was repeated many times to the firemen who worked with me during my time as Fire Chief.

Buck and I went to the opposite end of the pile and assisted the firemen until the hose was uncovered. Not noticing any damage other than some bruising on the outside of the hose, Buck said, "Mark it, and we'll check it in the daylight. Use it and if it springs a leak, take it out of service."

I followed Buck to the street entrance of the Elks Club. Borrowing a flashlight from a fireman at the head of the steps, we made our way down into the basement where we found Sarge and Tim Kurtz looking over the foundation with their hand lanterns. "What're you doin' in the basement?" Buck asked, looking at Tim.

"You old fart, I came down here to check on the bottom crawlers and here you come trying to convert Bill into the likes of you," Tim replied.

It was hard to see the complete bowling alley, but you could hear water running down from above somewhere toward the south end of the building. Always on the lookout for a good deal, Tim said, "Sure is a lot of nice wood. I wonder if they're going to refinish the lanes?"

"How's the ceiling look?" Buck asked Sarge.

"Not bad for having water on top of it. That must be what's draining in the back." Buck shined his flashlight toward the far wall but we weren't able to detect where the sound was coming from.

"Anyone down there?" came a shout from the head of the steps.

"Yeah," Tim replied.

The sound of footsteps could be heard coming down the stairs, and Jerome appeared and requested permission to wrap up the unused equipment.

"How are things in the lodge room?" Sarge asked.

"Looks good," Jerome replied. "Nelson finished on the south side and up the center. We covered the north side and up into what's left of the mechanical room."

"Did you get my ladder down?" Tim asked.

"Yep, Belford set up the aerial and they went up and got it. He said it was jammed into where the roof had sunk into the fire.'"

"Don't put it back on the truck until we check it out," Sarge ordered.

Jerome turned to leave. "I'm going to help Jerome, I said." Once we got outside, I said, "I noticed you didn't wait for Sarge to tell you to go ahead and wrap up."

"Its kind of a unwritten rule; I've been a paid man for three years now and kind of understand what he means when he says 'check' something. If he didn't want me to start wrapping things up, he would have said so. Thanks for coming to help."

Never before had I seen so much material that needed to be recovered. There were lengths of hose all over. It was one of the few times we could hand carry hose to the fire hall since it was so close. Back at the hall Walt Thiessen was supervising the live-ins as they placed the heavy, wet lengths on the hose rack, and inserted spacers separating the layers. "What are they doing that for?" I asked.

"Air circulates around the hose and it dries faster," Walt replied.

A siren made a short growl outside. "Open the door; that's Roxy," Walt said.

I folded back the overhead doors and Roxy began backing in the pumper. Once halted, he reached for the dash, and flicked a number of switches, bringing the engine to a halt. Climbing down from the cab he went to each side of the engine compartment and opened the hood. "What did you do that for?" I asked.

"It lets Walt know I haven't checked the radiator or oil," Roxy replied.

Axes, nozzles, ropes, the marked hose and questionable ladder were eventually cleaned and readied. The fire trucks were reloaded before everyone left for the evening. The men scheduled for fire watch were provided with a two-way radio and left to place barricades across the street.

It was quite an experience. *Something to tell my kids about when they get older,* I thought.

Now I was tired. *"How do those guys do it?"* I said to myself.

CHAPTER 5

LENTZER'S SURPLUS -

THE HORSESHOE DIAMOND

Early Saturday morning, January 16, 1971, plumbers were doing their annual thawing of the water lines at Lentzer's Surplus Store in downtown Devils Lake. When their torches ignited combustible material in the basement of the store, the fire department was notified of a fire in the only remaining wood structure in the uptown area.

The phone in my basement office rang with a sense of urgency, and the desk clerk in the lobby above informed me of sirens sounding outside. I rushed up the steps and through the front door of the hotel and saw volunteer fireman Harold Armentrout leaving Mann's Department Store. He headed east down the street toward the area where all the smoke was coming from.

As I approached the two-story building located between Fab & Trim and Carlson's Bakery, I saw Harold climbing the aerial to the roof of the bakery. On the sidewalk in front of the plate glass display window the Lentzers were watching their business and the belongings in the upstairs apartment being destroyed by the ravages of fire.

Smoke was rolling from every corner of the building, but the fire hadn't ventilated itself through the roof yet. Mike Eresman and I must have thought about the Lentzers at the same time. We approached them from opposite directions with intentions of removing them from harm's way. "Com'on," I said to Kopel, "we've got to get you out of here."

Turning the slightly built, elderly man and grasping him by the elbow I began leading him across the street when there was a loud 'BOOM' and glass flew everywhere, some striking me in the back as I leaned over the diminutive Kopel, doing my best to protect him. When we reached the curb I looked back to see smoke and fire coming through what had once been the display window. Mike was guiding Mrs. Lentzer through the front entrance of Fab & Trim. "Mama's okay," I said to Kopel. "Mike's taking care of her."

The door to the Lakeside Café opened and a customer helped Kopel through the front entrance. Once inside I asked him if there was anything I could do for him.

"No, as long as Momma is okay, it will be good," Kopel replied.

Returning to the aerial ladder I climbed to the roof of the bakery in time to see sparks flying from various electrical wires strung above the burning building. Since the Elk's Club Fire, I'd had the opportunity to attend State Fire Schools, and hours of training at the fire hall. For a couple of years, I even taught architectural drafting at Lake Region Junior College. All of these taught me a lot about building construction, and now I was especially observant whenever I stood on a roof.

It had been only a few minutes since I'd left Kopel across the street, but now the flames had eaten through the flimsy roof structure and fire roared from inside the building. Two hose lines were now working into the roof area, and at the front of the store a hose team was attempting to force their way through the front entrance. Through the blaze I could see Jack Voiles watching the happenings from his apartment window in the Fab & Trim Building.

"Turn your nozzle on fog," I coached Harold. Sparks were flying in every direction, and fear of electrocution was evident in the way the firemen were operating their nozzles. The other nozzle man heard me direct Harold, and adjusted his nozzle accordingly. I found myself looking around for someplace to make myself useful when someone yelled, "It's coming out the back!"

As the fire gained momentum more of the roof gave away and flames began climbing up the opposite wall. "Get some water over there before the fire gets into Fab and Trim!" I shouted, pointing toward the wall below Jack Voiles' window. Immediately, Harold and Jerome directed their hose streams into the roof opening below the window.

The smoke and smell of burning tar from the roof was nauseous, and eventually we dropped to our knees trying to avoid the smoke, as we continued to fight the fire. I took the nozzle from Harold and suggested he leave the roof. Not having taken the time to put on his turnout gear, his sports jacket and trousers were a mess. *He's fortunate to have Adin Mann for a boss,* I thought, *his clothing will be replaced for nothing.* (Adin was a long time fireman and current secretary for the volunteers; Harold worked in the men's department at his store.)

Harold was just swinging off the roof onto the ladder when I heard rushing water coming from the street side of the store. Tim Kurtz was directing a heavy stream from the aerial ladder nozzle into the Lentzer's apartment directly above the store area. That'll drive the fire out the alley side. A shout from the alley proved my guess to be right.

Harold and Sarge were conferring on the street next to the truck cab of the aerial ladder. Harold waved his hands and arms in the air, expanding on the fire activity. Occasionally Sarge would look up and smile. I wonder what that's about.

With all the water being poured on and into the structure, it wasn't long before the fire diminished and entry teams were moving into the building. From my position on the roof, I could hear the sound of boards breaking, and occasionally saw water coming up past the damaged edges of the roof. Jack spotted me and with obvious relief waved and gave the universal thumbs up signal.

Bob Mahanna shouted down to the crew in the street and moments later the hose lines began collapsing as the pressure was relieved. Lifting the nozzles in the air, we did our best to keep water from falling onto the Carlson Bakery roof. "Lower the hoses over the side, we'll roll them up on the ground," Bob instructed. Once the lengths were on the sidewalk, we climbed down the ladder and began rolling hose and loading it into the pickup.

I was rolling hose in front of the Montgomery Ward store when I bumped into a figure standing in my way. I was about to proclaim something derogatory when I looked up to see Sarge smiling at me. "You sure know how to upset Harold," he said.

"He was on the roof without fire gear," I replied.

"I know," said Sarge, "so were you. You've only been on board for a couple of years; until you've got more time under your belt, talk to me, I'll handle it. Harold's been ruining his clothes for years, and he knows better; I'll talk to him when the time is right." At the time I didn't fully understand the merits of politics; eventually I became proficient in recognizing the use and need for it.

I continued rolling hose and considered how to go about apologizing to Harold, when I heard a page over the outside speaker of the aerial ladder calling Iver Johnson to the fire hall. Jerome and I were just placing the last roll of hose in the back of the pickup when someone shouted, "Bill!" It was Iver waving at me from across the street. "Come with me," he said.

"What's up?" I asked.

"Sarge wants to see us; something about Kopel Lentzer."

We cut through The Stables Bar and across the alley to the fire hall. Inside the hall firemen were loading hose onto the drying rack and Walt Thiessen was overseeing the loading of replacement hose onto the pumper trucks. I followed Iver into Sarge's office and was told to close the door.

"Kopel has something he wants you to search for when things settle down. He'll go with you two tomorrow and give you directions," said Sarge. "I'll give you a call."

I returned to the Surplus store where Jerome and I boarded up the windows and entrances. As I unloaded a traffic barricade Jerome asked, "What do you think of old Lentzer?"

"He's a wheeler-dealer," I said. "I've bought a few things from him; he likes to haggle."

"I went in to buy a jacket, and he threw in a pair of leather gloves," Jerome continued.

"Probably did that because you fill his extinguishers," I replied.

"I don't think so," Jerome said with a grin. "He pays the same one cent over cost per pound of powder everyone else does."

"Is that all you make on servicing an extinguisher?" I asked.

"It's a good deal all the way around. I make a building inspection at the same time I pick up the extinguishers, and the owner gets a good deal. Besides," he said, "there's nobody else in town that does the work."

I put out the last barricade and went to help Jerome nail the last sheet of plywood over the doorway leading up the steps to the second floor. The stairway to the second floor apartment was almost completely destroyed. I wanted to get upstairs and look around, but realized I'd need a ladder. As if he had been reading my mind, Jerome said, "I wish we could get upstairs and look around."

"Me too," I replied.

The next morning, I was in my office at the hotel doing bookwork when the phone rang summoning me to the fire hall. I called Mary and let her know I wouldn't be going to church with her and the boys, and would be helping Kopel Lentzer find something in his burned out building. Previously that call would have met with a critical response from my wife. Since I had quit drinking, Mary realized my need to help others and if I could help Kopel find what he was looking for, it was okay. "Be careful," she said.

Iver and Kopel were sitting in the ladder truck visiting with Sarge when I arrived at the hall. "Get in, and go with Iver," Sarge said.

Iver drove to the front of the burned out structure and showed me how to position and raise the aerial ladder. Swiveling the big ladder into position at a window opening on the second floor Iver turned to Kopel and asked, "Is that okay?"

"That's fine," said Kopel, "but I can't climb the ladder." He held up his hand displaying the missing fingers.

"That's okay," said Iver. "Bill can go inside and I'll talk to you from the window."

I recalled hearing a story about Kopel's misfortune when I first came back to Devils Lake in 1963. Mike Eresman had told me that in Latvia where Kopel and his wife had come from, the Nazis had chopped off Kopel's right hand and three fingers from his left hand trying to get him to talk about his fellow Jews. After they had done their dirty work, they left him to die on a prison floor, and other cell mates bandaged him and saved his life. After the war the Lentzers migrated to the United States and eventually ended up in Devils Lake.

Climbing onto the ladder base, I reached down to assist Iver and together we climbed up to the second floor. Stepping cautiously, I felt my way into what appeared to be a living room/kitchen combination. "What a mess," Iver said, as he looked into the room from the top of the aerial ladder. Everywhere was evidence of the flimsy wooden construction.

"Look over by the kitchen cupboard and see if you can find a wooden chest with silverware in it," said Iver.

Debris was scattered everywhere, but it wasn't hard to see what looked like a wooden box lying on the counter next to the sink. To get there required moving a kitchen table, a number of chairs and a bookcase. Inside the box was smoke-stained silverware. "I've got it," I shouted to Iver.

"He found the chest," Iver called down to Kopel.

I made my way along the wall back to Iver and handed him the chest. I was about to climb onto the ladder, when he pointed and said, "Go to that closet, and you'll find a couple of suits; pull out the navy blue one."

Closets are pretty secure when there is a fire in a home. Clothing is packed so tight in most closets that damage is only on the fringes of the clothing. That was the case in the Lentzer's closet and shortly I was able to reply, "I've got it."

Continuing, Iver said, "Two pair of pants should be hanging inside the jacket. Inside a pocket of the second pair is a box being held in place by two safety pins. Bring me the box."

Feeling the pockets, I discovered the two safety pins. A little further into the pocket I detected a small box. Removing the pins, I was able to withdraw the box. I wanted so desperately to open that tiny box, but thought better of it when I saw Iver looking my way.

Looking down at Kopel and holding the tiny box high Iver asked, "Is this what we came for?"

"Yes," I could hear Kopel say. "Thank you, thank you."

When we got to the ground, Iver showed me the proper way of bedding the ladder and storing the outriggers. When we were done, Kopel said, "I want to show you something."

He reached into his pocket and retrieved the small box and opened it to reveal fifteen diamonds in the shape of a horse-shoe. "In the old country," Kopel began, "when two people got engaged, you were not allowed to give your girl an engagement ring. But it was necessary to prove your wealth and commitment. The best things were made of diamonds or gold. We were planning to go on the train tomorrow to visit the boys in Washington. I would pack my suit, and when we got there she would put on the brooch and show it to the relatives. I am glad you found this for us, it means a lot."

I watched Kopel reach for Iver and give him a hug. Turning to me and with tears in his eyes, he motioned for me to bend down, kissed me on the cheek and said, "Toda."

After the fire Kopel and 'Mama' Lentzer stayed at the hotel for over a month until the insurance was settled. Before he left Devils Lake he asked me to accompany him to Ramsey National Bank and help arrange for a Cashier's Check to close out his account. "The boys are coming to take us to their home in Washington," Kopel said.

The bank was quiet that morning as we approached the counter, and when the teller saw us she signaled bank president Fred Hoghaug.

Fred was a good friend to my family. He had started as a teller and over time had purchased the bank. He was well-liked by everyone, as he had gotten to where he now was by hard work and community commitment. I was privileged at a young age to be goose hunting with him and his sons when I shot my first goose. When my dad passed away in 1963 he was the first to comfort the family. It was not a selfish motive, it was because he cared.

"I've got your check ready for you," Fred said, holding out the check and reaching to shake Kopel's fingerless hand.

"Thank you, my friend," Kopel replied.

Kopel's business with the banker was his own, but when he showed me the check, I couldn't help but look at the amount: $90,000. "Have I done all right with Fred's help?" he asked.

Surprise must have been evident, because I noticed Fred smiling when I replied, "I would say you've done real well with Fred's help."

Prior to boarding the train for their return to Seattle, I had the opportunity to visit with the sons as to the welfare of their parents. One thing led to another and I asked about the brooch I'd been privileged to view. Frank said, "That's a story in itself."

"What do you mean? Is it worth a lot of money?"

"It's only worth about a $1,000 a stone, but after they cut him up and left him for dead, he got well and used its whereabouts to get free from their clutches. He and an SS Officer went to where my mother was living and dad asked her for the brooch. A Polish Officer had befriended the family and was in the kitchen waiting when the SS came into the house. Mama led the SS into the kitchen and the Polish Officer cut his throat. Dad said, 'It was either that or the Nazi would have shot the Polish.' Mom and Dad escaped with the help of the Polish Officer and hid out with friends until after the war, and then they came to America."

The Lentzers had been gone for almost a year and Christmas was approaching when to my surprise a box arrived for me from Seattle, Washington. Opening the box I withdrew a chrome-trimmed, folding serving cart. Attached was a note which read, 'Thank you from Mom and Dad for all you did for them. Merry Christmas, THE LENTZERS.' To this day, that same item occupies a special place in my home and in my heart.

WILLIAM OEHLKE

Looking at it reminds me of the little Jewish surplus store owner and his beloved 'Mama.'

CHAPTER 6

BROKEN RULES BRING SUCCESS

In the fire service, as in any other governmental situation, there are a few individuals that don't let micro management bother them, and consider right is right, full speed ahead and to hell with the consequences. Such was Walter Thiessen, the fire department's Chief Engineer. A great fireman and individual, he was determined to do what was right for the fire department and the City of Devils Lake.

Walt was on duty that Christmas Day evening in 1971 when a fire was reported in a house on 4th Street.

In those days, you were to contact the Fire Chief prior to leaving the fire hall. You would then pick him up at his house on the way to the call no matter which direction you needed to go. Although he lived close to the fire hall, stopping for him and starting again added to the response time.

When Walter received the call to a fire on 4th Street, he told Don Erickson, the duty live-in, to, "Call Sarge and tell him where I'm going, and alert the volunteers." Walt drove directly to the fire scene without stopping to pick up the Chief.

I lived only six blocks away, but when I arrived the fire truck was already on the scene. A booster line led from the rear of the Seagraves pumper toward the front of the house, and ended with the nozzle lying in the snow at Walter's feet. Light colored smoke was drifting out through the opening, and Walter was peering over the window sill into the living room.

Shrugging into the harness of a breathing apparatus I hurried to Walter's side. Smiling, he said, "How do you like them apples?"

Gesturing with his hand Walt said, "I made a U-turn on 9th Avenue, put the truck in pump, cranked the throttle up a couple of turns and dragged the booster line to the front yard just as the window blew out. Glass flew all over and flame came out of the window over my head. I shoved the fog nozzle through the opening just as the fire sucked back inside. The water turned to steam, and the fire went out!"

A voice behind me exclaimed, "Good job!" Bud Johnson had shown up as Walt was explaining what had happened. Walt was really excited, and I couldn't blame him. You sometimes read about steam putting out fires; they produce movies involving this type of scenario, but seldom is it as evident as it was in this home on 4th Street.

"Come with me; let's go inside," Bud ordered. We went through the door into the living room. Everything above four feet from the floor was destroyed. Anything constructed of plastic was sagging from its anchor; pictures, wall phone, floor lamp, etc. Wood charring indicated a fast, hot fire. The Christmas tree was bare of needles, the cords and bulbs sagged between what remained of the branches. The upper window casing and paint next to the tree was almost completely gone. *What a mess,* I thought.

Shining his flashlight on the wall by the front window, Bud said, "Look here." I could just make out the heat line leading away from the Christmas tree toward the stairway. "Do you think it could have been a Christmas tree bulb, like at Majestic Cleaners?" I asked.

"Could be," Bud replied in muffled voice. "We'd better go upstairs and check the bedrooms."

Most of the firemen had rubber fire coats with wool linings that trapped the heat. The further up the steps we climbed, the more unbearable the atmosphere became.

There were a number of bedrooms on the second floor. Bud and I parted ways to inspect the bedrooms and bath. This was my first time searching for victims, and I was concerned as to what I would find. During our last training session, Bud had explained the need for a thorough, but quick search. My adrenaline was pumping as I turned the knob to enter the first of my assigned rooms; I turned on the light switch illuminating the bedroom. Suddenly like a flashing neon sign, Bud's statement, "Don't turn on the lights, use your flashlight," passed before my eyes. I stood waiting for something to happen. When it didn't I thought to myself, *you've got to think and remember.*

When I reached under the bed and didn't touch anything, I felt some relief, and then I realized it was a bigger space than I could reach and decided I would have to shine my flashlight beneath the bed to complete my search. Fearing the worst, I shined my hand light into the void, and after scanning the emptiness realized I had a couple of other places to look before my search was complete.

I carefully opened the bathroom door and illuminated the interior with my flashlight. Everything appeared to be in order: *no bodies or pets,* I thought. I glanced toward the closet door, and realized it would be next after I checked behind a dresser that had been pulled away from the wall. Nothing here, closet is next. With some anxiety I opened the closet door expecting to find a victim. Clothes were hanging neatly from the rod, but bed clothes covered the floor. Gingerly reaching through the pile and finding nothing, I thankfully returned to the hallway where I was confronted by Bud. In a muffled voice he said, "You've got to get through a room faster. Come with me."

At the south end of the second floor was the last room to search. Bud opened the door and shining his light into the interior motioned for me to come over by the window. I wasn't sure how Bud was taking the heat, but I knew it was tough on me. He set his hand light on a nearby table and said, "Let's get rid of some heat."

Raising the interior window exposed an ice covered metal storm window. The ice began melting immediately leaving a puddle on the inside sill. Within seconds the glass was free of ice and we were able to open the bottom section funneling heat out into the night air. "Wow, tell me it's not hot up here."

I looked around and saw Bud rummaging through a closet. "Look under the bed," he ordered.

Again I swept under the bed, and finding nothing shined my flashlight into the void. The heat radiating from the floor was unbelievable. *It's almost like it's on fire; I've got to be right above the Christmas tree,* I thought. Feeling a presence behind me I looked up to see Bud standing above me. "Let's see if we can find the fuse box," he said.

At the bottom of the stairs we were confronted by Chief Reardon. "Did you find anything upstairs?"

"No," Bud said. "We checked the rooms and opened a window. We're going to turn off the power."

Trudging through the snow, we circled around the house to the back and were greeted by a rush of heat coming through the back door opening. On the floor holding the back door open was a fish bowl. Inside the bowl were two mud-turtles covered with soot. *Hot even close to the floor,* I thought.

"Let's go to the basement and check the fuse box," Bud said.

I had been caught up in my thoughts and hadn't noticed the whining coming from behind the door leading to the basement. Two large white poodles were waiting as I opened the door. When they saw Bud and me in fire gear their whines turned to snarls. Jerking the door from my grasp Bud kicked out sending both dogs retreating down the steps. He quickly closed the door. Bud smiled. "I wonder what they would have done if we'd had our masks on."

Bud shut the back door, and we walked through the kitchen and down the hall toward the living room. Two floodlights now illuminated the living room, and a heavy extension cord led outside to a generator. Below what remained of the Christmas tree Jerome was sifting through the debris.

"What are you looking for?" Bud asked.

"I was trying to find the plug-in cord before we take some pictures."

Outside Sarge was talking to Walter. I imagined Walt was updating Sarge on what had happened. Behind me Bud said, "Lets save Walt." I found out later that Bud guessed what was happening and hurried out the front door to where Walt and Sarge were standing.

I followed Bud, expecting to hear him give a report. Instead he placed his gloved hand on Walt's shoulder and said, "Good show, Walt; the steam put out the fire. We'd have had one helluva mess if he'd been any later," he said to Sarge.

A shout from down the sidewalk drew our attention. Coming on a run was Dennis Clemenson, son of the homeowner, and his girlfriend.

"What happened? We just went for a walk."

Sarge's normally gruff exterior seemed to mellow when he addressed the couple. "Do you remember the Christmas tree fire at Majestic Cleaners a couple of years ago?"

I watched Dennis as he tried to fathom what Sarge was leading up to.

"It could have been a bulb on the tree. When it burst, it set the tree on fire. It only takes a few seconds to burn up a tree, especially if it's close to a heat duct or not very fresh. Mr. Johnson will take you in the house when it's safe."

Bud looked at me and rolled his eyes at the reference to 'Mr. Johnson.' Looking past me he said, "The dogs are okay, they're in the basement. They definitely don't appreciate firemen."

Back at the fire hall, Bud explained the reasoning behind his behavior. "If I hadn't complimented Walt on his actions, Sarge would have given

Walt the silent treatment for a month. Wilbur Clemenson owns the house and runs the radio station. Good publicity for the fire department never hurts." Looking around to see who was listening he continued, "Sometimes you have to forget policy and do what has to be done. I don't know how the person sounded when they called, I'm sure they were excited. Don't ever think Walt was wrong; I'm sure after Sarge thinks it over, he'll agree with Walt's actions, although he won't talk about it, except maybe to Wilbur. He's a good friend to the department."

Now I understood how Bud's comments had saved Walter from an ass chewing, and with Wilbur Clemenson running the radio station, the fire department would be sure to receive a positive review.

It's all politics, I thought, *and it will definitely be a fire to remember.*

CHAPTER 7

SNOW AND 55 BELOW

It was the 10th of January 1975, the snow was 33 inches deep, and the wind was gusting 30 miles per hour. Visibility was almost zero as I peered through the windows of the overhead door. It was the worst storm in nine years. In the fire hall with me this morning were Jerome Hoffart, Al Janzen, Alvin Schroeder and Rich Klindtworth. They were shooting baskets on the apparatus floor when the phone rang.

"There's smoke coming from the vents in my house!" a lady screamed.

"Who's calling?"

"Margaret Schumacher, we live at 302 Pitcher Park."

"Get out, and go to the neighbor's house." *Dear God*, I thought, *help them to get out.*

"Rich, you're staying back and working dispatch. Page out the volunteers and have them respond to the fire hall."

I quickly put on my fire gear and climbed into pumper 201 for my first serious fire emergency as Chief of the Devils Lake Volunteer Fire Department. Al Janzen was at the wheel, and Alvin and Jerome were on the tailboard as we drove out of the fire hall into the storm of the decade. Turning at the First National Bank corner, we drove south toward the railroad underpass. The farther south we traveled the bigger the drifts and the worse the visibility. Rounding the corner next to Jerome Candy Company, Albert slowed the big pumper and glancing down toward the opening under the tracks, I could see a suburban almost covered in snow. There was no way we were going to get through that.

"Let's take the 8th Avenue crossing," Albert said, looking my way for approval.

"Go for it," I replied.

Turning at 8th Avenue we encountered a humongous snow drift stretching across the road. Without hesitating, Albert drove the big pumper through a taxpayer's yard and back onto the unsheltered roadway. Immediately in front of us the railroad tracks stretched east and west. The next shelter was about 300 feet away on the other side of the tracks. The wind-driven snow struck with the force of water ski spray as we left the shelter of the taxpayer's yard. In order to give Albert some protection, I kneeled on the seat until we got over the tracks. *God its cold*, I thought. *The next thing we're going to do is buy a truck with an enclosed cab.*

Heading west on 5th Street South we plowed through a big snow drift at each intersection; after six miserable blocks we turned south on Highway 20. Once again in the open, visibility dropped to zero. Occasionally I could see 10 feet in front of the pumper, but most of the time we had to use our imagination because we couldn't see anything. *I bet we are the only ones out in this crap.*

A quarter mile down Highway 20 opposite Western Area Power, we heard a shout of, "Go to the right a little."

"What?" Albert shouted.

"Go right a little; we're watching the center of the road."

"They can see better out the back than we can see out the front," Albert shouted.

"Is that the turnoff?" I asked.

"Sure looks like it; I'll give it a try."

For just a moment the approach had been visible. Turning the big steering wheel and proceeding ever so slowly, Albert edged the big pumper around the corner. I cracked open the door so I could watch the tires as we moved through the curve. Behind us a culvert came into view. *O shit, we almost drove into the ditch!*

Turning east at the Coca Cola warehouse the shelter belt on the south side held back the blowing snow and we could see the outline of the tree-sheltered trailer court in the distance. As we entered the trailer court Albert shouted, "There's the turn, but I'm not sure if I've got enough hose to get back to the hydrant."

"I loaded an extra 250 feet of two-and-a-half inch hose this morning," Jerome yelled from under the hose cover.

Pressing the mike key on the radio, I heard the dynamotor begin whining. *I can't believe it's still working*, I thought.

"Fire Station—217."

"Go ahead."

Again the dynamotor whined as I asked, "Did anyone get to the station yet?"

"10-4, we've got snowmobiles and firemen ready to head your way."

"Send a half dozen firemen this way, and keep the rest in town."

"Ten-four," replied Rich.

For just a moment I could hear the tire chains rumble on a section of clean pavement and then it was quiet once more as they bit into the snow on the way to the burning mobile home. Albert had shifted down and once again we were crawling along, when through the driving snow I could see what remained of a burning trailer.

"Fire Station, we're on the scene."

"You'll get warm now!" Albert exclaimed.

It was hard to believe; we'd made it to the scene in 15 minutes. It seemed like an hour. Albert could really drive.

Albert jockeyed the big pumper back and forth until it was pointed back the way we had come. Jerome and Alvin off-loaded the hose and Albert drove off to the hydrant we had passed on the way in. *I hope he makes it,* I thought, *we're going to need more than the 260 gallons in the tank.*

Except for a small portion of wall next to the front entrance, the majority of the trailer was already destroyed. The burning trailer was typical of a seventies model as there was only lightweight paneling covering the walls. Later codes upgraded wall covering to include sheet rock, making mobile homes less likely to be totally destroyed in a fire. The wind was blowing so hard, I could see where heat from the burning trailer had melted snow across the yard and scorched the paint on Horner's mobile home 30 feet away.

"Go next door and see if the family is there," I said to Alvin.

Alvin and Jerome had just finished separating the skid load when the radio barked, "Water is on the way."

In a few moments the hose began stiffening. Jerome opened the nozzle and began spraying water on what was left of the mobile home. "There isn't much pressure," he shouted.

"201—give us more pressure," I radioed.

"Pump's frozen; you'll have to work with hydrant pressure," Albert replied.

"217," Alvin radioed. "Margaret and her daughter are next door, they're a little shook up but they'll be okay."

I had been pulling burning debris from the trailer and throwing it into the snow banks for over 20 minutes when I heard the unmistakable sound of snowmobiles. *Great! Help has arrived.*

In moments six firemen led by Jim Nelson appeared through the driving snow. Jim had been a paid fireman for awhile, and now had a full time business. They were true snow country firemen; under their fire coats they were dressed in snowmobile suits, masks, insulated gloves and thermal boots. Jim gave out assignments and enthusiastic firemen were suddenly scrambling over the chassis, using axes and a Halligan tool to remove burning material and throw it into the snow or wash it down with water from the hose line. *They must have stopped at 201 for tools.*

The inside of the Horner trailer was toasty warm. Perry and Pat welcomed us with a cup of hot coffee. Alvin was visiting with the bosomy Margaret and doing his best to concentrate on what she was saying. Her daughter was seated on the living room couch wrapped in a blanket. As I talked with Margaret I was able to find out a number of things. First, she had heard a roaring noise coming from the area of the furnace. She thought it was just the wind. A short time later she saw smoke coming from a floor vent. When it got worse she called the fire department.

"Did you hear a bang?"

"Yes, it wasn't long after the bang that the vents started smoking."

"It sounds like your chimney was blocked by ice."

"I could see flames right outside our trailer," Perry said.

"Snow melted right up to your trailer and scorched the paint," I replied.

"Have you cleaned the ice from your chimney?" I asked Perry.

"No. Why's that?" he asked.

"I think the bang Margaret heard was fuel oil building in the furnace because it wouldn't ignite without a draft. The chimney was iced over, the furnace filled with fuel and when it tried to ignite, nothing happened. Finally it fired up and got so hot from all the fuel everything around the furnace started to burn." Suddenly there was a bang, as Perry's fuel oil furnace backfired.

"That's the same sound!" Margaret exclaimed.

"Alvin, get up on the roof and knock the ice off the chimney," I ordered.

I went down the hall and turned off the furnace. Perry put on a coat and followed Alvin out the door. In moments I heard a commotion against the wall of the trailer as Perry helped Alvin up onto the roof. There was a rattling and scraping on the chimney, and Alvin shouted into the stack, "Ice is off the chimney."

I looked in the heat chamber, trying to determine how much oil remained. It looked pretty good, so I decided to give it a try.

"Put the vent cap on," I shouted, "I'm going to fire it up."

Turning the thermostat down, I started the pilot light. I held the door closed and called to Pat Horner, "Turn up the thermostat." In moments the sound from the furnace indicated it was burning.

"Come on down, I think we've got it," I shouted.

"As soon as the weather clears," Pat Horner said, "we'll get Margaret some help."

Thanking the Horners for their hospitality, we returned to where Jim and his crew were continuing to extinguish the fire. To the north 201 had been moved to the intersection and Albert was waving my way. My radio crackled and Albert said, "I backed the truck up to get it out of the wind; the radiator is freezing up."

As Jerome, Alvin and I struggled through the snow, I wished I had snowshoes. When we finally reached the pumper I was sweating. "I don't think I've ever worked so hard to go two hundred feet in my lifetime," Alvin said, looking back toward what was left of the burning trailer.

Albert motioned us over. "The heat gauge was climbing, the antifreeze was crystallized, and the radiator was marked 15 degrees above zero. I covered the radiator with a tarp and backed the truck over here out of the wind."

All around me was blowing snow. I wondered what Albert meant by 'out out of the wind'. "How are you doing?"

"I'm fine," Albert replied, "but we have to get 201 back."

"How's the temperature now?"

"Better, since I covered the radiator," he replied.

"You guys go into a trailer house and get warm. I'll stay with the truck." I crouched under the dash of the pumper and leaned against the fire wall to stay warm. *Our next truck will have a heater!* "Fire Station—217."

"Go ahead."

"Call the Young brothers and see if they can recover us."

An hour later I was looking up at the heat and gas gauges, and as I reached to switch the charging system to the other set of batteries, I heard a horn honking. I pulled myself up and was face-to-face with an oversized 4-wheel drive vehicle. Relief had arrived.

Albert, Jerome and Alvin came out of the trailer house when they heard the horn honk. I lowered my body to the ground and stretched my legs. 'Shorty' Young took my place in the truck and the rest of us climbed into the 4-wheeler. Even with oversized tires the 4-wheeler had difficulty maneuvering around and over the many snowdrifts. On the way back to the fire hall, Lloyd drove by the underpass, and the Suburban was completely covered. "Snow sure is deep," Albert said.

Anxious for details, firemen quickly gathered when we returned. I left Alvin to answer questions while I went to radio the Young brothers.

The firemen were discussing the fire and storm with Alvin when Jim Nelson and Gary Kurtz returned. As they began to warm up it was apparent Gary had frostbite and was a candidate for treatment. Alvin was leaning with his back against a steam radiator, and Joe Belford said, "Al's shaking like a cat shittin' peach seeds. Better get him to the hospital."

There was a flurry of activity as volunteers left on snowmobiles to relieve the firemen on the scene, and others began putting chains on the reserve pumper and the ladder truck in anticipation of another call. Within the hour a wrecker, used mainly for recovering semi-tractors and trailers, driven by Shorty Young appeared with 201 in tow. Rich opened the overhead door, and Shorty drove into the fire hall where his brother Lloyd disconnected the pumper. Noticing the surprise on our faces, Shorty smiled and said, "The wind let up, so we went and got her. I think the radiator is frozen—anti-freeze probably got too low. The hose is frozen, so we're loading it on a flat bed trailer."

Many events were to follow in the next 28 years, but it would be hard to top my first weather-related emergency as Chief of the finest volunteer fire department in the State of North Dakota.

CHAPTER 8

PIE, ANYONE?

Fire Commissioner Balzer Kurtz was making the rounds of the departments for which he was responsible and his final stop of the morning was the Fire Department. "How's it going?" he asked.

"Setting up the day's work schedule," Jerome answered.

As I waited for Balzer to come into my office the phone rang. "Fire Station."

"This is Darrel Maxson at the Lunch Box. I've got a fire under the grill."

"We'll be right there," I replied. "Com'on, B.K. Let's see what's going on."

As we left, I heard Jerome calling various firemen, and through the jumble of radio traffic, City unit 304, Jim Moe replied, "I'm on the way."

It was only two blocks from the fire hall to the Lunch Box, and I was surprised not to see anyone standing in the street or moving their cars. I did see Tim Kurtz, dressed in his shiny silver fire gear, enter the café. *He must have heard Jerome's radio call*, I thought. Pulling up behind the parked cars I ordered Balzer to, "Grab an extinguisher."

There were at least a dozen customers still seated throughout the small restaurant. Darrel saw me come in and gestured toward the grill where I could see a glow under the burner. *Same old crap*, I thought, *I wonder if he'll ever get the grill clean.* "Where's Tim?" I asked, glancing around.

"He went downstairs," Darrel replied.

Motioning toward the grill I told Balzer, "Put some powder on the flame." With a whoosh, powder went everywhere. Some trickled under the grill and put out the flame. The majority of the residue spread throughout the café and down the stairway to the basement, covering everything in a blanket of yellow. *Two hundred pounds of pressure can sure make a mess*, I thought to myself.

"What the hell is going on?" came a shout from below. Tim's heavy feet stomped on the wooden steps as he climbed up through the yellow haze. I could just make him out as he appeared above the railing. Nowhere in the room was the powder as thick as it was on Tim's silver clothing. His eyes and mouth looked like three wet spots in the middle of his powder-covered face. Seeing his brother holding the extinguisher he said, "Where in the hell did you learn how to use an extinguisher?"

"There was a fire under grill," Balzer replied sheepishly.

Everyone in the restaurant was coughing and gagging. Tim was doing his best to moisten his lips, and finally reached for an upended glass and filled it with water. Despite Darrel's effort at reassuring customers with glasses of water, the café quickly cleared out except for the four of us.

Having arrived in 304, Jim Moe came in the front door carrying an exhaust fan. "Wow! Who fired the extinguisher?" he asked as he started the fan, drawing some of the powder cloud into the street.

Since extinguisher powder can eat through vehicle paint and leave it spotted if there is moisture in the air, I didn't want to take any chances. "Grab the hose," I said to Jim. "We have to wash off these cars." Turning back toward Darrel, I said, "Call everybody that was here and tell them to wash their cars."

We returned to the station and Balzer handed the ten pound extinguisher to Jerome. As Jerome hoisted it to gauge the amount of powder used, a surprised look came over his face.

"Who fired it?" he said.

"He did," I replied, indicating the Commissioner. The handle was crushed and the safety pin bent out of shape. "Holy shit," I exclaimed, as I realized what had happened.

"Balzer," Jerome said, "you didn't remove the safety. You squeezed the handle and bent the pin when you fired the extinguisher."

I was watching Balzer as Jerome's comments sank in. He was completely serious when he said, "Would you teach me how to use an extinguisher?"

Later that afternoon Jack Voiles, a retired volunteer, came through the back door of the fire hall with a chocolate pie in his hands. "I'll cut the pie if you make the coffee," Jack said. He sliced the pie and served it up on paper plates. Whipping cream was piled high on the pieces and being naturally curious, I asked Jack, "Where did you get the pie?"

"There was a sale at the Lunch Box," he replied.

"Sure is good," Jerome said.

I don't think Darrel had time to bake any more pies, I thought, and scraping back some of the whipped cream I discovered remnants of yellow powder. I smiled to myself, knowing it was non-toxic. "Great pie. Thanks for sharing, Jack."

CHAPTER 9

THE MEAN OLD YARD COP

During the 1960-70's, activists protested the construction of missile sites in North and South Dakota, and the treatment of Indians on reservations in the United States.

Discontent was evident on many reservations, including the Fort Totten Indian Reservation six miles south of Devils Lake. Following the gunfight at Wounded Knee, a rumor saying, "We're going to burn down Devils Lake," was heard.

Discussion over coffee at the fire hall the morning of June 27th concerned the possibility of something happening in Devils Lake. Firemen were looking to me for a sense of direction. Even police officers who never came by said, "Just stopped in for a cup of coffee," and before long were asking what we knew about the rumor and what we were going to do.

"What can we do?" I asked. I knew full well there wasn't an answer except to keep our eyes open, and said so.

My tenure as Chief of the Fire Department was only six months old when an episode at Pine Ridge Indian Reservation took place. Needless to say, I was concerned for the well-being of the community and the constant barrage of questions regarding the rumor didn't help one damn bit. Teaching at the Junior College part-time prior to my appointment as chief helped me understand the feelings of the members of our local tribe. *I hope that'll help,* I said to myself. The only call we'd had since Pine Ridge was a garbage can fire in the alley behind the Eagles Club on 3rd Street.

Although it was my day off, I returned to the fire hall for coffee. It wasn't long before the conversation turned to the lack of manpower, and the fact that many firemen would be enjoying activities outside the city, making them unreachable in the event of an emergency.

Later that day as I puttered around the yard and contemplated taking my family to the swimming pool, my radio barked. "217—Fire Station."

"Go ahead," I answered.

"We've got a fire at the loading dock on Railroad Avenue by the Mayer Hotel. I'm toning out the volunteers."

Although this particular loading dock was important to some heavy equipment businesses around the community, we had access to another dock on the west side of town in the area where the old ice and roundhouse had been located. The Great Northern Railroad had a rail yard here in Devils Lake, and for many years all kinds of trains dead headed (free of encumbrances) here to be worked on or stored for awhile on one of the many sidings. Occasionally a steam locomotive with a shattered cab would be parked on the siding across the tracks from the loading dock.

The loading dock south of the Mayer Hotel was in the open and constructed of heavy creosoted timbers of various lengths and thicknesses. Ramp planks were the smallest, measuring 10x18 inches. The platform itself was constructed utilizing 2x2 foot creosoted beams. The size of the beams indicated the capacity of the platform to handle certain weight categories. The support structure was made of the same timbers, and anchored in cement. From the track side, supporting beams could be seen spaced every 10 feet the length of the platform. The openings provided by these spaces were known to harbor all kinds of activities, including sex and alcohol consumption.

Thank God, there's a 10 inch hydrant by Tubby's Gas Station, I thought, as I drove toward the loading dock and smoke-filled sky.

As I approached the depot from the east it was clear there was a problem. Brilliant yellow and red flames reached for the sky, and above the flames the oily, black smoke was being pushed up by the heat of the fire. A heavy hose line was already stretched across the street and the two men on the business end of the hose had their backs toward the flames. I blocked the intersection with my pickup, grabbed my gear, and jumped from the cab. It was clear then why the men were positioned as they were: the radiant heat from the oil-soaked timbers was overwhelming. From where I stood, it was hotter than hell!

To the east of the loading dock was a water tower. In the days of the steam locomotive, water was dispensed from the tower into a tender connected just behind the locomotive. In addition to water, the tender carried many tons of coal, and together they were used to produce the steam necessary to operate the engine. A large telephone cable above the fire was sagging toward the ground. *Going to cause problems for the south end of town,* I thought.

Past the hood of the Seagraves, I could see the heavy line filling with water. "If we had more help, we could stretch another line," said Don Erickson, the pump operator. "I've got plenty of hydrant pressure for more hoses."

"LEC—217, turn on the fire sirens. We need some help," I radioed.

The sirens began their donkey bray, and I was shrugging into my fire coat when someone shouted, "There's somebody under the dock!"

I headed for the loading dock with intentions of checking under the platform for a victim. *The hose would just have to wait,* I thought, and then I heard, "What do you need?"

Fire Commissioner Balzer Kurtz was pushing his way through the crowd and headed my way. "Help stretch another hose; I'm going under the dock," I shouted.

I ducked behind a water tower support leg to keep out of the heat and glanced behind me to see a couple of firemen, under the watchful eyes of the Fire Commissioner, connecting another hose line to pumper 201. *Good,* I thought, *we'll get something going now.*

The blazing heat from the oil-soaked timbers was unbelievable as I stepped into the open. *Damn it's hot!* I thought. Instead of running directly toward the loading dock from the protection of the water tower support leg, I ran out into the rail yard and then back north toward the dock.

Tilting my head and helmet for protection, I ran for an opening under the loading dock and after a few feet, felt a wetness surrounding me. It was too damn hot to look up. I could only guess that a hose team was trying to help by spraying me with water. The heat was radiating out over the tracks, and the flames were crackling from the timbers of the 150 foot dock as I crouched and scurried toward an opening under the platform. As I reached the opening, I glanced up and thought: *that's some fire; we'll play hell putting it out.*

I ducked under the dock, and immediately snagged my fire coat on a gas fill pipe that led to a underground storage tank across the street at Tubby's Gas Station. Working to untangle myself, and in a rush to get into the confines of the loading dock, I hadn't noticed the heat diminishing. *Maybe it'll be better underneath,* I thought, *if I can just get loose from this damn pipe.*

I was finally able to dislodge my coat and rescue rope from the fill pipe and crawl under the loading dock. I headed north into the semi-blackness of the loading platform and after about 15 or 20 feet decided

Damn, there's nobody under here. Backing up a few feet to where I could look under the support beams to the neighboring open space, I couldn't believe my eyes. The darkness of the adjoining elevation was broken by the flickering flames of dripping creosote. In the flames I could see a body stretched out as if it were in a coffin. Flaming creosote was falling on and around the body; next to his left hand was a brown paper sack. *"Holy shit!"* I said to myself.

I pushed myself backwards until I could crawl and make my way past the fill pipes to the adjacent opening, hesitating for a moment as I felt the refreshing spray from a hose line.

I'd seen someone across the tracks when I hesitated, and now that I was in the semi-darkness of the crawl space I looked back and recognized the round and dumpy figure of the yard cop known as Deadeye. He was watching the activity taking place above me, but I knew he saw me move to the next opening. I had learned to become suspicious of everything when it comes to unexplained fires, and seeing Deadeye gazing my way piqued my curiosity as to what was going through his mind.

As I pulled myself toward the body, the slope of the platform made the crawl space smaller. *Why in the hell did he go this far up?* I asked myself.

Finally I made enough headway so I could reach past the body and grab the sack. Peeling the wrapper back revealed an empty wine bottle. *Stands to reason, I thought; some people buy a jug and hide while they're drinking this cheap crap.* Although it was dark, the burning creosote provided just enough illumination for me to see where it had melted the victim's trousers and jacket. It sure looks like a man's shoes, I thought, and grabbing him by the ankles I struggled to drag him out from under the dripping creosote. I'm not kidding when I say it was the shits trying to drag a limp body backwards with clothing snagging on everything. I had maneuvered the body back toward the tracks about ten feet when I felt him stir. Pulling harder, I heard a muffled voice utter, "Wha'da hell?" Catching me by surprise and unable to rear back, I shouted, "What the hell you doing under here?"

I was both relieved and upset. Relieved he was alive and upset that he had placed me in such a crappy position. "Jesus Christ, wha'da hell, I'm burnin'!"

"No shit," I said, and with renewed vigor dragged his ass closer to the tracks. Damn I was mad. Now the adrenaline was pumping and I wanted to get him into the open so I could see who it was. He kept mumbling as I dragged him far enough back so I could crawl close to his head and see his face. It was Abe Redroad! "God Dammit Abe, what the hell are you doing under here?" I shouted.

"I hid up here so Deadeye couldn't see me. He's one mean son of a bitch. I had a jug once and he broke it on my head. Man, he's one bad dude," Abe replied.

It was hard not to smile at the forlorn figure in front of me. Abe had worked for me at the hotel. He was a hardworking individual when he had something to do, and went the extra mile to please his boss. Thinking back to when I first spotted Abe, I asked, "Did you start a fire under there?" "

"Yeaaaaaaah, I was cold so I lit a little fire."

"Christ Abe," I said, "its 76 degrees. Look at your clothes; they're melted and you set the loading dock on fire." Across the rails I could see the yard cop looking in our direction. "I think you're in real trouble now."

Abe looked across the tracks and immediately backed out of sight under the platform. "Don't tell him," Abe said, returning to a position directly behind me and out of sight.

"Why not?" I asked.

"He's mean; he don't like Indians," Abe replied.

I understood Abe's fear of Deadeye. Rumors had circulated for years about the abuse of Indians, and one individual always mentioned was Deadeye. Seeing Deadeye across the tracks looking our way reinforced my understanding of Abe's fear of the yard cop. From what I had heard and the fear I could sense in Abe's voice, that guy was a vindictive individual, and I needed to protect Abe from retribution. I doubt if the fire's radiating heat will stop him from moving closer if he knows Abe is under here with me. I continued facing toward the tracks watching Deadeye, and meanwhile talked loud enough for Abe to hear.

From somewhere above I heard, "Chief, you okay?"

"Yeah," I shouted, "I'll be out as soon as I finish checking."

"Tell you what," I said to Abe, "when the fire dies down, you come with me and I'll get you out of here. Move over here," I said, pointing to a heavy timber laying crossways as part of a large X which supported the track side of the platform. "I'm goin' to check more of the platform; I'll keep a watch on Deadeye."

Carefully, Abe moved behind the timber and pulled his legs into a fetal position.

The spray above had lessened as I crawled out and down to another opening under the loading dock. This time I used my pocket light to examine the far reaches of this cavity and didn't find anything more than some condoms, a pair of shoes and a bunch of brown paper sacks. *Probably wine bottles*, I thought.

Before I crawled to the next opening, I glanced over the edge of the platform. Thirty feet across the platform two hoses were working to extinguish the oil-fueled fire. Across the street a crowd had gathered and were shouting and laughing. I guessed by their behavior they had just come from the Mayer Bar or VFW Club. Comments were being directed toward the Fire Commissioner fighting to control the two-and-a-half inch hose line. Uneducated in hose handling techniques, he struggled to control the heavy water stream and look professional at the same time.

Across the tracks Deadeye kept looking toward the opening where Abe was hiding. Suddenly I heard swearing coming from across the street. Looking back, I saw Balzer sweep the crowd with a stream of water! "Hey," I shouted, "don't do that."

Balzer turned back, bringing the nozzle to bear once again on the burning timbers, and out of the corner of my eye I saw Abe leave the opening and run down the tracks toward the depot. *Oh, shit,* I said to myself, *Abe thought I said, 'Take Off.'* Abe was really moving but hadn't quite reached the water tower 50 feet away when Deadeye spotted him and stumbled across the tracks after him. You could hear whistling and shouts of, "Go!—Go!—Go!" from the crowd across the street. The two of them made quite a sight; Deadeye waddling like a duck and shouting, "Stop, God damn you, Stop!", and Abe doing his best to keep out of Deadeye's grasp, and running down the passenger ramp of the train depot.

For a moment I watched Abe run and knew in my heart that I'd done the right thing, and Abe would never be caught by 'The Mean Old Yard Cop.' I couldn't possibly tell anyone that a fire had been started under the loading platform because someone was cold. They wouldn't believe me anyway.

I completed my investigation of the remaining openings and found more garbage but no occupants. Toward the end of my investigation, I became increasingly aware of the quietness above me. Carefully I peeked over the edge of the platform, and much to my surprise there was only one hose operating. The other was being rolled and loaded into my pickup.

"Where did Balzer go?" I shouted.

"He just laid the nozzle down and left after you hollered at him," Harold replied.

"Hey, Chief." Pete Aman was waving from across the street.

"Com' on over," I shouted.

Pete and Steve Chepulis were linemen for the telephone company, and stayed at the Rural Fire Department. They were dressed in fire gear, and from appearances had been assisting our city volunteers. "Thanks for helping. How's it going?" I asked.

"Steve and I were bullshitting, heard the siren, and came to help."

"Looks like fire melted your cable."

"I guess we'll be getting a little overtime tonight," Pete replied.

"Do me a favor, will you guys?" I asked. "You've heard the rumor: 'Burn Down Devils Lake'?" I watched as they acknowledged me with a flicker of interest in their eyes, and continued, "You'll probably be splicing cable most of the night. Give us a call if you see something unusual. Word has it that something is going to happen, and the cops need additional eyes."

Smiling, Pete said, "Be glad to. They need all the help they can get."

It's going to be a long night for those two guys, I thought, looking up at the sagging cable. "Thanks guys, I hope nothing happens, but if it does, we'll have gotten some sleep."

Extinguishment of the loading dock fire had been accomplished as we were talking and the last length of hose was being thrown into the back of my pickup. I was turning to leave when Pete called, "Tell you what. We'll take a break every half hour and drive the streets and alleys uptown."

I'd trained Pete and Steve for over two years, and knew they would keep an eye on things until daylight even if they were done splicing. *Besides, they wouldn't have to punch their time cards until they returned to the office!*

CHAPTER 10

MAE'S BEAUTY SHOP—

IS THE RUMOR TRUE?

I lay in bed thinking about the loading dock fire. It had been a busy evening, and if there had been more firemen, someone else could have crawled under the dock. I wondered if Deadeye had caught up to Abe. It was pretty funny watching the two of them: Abe running down the cobblestones with Deadeye stumbling after him. I wondered why Balzer dropped the nozzle. Good to see Steve and Pete, they'll keep an eye on things for us.

It was 1:00 a.m. and I should have been asleep, but instead kept think-ing about responding to different areas of town, with regards to the rumor, (burn down Devils Lake), when a click from my radio indicated the open-ing of a mike for transmission of a message. *Oh, Shit!* Pulling on my boots and trousers I grabbed my radio and turned down the volume so as not to wake Mary, and headed out the door.

"217—Pete called and said there's a fire in Mae's Beauty Shop! I'm going to tone out the radio receivers."

Hurrying west on 4th Street I couldn't help but think about the earlier lack of manpower. On top of that, I couldn't get that damn rumor out of my mind. *What if this is the beginning of a bunch of fires?* I thought. *What should I do?*

"LEC—217, tone out the volunteer radio receivers again, and contact the rural fire department to come to the scene."

"10-4," dispatch replied. *One thing about Loydene handling dispatch,* I thought, *she'll get everybody going.*

As I got closer to the uptown area, the shorter distance between street lights made visibility easier and I was able to look into store fronts on my way to the beauty shop. *Nothing so far,* I thought. Ahead were the flashing lights of a police car and Officer Dallas Carlson facing my direction signaling me to stop. "I'm the only one on patrol," Dallas said. "Trade places with my patrol car and I'll get back to checking buildings." *He'll keep an eye on things,* I thought.

Across the intersection Joe Belford was positioning the snorkel in front of the two story brick building housing Mae's Beauty Shop. About 50 feet away, other firemen were hooking pumper 201 to the Huesgen Corner hydrant, and two others were dragging hose toward 204. Two heavy lines snaked their way down the Avenue toward the alley where 201 had dropped them off. *Looks like a better manpower turnout than earlier at the loading dock,* I thought.

Parking my pickup, I grabbed my coat and helmet and followed the hose lines to the rear of the beauty shop. The back of the building was set in from the alley about 20 feet and shared walls with the Gambles Store to the west and the Rexall Drug office building to the east. The basement of the building contained some used furniture and display racks; the ground floor housed the beauty shop, and eight apartments occupied the second story. A freight elevator at the rear of the building served all three floors.

Through the smoke, I spotted Wayne Brown, the department Chaplin, doing his best to hold onto an attack nozzle while tightening the straps on his breathing apparatus. At the rear of the beauty shop Harold Armentrout was about to strike the door with an axe, when I hollered, "Try the door knob." *This'll give us a lead on whether or not someone got inside and started the fire,* I thought.

Harold waved, acknowledging he heard me, and took out his flashlight. He passed the light beam over the door casing checking for pry marks. Grasping the door knob he attempted to gain entry. "It won't open," Harold shouted. He retrieved his axe and swung until the door splintered and moved inward.

From inside the building came a deep moan and suddenly, dirty brown smoke, accompanied by bright yellow flames, rolled out through the doorway. Caught off guard by the sudden rush of smoke and fire, Harold stumbled backwards and fell to the ground. Windows above him exploded, showering glass everywhere.

"Hot damn!" Wayne shouted, followed by, "Holy shit!" from someone on the Gambles Store roof. Through the smoke, I could just make out two firemen, who later turned out to be Jack Nash and Gayle Hovdeness, huddled against the wall next to the ruptured windows. *Damn that was close.*

My thoughts hurriedly turned to Harold's welfare and as I was approaching he rolled over and got to his knees. Slowly he got to his feet and looked himself over. "Are you okay?" I asked. I placed my hand on his shoulder as he looked up at the broken windows, and then to the ground around him. Pointing to a piece of glass sticking up from where it had been driven into the gravel he said, "Damn lucky I didn't get speared."

Shrugging from my hand, Harold put on his mask, scurried under the flame and smoke and took the nozzle from Wayne Brown's hands. Together they maneuvered forward toward the open doorway, their helmets tilted toward the rush of heat. Ducking low, I watched Harold peek around the corner and turn back towards Wayne. In just seconds, Harold opened the nozzle and began crawling through the blazing opening with Wayne close behind.

"204—How's it looking up front?" I radioed.

"Smoke's pretty thick," Joe Belford replied, "but the windows haven't cracked."

"They probably won't," I said. "The fire just vented out the back of the building."

At the back of the second story just above the flames reaching for their boots, Gayle and Jack were working a hose stream through an apartment window. *There's an elevator shaft next to that apartment*, I thought, *it'll be like a chimney.* "Watch out for the elevator shaft," I shouted.

Without taking his eyes from Gayle's back, Jack waved his hand and relayed the information. Upon hearing me shout, two additional firemen climbed the ladder and assisted with the repositioning of the heavy line. I watched as Gayle, always safety conscious, glanced back to make sure everyone was braced before reopening the nozzle. The force of the stream made a ripping noise on the walls as Gayle did his best to maneuver it toward the elevator shaft.

"217—204."

"Go ahead, Joe."

"A front window did collapse, should I send in a crew?"

"Not for a while; work from the sidewalk . . . there's a team working in from the back on the ground floor. You can send a team into the second floor. Be careful, Gayle's working from this end."

"10-4," he responded.

Brilliant flashes of color showed through the smoke as aerosol cans exploded inside the building. It was like the Fourth of July as a flaming can came hissing through the air and struck the cab door of the aerial ladder truck. *Oh shit,* I thought, *I'll bet Harold doesn't know about the elevator shaft.* I ran to the doorway and reaching in, jerked and pulled on the hose line.

"What, the hell?" came a muffled response.

"Come here," I shouted.

With one hand on the hose so as not to lose his way, a fireman came crawling out the doorway. "What's goin' on?" he asked in a muffled voice.

Surprised to see someone other than Wayne or Harold come through the doorway I asked, "How many guys are in there?"

"Four," he replied.

"Tell the guys there's an elevator shaft in the southwest corner of the ground floor."

"Harold thought the floor was shaking," the fireman responded.

"Pull him out," I ordered. He turned and disappeared into the smoke and moments later returned followed by the other three firemen. As Harold came through the doorway I grabbed him by the shoulder and said, "There's an elevator inside the back door, that's what was shaking." I was close enough to see the change in expression on Harold's face when I told him about the shaft. *This is bullshit,* I thought, *we need more radios.*

"217—219."

"Go ahead."

"Bill Eisenzimmer and I are going in the second floor, smoke's pretty heavy."

"Watch for Gayle and Jack, they're coming from the back."

Thinking about portable radios, I began formulating my appeal to the City Commission. If the Fire Commissioner would just show up he could see what we are going through.

"204—217."

"Go ahead."

"How's it looking out front now?" I asked.

"I just sent a crew in the front door a few minutes ago; they haven't found much fire, but there's a lot of smoke. It must be on the south end of the building."

Assistant Chief Walt Thiessen appeared carrying full air bottles. "How are we doin' for air?" I asked.

"We've used 36 bottles; I filled the cascade system yesterday, and the rural fire department brought up their spares," Walt replied.

Walt was a career fireman. Despite a 12 year difference in ages, he was respectful of my rank. We had worked together installing extinguishing systems in café kitchen hoods a number of times when I was a volunteer. Following the forced retirement of Sarge Reardon, Walt maintained his friendship with the ex-Fire Chief, visiting with him in his shop where he repaired locks. Because of the bad feelings associated with his departure, Sarge no longer visited with me, and Walt was instead confronted with, "How's the kid doing?" Others in their presence had told me that all Walter ever said was, "Why don't you call and ask him yourself?" Walt's allegiance was to me now, as it had once been to Sarge.

"What do we need more," I asked Walt, "radios or a high pressure compressor?"

"Depends on how much it costs," Walt replied.

I could always depend on Walt. We wouldn't be pissing money down the drain if he had anything to say about it. "Wouldn't hurt to get some more portables," I baited.

"Now you're talking," he said with a smile.

Walt half hitched his rescue rope around the necks of a half dozen empty air bottles and started down the alley. "Are you using 205?" I hollered after him.

"Nope, I'm using your pickup to haul stuff around. I parked 205 at the intersection, it's got better lighting."

Both crews on the south end had switched air tanks a number of times from the spares on the tarp at the rear of the building. Smoke was diminishing, aerosol cans had quit exploding, and walking around to the front of the building I noticed the crowd of onlookers had been reduced to a few individuals sitting on the curb across the street.

"218—What's your status?" I waited a few moments before repeating my call and was rewarded by Gayle's reply.

"We worked the upper elevator shaft and we're halfway down the hall. I don't see any indication of the fire getting any further than the elevator shaft," he replied in a muffled voice.

"219—How are you doing?"

"We're downstairs inside the shop. Tim said to pull the ceiling."

Since a 4x8 foot piece of this type of ceiling material was valued at $250, I advised, "Don't remove any more than you have to."

It was beginning to turn daylight when I realized I still hadn't seen the Fire Commissioner.

"LEC—217."

"Go ahead."

"Would you send an officer to Commissioner Kurtz's house and bring him to the scene?"

"We tried earlier," Loydene replied, "but no one came to the door. I'll have an officer try again."

Later inside the building, I was sifting through debris looking for the point of origin when I heard a voice say, "I thought the guys I sprayed last night were setting me up. I didn't dare leave home before daylight."

I looked up from where I had been examining the floor to see the Fire Commissioner standing just inside the door. Balzer Kurtz was a big man, had boxed Golden Gloves for years and was not to be reckoned with. I found it hard to believe that his spraying of water would have caused any serious retribution. If it had, I was sure he could have handled it. "Do me a favor. See if you can find Mae Keogh and keep her company until I get done," I said.

I resumed sifting through the debris-laden floor in the area pointed out by a blue/white heat line and discovered the plastic base of a waste basket. Clearing the area around the basket gave me room to empty the remaining contents for inspection. Carefully using my knife, I peeled back what remained of the wastebasket, and discovered the point of origin. Before disturbing the items, I took a series of pictures leading up to my discovery. On the way out the back door, I was met by Jerome.

"Everything looks good. Gayle was in all the apartments and the attic, and we only damaged a couple of pieces of the tin ceiling out front." Behind Jerome, Balzer was visiting with Mae Keogh, owner of the beauty shop. Seeing me standing in the doorway she asked, "What about the fire?"

"It started in a wastebasket at the back of the store."

"What do you mean?" Mae asked.

"I found cigarette butts in a wastebasket at the back of the store."

"You're shittin' me!" Mae exclaimed.

"Nope, that's where it started; I looked through everything. Appears it began smoldering three or four hours before we got the call. I'd guess the butts were part of the clean-up last night."

"Who called it in?" Mae asked.

"A telephone repairman working on some phone lines that melted during a fire we had last night." Continuing, I asked, "Was anyone living upstairs?"

"No, I haven't rented apartments for two years. What's going to happen now?"

"It's a mess, but we'll get you inside when we're sure it's safe."

Harold and his crew had been waiting for me to finish my investigation and now they came out through the back door dragging a hose.

A short time later Gayle's team began backing their hose down from the second floor and loading it into the back of 205 for transport to the fire hall. I took Mae and Balzer inside to where the fire had originated and explained to them what had happened. Mae admitted she had done the clean-up at closing time, and it was hard for her to admit she had deposited the cigarette butts in the wastebasket.

Watching 205 back down the alley I thought about the fire that had been fought, and the fact that despite various incidents, was relieved that I would be able to mark "no" in the injury column of my report.

Maybe that's a bullshit rumor about burning down the town, I thought.

CHAPTER II

LAKE LUMBER—

DUTY AND HONOR

Some fire departments receive their emergency calls by telephone while others are dispatched by a 911 Center. Large departments such as those in New York, Chicago, Los Angeles, etc. are dispatched by their own fire alarm dispatch centers. Emergency calls in many localities are dispersed by the use of radio traffic to volunteers, who respond to the fire hall and drive the various pieces of equipment to the scene of an emergency. Medium size departments have a duty man who responds to emergencies with individuals who live in the fire hall. Live-ins might be students at a local college, or have full time jobs in the community. Large communities have a number of stations and full time staff. Some metropolitan communities are served by all-volunteer departments. They utilize drivers from police departments headquartered in the same building as their emergency equipment. Upon arrival at the scene of the emergency, volunteers take over operation of the equipment and the drivers provide crowd and traffic control. When the emergency is over the police officers return the vehicles to the fire department and volunteers on duty for that week ready equipment for the next emergency. All maintenance work is done by local truck dealers and pump testing certifiers who keep a set of records.

When receiving a call the dispatcher at the emergency call center will ask a number of questions, such as: Who's calling? What's your address? What's the emergency? When dispatch is satisfied with the answers to the questions asked, emergency responders are alerted sending them on their way.

It was early morning September 19, 1975, when a radio call indicated a fire at Lake Lumber Yard on the north side of Devils Lake. Jim Fitzpatrick had reported the fire.

Walt said, "The thunder woke him up, and he looked out the window and saw fire by Lake Lumber."

I pulled on my fire pants and sweatshirt, and opened the door to a driving rain. As I hurried down the sidewalk to the garage I could see a large puddle of water in the low spot where the concrete driveway ended and entered the gravel-covered alley. *It's going to be messy this morning,* I thought.

The garage door was open by the time I got there and the cold seat of my pickup helped awaken my senses and prepare me for what lay ahead. I wondered if the neighbors could see my emergency lights as I drove away through the downpour. Lightning and thunder hadn't awakened me, but they might not have been so fortunate. It was a raging thunderstorm.

The sight of flashing blue lights penetrating the rain as volunteers responded to the emergency gave me some comfort: help was on the way. As I drove 10th Street toward the fire, I remembered what Roxy Caye had said years ago about thoughts that go through volunteer's minds when they are responding to fires. Roxy had said, "After awhile, everything becomes second nature. The duty man has to concentrate on driving, and what hydrant he should use. If he's responding by himself, his stomach is full of butterflies until he sees a blue light in the area. Up to then, he's not worried about weather; he's concerned about the availability of manpower; especially if he sees flame."

"What's Christie think about?" I had asked.

"His is a bigger role in the whole situation," Roxy had continued. "Besides manpower and weather, he considers exposure, protection, who's on vacation, equipment maintenance, water flow in the area, evacuation, hazardous materials, training the new personnel have had up to this point, etc."

All these thoughts were running through my mind as I turned at the 2nd Avenue intersection and drove north toward the wooden storage building. Fire was coming from the opposite side of the building next to the 18-unit low income housing apartment complex. From this angle it looked like fire was coming from the apartment building. I'd just crossed the railroad tracks when I saw 201 heading my way after dropping off his hose load at the front of the 75' x 200' structure. I drove around the big pumper and parked across the street from the lumber yard.

A couple of live-ins who had ridden with Walt were at the front of the building donning breathing apparatus. Seeing me pull up, the one named

Wade pointed toward the back of the structure. "It's burning inside the building," he shouted. I could just make out the flame coming from the wall, about 75 feet from the corner of the building. Suddenly it seemed the rain had gotten worse.

I radioed the Law Enforcement Center and asked for traffic control. It was customary in serious situations such as these to also contact the utility companies and to request that the ambulance stand by. They also had the capability to tone out the volunteers so all manpower would respond. "Were going to need more help up here; you'd better contact Rural. Have them come in on Josephine Street and park in the lot across the street from Lake Lumber."

"I'll be responding with 202," Jerome radioed. "I'm leaving Don Erickson at the hall."

"Park across the street, and take over as staging officer until Rural is on the scene."

The first unit on the scene had been a 1946 open cab pumper. It had dropped hose and equipment at the scene and narrowly missed me as Walt drove back toward the high service hydrant at the intersection in order to make full use of the pumper's 1000 gallon per minute pumping capacity. Help had arrived and was connecting the pumper to the hydrant.

All fire trucks have distinctive sounding sirens including 201 and 202. The snorkel had a definite growl, and could be heard from a long distance as it drove carefully toward the scene of an emergency. The aerial ladder was a light weight unit. Its 55' length had been placed on a farm truck chassis. Bangor, extension, Pompier, wooden and single length ladders hung or were sandwiched away on shelves under the aerial; the rattle of ladders played accompaniment to the fender-mounted siren. It wasn't hard to figure out where that unit was coming from. Considering all this and the fact that we only had one radio frequency, I could position each of the arriving vehicles using a minimum amount of radio conversation, thus avoiding interrupting fire ground communications.

This morning, I could hear the snorkel coming from the area of 5th Avenue, and the faster units 202 and the aerial approaching from College Drive. That rattle of ladders is sure distinctive. "204, when you get to the intersection, drop a couple of lines, hook up to 201. Bring your truck up here and put it between the lumber yard and Low Income Housing."

"10-4," replied 204.

In years to come, my communication to <u>others</u> would be of a more personal nature, basically using first names. I had found by using first names others on the scene heard us and knew volunteers with certain talents were arriving or were on the scene. Some of these specialties included electricians, plumbers, engineers, etc.

"203, park your aerial in the parking lot across the street from Lake Lumber and take a hose line through the front overhead."

"10-4," replied Tim Kurtz.

I shifted my gaze back to the front of the building when I heard Gayle radio, "201, charge our hose line." *Damn rain, I can hardly see what's going on.* At the office entrance I could just make out what appeared to be one of the firemen prying on the door with what looked like a Halligan Tool. "Hold on a minute!" I shouted. "Gayle, come over here."

Gayle had just finished putting on his breathing apparatus mask when I shouted. He reached out to halt the fireman prying with the Halligan Tool, removed his mask and came my way. "What's wrong?" he asked.

"Try to protect the file cabinets and safe. If the fire is coming through the wall, have your crew remove the records."

"I thought if we went through the office, it would give the guys some protection and get us further into the fire," he said.

"Good idea, but wait until there's a hose line operating in the lumber yard before you open the office door."

Gayle hurried back to the office door, trying to hold onto his helmet while he put on his face mask. He reached for the Halligan Tool and began prying on the door jamb. I saw him reach for the door knob, look back and crouch down; slowly, he pushed the door open. As the hose was advanced through the doorway, Gayle continued holding the door open and once the nozzle man and two other firemen had advanced into the room, he waved and disappeared into the smoke-filled office and showroom area.

To the south near 201 I could see the big chassis of the snorkel, and rounding the corner to head my way 203 had come to a stop. Firemen were busy toward the rear of the snorkel, and one fireman climbed down from the cab of the aerial ladder, went to the rear of pumper 201 and began dragging a heavy hose north toward me. The flashing lights of 203 grew in intensity as it came my way, and just before it reached the lumber yard turned into the parking lot across the way. A moment later 204 appeared and when it got closer, I stepped to the side; now I could see a pair of hose lines leading back toward 201. About 50 feet back, two firemen were standing on the uncharged lines, hoping with their added weight they would be able to assist removing the remainder of heavy hose from the hose bed of the snorkel.

Behind me someone shouted, "What happened?"

Over my shoulder I saw Tim Kurtz and said, "I'm not sure Bear, could have been lightning."

Tim had been with the department for over 20 years now, and had mixed feelings about my taking Sarge's place as Chief of the department. *Now is the time to change that mindset, and give him more responsibility,* I thought.

"Gayle's got a crew in the office. I want you to get a crew and take a hose line through the overhead door." I could sense his astonishment, but chose to turn back to watching through the office door. In moments Tim was barking orders and taking the lead in getting ready to advance through the overhead door.

From behind the elevator across the street 202 was approaching with Jerome in the front seat. Another open cab post-war Seagraves, it maneuvered around the aerial ladder and came to a halt next to me in the middle of the street. "Do you want me to hook up to Lange's hydrant?" Jerome asked.

"No, just park it and get to work; we can always hook up if we need it."

Glancing south again, I could just make out the dark red chrome-trimmed pumper glistening in the rain under the street light. With hoses leading every direction it reminded me of the squid's tentacles in Jules Verne's novel 20,000 Leagues Under the Sea. One of the hoses was still uncharged and was being advanced toward the lumber yard, where Tim was standing by the overhead door with an axe in his hand watching the entry crew drag the hose. It was about a 500 foot haul for the uncharged line, but within moments it had been advanced to a position next to the overhead door and personnel were waving back toward 201 indicating they wanted the line charged.

Tim reared back, and swung the axe, and chopped a hole in the overhead door. Working the axe he increased the size of the opening to about 2x4 feet. Now it was possible to see fire illuminating the inside of the lumber yard. The door began to rattle and bow as it pulled in oxygen to feed the fire. The entry crew struggled to position the hose and open the nozzle into the opening. One by one they began climbing through the opening. Suddenly my radio barked, "There's lots of smoke coming from the back of the building. I think the east door collapsed."

The first two firemen had climbed through the hole, and the third fireman indicated his mask wasn't working. Tim had been watching the entry crew as they donned their breathing apparatus and noticed the third fireman and his nervous behavior. He reached down and opened the fireman's air tank valve all the way and slapping him on the back, shouted, "Get in there, it's venting out the back. Don't open the overhead door," he continued, as he fed hose through the opening to the entry team. *It won't be long before he gets inside himself,* I thought; *he likes to be in the thick of things.*

As I backed away from the front of the building, I could see smoke and flames rolling from the rear of the structure. "204," I radioed, "an entry team is going through the front door, watch out for them."

Apparently Joe had depressed his mike key to answer, but everyone with radios including the Law Enforcement Center heard, "Oh shit, it's coming through the wall!"

Tim met me at the side of the building. Fire pushed through an opening in the storage yard wall toward the snorkel. "I'll get some help," he said, as he made his way back around the corner.

"Hold on a minute, look at this," I shouted. Cliff Ludwig was struggling to get his blocky frame under the snorkel boom. I almost wished I hadn't stopped Tim, and then I saw Cliff complete the maneuver and reach for the booster hose nozzle. In just seconds, the hole in the wall had doubled in size and now the snorkel appeared to be in danger. Stuck in the mud, there was no way to keep it from being scorched. With the fire getting oxygen from inside the storage yard, it was really rolling when Cliff turned on the nozzle.

"Cliff sure has his shit together," said Tim.

"Check the lenses," I said.

"Wow," said Tim, "it melted one of the cab lights!"

I looked up to where he was pointing and could see one of the revolving lights had stopped. Making my way through the muddy wheel ruts I reached into the cab and turned off the emergency lights which brought Joe to the front of the truck. "Who turned off the lights?" he asked. Tim pointed toward the cab light, and smiled. Joe looked up at the warped lens, pretended to be wiping his forehead, and returned to the rear of the snorkel and his control panel. By this time, Cliff had sprayed enough water from the booster nozzle that he was able to hold back the fire from getting any bigger.

I was back on the street when a radio call from Gayle indicated they had found a deposit purse and would be sending it out. "Everything else will be okay; the guys in the yard cool off the wall every once in awhile." *I hope Gayle's right,* I thought. Looking through the opening in the overhead door I could see flames everywhere. It still looked like a lot of fire to me.

A short time later Tim donned a breathing apparatus and headed for the showroom. I guessed that the big guy was going to sneak out to his entry team, and as I watched through the hole in the overhead door, I saw him exit the office door into the lumber yard storage area. There was no one with him; Gayle and his team were still in the office.

"218—Bring your team outside and take them through the south side entrance."

Hearing commotion, I turned to see "Ike" Burdick and some of his Rural firemen coming across the street. "Where do you want us?" he shouted.

"Spell some of our guys, and give them a rest."

Although the overhead door entry team was able to prevent fire from entering the office area, they weren't having much success getting further. "203," I radioed, "I've got some fresh bodies out here; I want to switch your crew." I wasn't worried about Tim, he hadn't been inside for too long, but his entry crew was something else. Each one of them had switched air tanks at least three times and by now they were feeling the effects of heat and smoke. Jerome had motioned toward a couple of firemen making up the recovery team and together they entered the lumber yard to relieve members of Tim's entry team. One by one the first team came out through the office door and started toward the railroad tracks where they could rest and drink some water. "How's it going in there?" I asked.

"Its one hot mother!" Jack Eisenzimmer exclaimed.

"Rest up over by the tracks, there's some grub over there."

One thing a fireman always needed was something to drink, whether it was water, coffee or pop. In later years, pop and water were the mainstays.

Looking up I saw Gayle's entry team was just leaving the office and dragging their hose around to the south side, when I heard a crash.

Through the smoke and flame I could just make out the south over-head door hanging at an angle. From time to time the smoke cleared, and I could see fire eating at the fascia outside the opening. *Must have burned off the rail hangers,* I thought. Hurriedly switching their air tanks, the entry team began advancing the heavy hose into the burning building.

As the hose advanced into the building there was another crash, and the forward movement of the hose came to a halt. Heavy black smoke had been rolling out through the opening, but for a brief moment following the crash I had seen what appeared to be a section of roof framing lying directly across the opening the entry team had taken to get inside. Once again the smoke increased in intensity obscuring the doorway. The re-covery team should have been next to the building ready to go inside, but when the crash occurred, they were by the railroad tracks talking to the members of the overhead door entry team. Hearing the crash they turned and rushed toward the building. I was on the verge of transmitting 'Man Down' when I heard, "We're okay, we're coming out."

As the entry team scrambled out I waited for Gayle to appear, and pulling him close asked, "Didn't you look above you when you went into the building?" I was pissed and thankful at the same time. Without wait-ing for an answer, I looked around at the firemen and noticed they had removed their air masks and were watching me. Turning back to Gayle, I said, "Take your team back inside and put out the fire!" Gayle looked like he was ready to respond when I added, "If you guys can't do it, I'll get a group that can, but we're going to put that fire out." The challenge worked. Once again they began their push through the door opening. Watching the hose slowly advance, I was glad to see they weren't hurrying this time.

Back at the front of the building I saw that Tim's crew had enlarged the door opening and Gary, Tim's son, was feeding hose into the build-ing.

"How are they doing?" I asked.

"Not so good," replied Gary. "I don't think they've moved more than 40 feet."

"They'll make some headway now; another team is coming in from the south. You aren't learning much out here are you?" I asked.

"No, Dad didn't want me inside."

"I'll talk to him. The only way you're going to further your education is with hands-on training. I want you to remember, what you're doing is important; it's the lifeline to the guys inside."

I watched Gary for a while and when the hose begin moving he turned and smiled. I gave him thumbs up and thought, *they're tying in with Gayle's crew now.*

"217," Jerome radioed, "there's a vehicle in here."

"What kind of shape is it in?"

"Completely burned out, even the tires are gone," Jerome replied.

The rain had stopped falling, and the sun was beginning to peek over the horizon. I found it hard to believe we'd been working for more than four hours and Mike Kurtz (owner) hadn't shown up to see how things were going, when I heard, "How's it going? Did you get into the office?"

Mike was a demanding individual. He owned the lumber yard, a cement plant, motel and a construction business. He had learned how to read blueprints from an older partner Frank Risovi, who had since passed away. Frank was the complete opposite of Mike in that he was pleasant and willing to listen, whereas Mike felt it was his way or no way.

I understood politics from the years I managed the hotel after dad died, and knowing Mike's following, carefully responded, "Here's your stuff," handing over the bank deposit material.

"Did you open it?" Mike asked.

"No, Michael, I didn't open it. And in response to your first question, it's going as well as can be expected." I felt I had gotten the upper hand, but I should have known better.

"I'll check this out when I get back to my office," Mike said.

Mike Kurtz stood around for a while longer without speaking. Eventually he returned to his vehicle and left. No sooner had he left, and Joe radioed, "217—204."

"Go ahead."

"The fire is out on this end of the building."

Hearing a metal-on-metal ripping noise, I looked east and saw the silver-clad figure of Tim Kurtz come through the opening dragging the fallen sections of overhead door. Now what, I thought as Tim removed his mask, looked around, and headed in my direction.

"How's it looking?" I asked.

"Good, we've just about got it. We'd never have made it without the other teams."

"What other teams?"

"The two teams you sent in to help."

"It was just one team, Tim. I gave them hell for not paying attention; they must have taken it personally."

Tim looked at me with wonderment in his eyes. "Sure seemed like it was two," he said. "Give us another half hour, and some fresh meat, and we'll be done. Is it okay if we roll up some hose?"

"Go ahead," I replied. As he was turning back toward the building, I remembered what I had promised his son Gary. "Hold on a minute."

Tim hesitated and then turned back to face me. "Gary and I had a little talk; he wants to get into the middle of things. Do you think he's ready?"

After a few moments, Tim lifted his gaze from the ground and replied, "Yeah, I guess so. A while ago he told me to back off and he'd take care of himself. It's probably time to let go."

"I'll transfer him to 202 and give you one of their personnel."

"No," Tim replied. "Give me a newbie, don't transfer a pumper man."

Tim turned and went to the equipment pile and grabbed a couple of air tanks. As the big Dutchman walked back toward the building, I couldn't help but wonder how I would have responded in that situation.

To the south a group of firemen had discarded their Styrofoam cups and were readying themselves for the final push inside the lumber yard.

It was 6:30. Entry teams had exchanged personnel three times and the fire was almost extinguished except for the tar-impregnated "Buffalo Board" (insulated fiber board). This large pile would cause us to return a number of times during the day. After Adin Mann's funeral we borrowed a tractor from Lake Region Grain and spread out the pile in order to complete extinguishment.

I was just outside the south entrance watching wrap-up, when a call from Jerome took me inside the warehouse to examine the burned up truck. *Surprising how little light there really is in here,* I thought, as I adjusted my flashlight beam from direct to broad. Stepping through the overhead door opening, the first thing I noticed was the lack of structural integrity at roof level. On the floor of the warehouse were a number of pieces of what appeared to be rafter material. Immediately to my right was the section of roof material that had fallen after the entry team had first gone in to assist Tim's crew.

Climbing over the debris and directing the beam toward Jerome, I could see what he meant by a burned out vehicle. I could tell from 40 feet away that there was nothing left of that rusty looking hulk behind Jerome. The roof and part of the wall was gone; hanging above his head were the remains of various sizes of electrical cable, often referred to as Romex. Through the roof opening I saw the remains of a power pole, probably what Jim had seen burning. *That's one helluva pile of debris,* I thought; *probably where the fuse box is located.*

"Jerome, would you see if you can find the fuse panel in that debris pile?" I asked.

A number of firemen had finished rolling hose for Tim and were close by, so Jerome was able to enlist their assistance with a wave of his hand.

Chances are it is at the bottom of the pile, I thought, *but with a little luck they'll find it.*

One fireman left and returned shortly with a scoop shovel and rake. Others began removing the larger items and on occasion a flash indicated a camera was being used to catalog evidence.

While they were working the debris pile, I began examining the truck. Already turning red from rust, it looked miserable. The hood and cab were dented from falling rafters; the wooden truck bed was gone; glass was inside the doors (windows rolled down); all that was left of the six tires were the stranded wire cores, and the gas cap was melted and hanging by a thread of plastic. Prying the hood up, I could see that fire had consumed anything combustible including the battery, leaving a puddle of lead that had once been the plates from the battery. The cab of the truck was also void of anything combustible. I had just about completed a second examination of the truck when I heard Jerome say, "We've got it."

Looking over to where Jerome was shining his light, I could see what looked like an ITT electrical panel. "Hold it," I said. I looked at their find and mentally measured the distance from the north wall to where the electrical panel laid in the debris. "Take some pictures, and be careful removing the wiring." Struggling to remove the panel in one piece with attached wiring, it was some time before they had removed all the debris. Eventually they were able to lay it in the open for me to examine.

I smiled, watching the firemen's eyes follow mine when I looked in various directions. I spent some time looking over the panel, the hanging cables, positioning of the panel and the remains of the debris pile where it was found.

Satisfied with my theory I begin to explain: "Holes in the panel indicate high heat, maybe thousands of degrees. It looks like lightning hit the pole, followed the cable inside and blew out the electrical panel. Hot metal flew all over, probably started a number of fires in all this lumber."

"How did the vehicle catch fire?" asked Jerome.

"Hot metal flew everywhere; I'm sure it went through the cab windows. The debris pile was burning, and it radiated heat toward everything around it including the pickup. Nobody recalls hearing any bangs, and the tires are gone. That tells me the fire had been burning for a while before we got the call."

I left Jerome and the firemen looking over the area of origin doing their best to understand what I had explained to them. Stepping out into a bright, cloudless sky, I heard what sounded like swearing at the front of the lumber yard. Joe was standing at the rear of the snorkel. Getting a better look I could see the snorkel stuck deep in the mud. Breathing a sigh of relief, I said, "Bring 202 over here and we'll pull it out."

In addition to being remembered as the day of the Lake Lumber fire, this day would also be significant in that a longtime fireman was to be buried. Salvage continued for a couple of hours at the scene, and 201 was returned to the station and readied for its secondary duty of the day, transporting the casket of beloved Adin Mann. The funeral service had just finished, and outside a pumper siren indicated a crew was on its way to another emergency call: a fitting tribute to the passing of this fine gentleman.

CHAPTER 12

THE COLONIAL HOTEL FIRE

Thursday morning, June 9, 1977, found me standing in front of the Colonial Hotel directing a rescue and suppression operation. The 50 room hotel was a three-story brick structure. The initial call had come in at 1:30 a.m. from the desk clerk indicating a fire on the third floor. Since a number of previous calls from the Colonial had involved cigarette burns in the carpet, Walt initially responded with one man and the mini-pumper.

The first indication I had of the fire that morning was when Walt contacted the Law Enforcement Center by radio. "LEC this is fire department 220, we are responding to a call at the Colonial Hotel."

"10-4; LEC clear."

As Walt's backup, I got dressed and started for the fire hall with intentions of doing dispatch duties. As the hotel was only two blocks off my route, I decided to do a drive by on my way to the station. Approaching the hotel from the east I realized that this was more than a cigarette burn in the carpet. A lifeless victim was hanging from a second floor window and there was a glow in a third story-window. "LEC—217," I radioed. "Alert the volunteers, ambulance and rural fire. Have police block off the area around the Colonial from Railroad Avenue to 4th Street."

As I climbed from my pickup I heard glass breaking and someone screamed, "Save me!" *It's going to be one helluva night,* I thought.

Just then Walt and Wade Christianson, one of the live-ins, came out the front entrance dragging a hose from the mini-pumper. "The third floor is on fire!" Walt shouted.

Hearing our radio conversation it was only moments before the remaining live-ins responded with 202, the inline pumper for the month. "Hook 202 to the Huesgen hydrant," I radioed. "Walt, I shouted, "take care of 202 until Nakken gets here."

Early arriving firemen had been monitoring the radio conversation on their receivers and were on the scene in a matter of moments. After tone alert from the LEC, the remaining firemen arrived a short time later. In less than ten minutes, all of our 36 firemen were on the scene.

I watched two firemen drag a heavy hose toward me from 202. Other firemen and live-ins were donning breathing apparatus and starting to advance a couple of additional lines from 202 to the front of the hotel. As the first hose line began to stiffen with water pressure, I looked toward 202 and saw a Montana-Dakota Utilities pickup park across from 202. Don Nakken climbed from the cab and hurried to the operator's panel of 202.

Moments later Walt come down the sidewalk and met up with Gayle who had just shut off the gas meter; they went to the mini-pumper and donned breathing apparatus. As they tightened the straps I realized none of them had ever been in a big fire. *Hell, we've never had a fire this big in Devils Lake,* I thought.

Being the leader he was, Walt grasped the nozzle while the rest of the firemen picked up the hose. Glancing warily at the blood running down the wall above their heads, they followed Walt through the doorway into the burning structure. On the way one of the firemen blocked open the entrance door, and I saw the team donning their masks before climbing the stairs. *Quite a crew,* I thought, *not one of them backed down.*

Hearing sirens I looked to the north and saw aerial ladder 203 turning onto 4th Avenue and from somewhere beyond came the growl of snorkel 204. *Oh shit! I remembered taking a set of batteries from the compartment on 204 for load testing.* I looked around and noticed the mini-pumper parked across the street. *Lucky the snorkel runs on one set of batteries, we'd never have gotten it started. We'd better hook up the mini to the empty slot,* I thought.

In moments 204 was being positioned at the front of the hotel, and when Joe climbed from the cab, I explained to him the situation. He sent Cliff Ludwig to get the mini-pumper and connect it to the empty battery cables. In the meantime pumper 201 had radioed that it was connecting to the high volume hydrant down the street at the Great Northern Hotel corner and would be dragging hoses to the snorkel.

All the fire fighting equipment we had was on the scene: two pumpers, a 55' aerial ladder and the 65' snorkel unit. During the two and one-half years I had been their chief, we had preplanned fire fighting activities at various buildings around town. One of the buildings we had discussed was the Colonial Hotel. As I looked at the activity taking place, I noticed two things out of sequence: the biggest pumper, 201, was second-in and the mini-pumper was parked next to the snorkel with battery cables connecting them together. Everything we had trained for, but didn't want to happen, is being put to the test. *We're all learning from this one,* I thought.

In order to avoid running over hoses, 203 had backed down the alley from the west. Tim raised the aerial ladder to the third floor fire escape, being careful not to collide with the power lines. "220—how's it going up there?" I radioed.

"We're at the 3rd floor landing," Walt replied in a muffled voice. "The fire is in the attic, and some of the ceiling has fallen down in front of us."

I was considering taking a defensive *'surround and drown'* stand when Walt radioed, "We're going to stay awhile."

Joe had the platform operator wash the blood from the wall before moving in to retrieve the body hanging over windowsill. The noise people made in the street behind us was typical of sidewalk supervisors. One moment they were shouting suggestions, and the next they applauded the firemen. The seriousness of the situation brought all types out of the woodwork.

From the middle of the street, I could watch both the platform and the ladder crew raising the Bangor ladder in an attempt to rescue the screaming occupant. As the ladder began its ascent, I could only hope it would reach the window in time. I saw Jesse the custodian standing in the crowd and yelled, "Get over here." He came running to my side and immediately started to explain what he saw from his room just before he hollered *'FIRE!'* Still shaking, he told how he saw fire coming through the door of room 304, pulled on his pants, and climbed down the fire escape. Motioning for Jesse to stay by my side, I backed up to get a better look at the third floor and saw fire glowing behind the hotel. *My God, it looks like the fire is spreading,* I thought.

The crowd suddenly shouted, "Don't jump!" The ladder had almost made it to the window ledge with a fireman beginning to climb it, when suddenly the fire behind the occupant grew and I heard **"Look Out!"** Firemen ducked behind the ladder as the subject became the victim. "Holy Crap, he jumped!" someone in the crowd exclaimed.

I'd never been witness to this before, and with bile moving upwards, I started towards the victim, and stopped. Firemen had begun gathering around him, shielding the view from bystanders, and I saw one fireman kneeling on the ground. Other firemen rushed from the alley where they had been throwing up and took their place in the outward-facing circle. It reminded me of elephants protecting their young. I don't think any Fire Chief could have been more proud than I was at the sight.

Earl came running with a body bag in one hand and a medical bag in the other. He unfolded the body bag as the crowd parted to let the ambulance through. I wondered just how many firemen would quit over this incident. *Dear God*, I thought, *we've only been on the scene for a few minutes!*

The crowd was quiet as the firemen loaded the black bag into the ambulance, turned, and finished raising the ladder to the broken window of 306. Two firemen could be seen climbing through the window of the third floor fire escape from the aerial ladder.

As the crew on the Bangor darkened down the fire in 306, fire began rolling out of the fire escape window just over Bill Eisenzimmer's head. Ducking low he continued spraying water through the opening. At the opposite end of the hotel, Cliff was climbing from the platform through the second floor window where the body of the first victim was hanging over the broken glass in the window frame. Ray positioned one of the floodlights to shine into the room, revealing another subject. In moments both Cliff and the room's occupant appeared at the window and passed a black body bag to Ray on the platform.

Sometime later Cliff said, "When the roommate saw his buddy, he broke down and wasn't a lot of help. I finally told him we'd have to get going, because there may be others who need help."

The snorkel was working through the different rooms when a shout from bystanders got my attention. "Save him! Save him!" At first I couldn't see what they were shouting about. Joe yelled, "I think they mean on the roof."

Sending the platform to the roof, I heard a reply over the intercom: "There's a nude guy up here and he just ran across the roof." I wondered how people on the ground knew there was someone on the roof. Looking around, I spotted Bill Witthoff leaning out from a third story window taking pictures. In answer to my curiosity, Bill waved down to me. Meanwhile the platform had come to the ground and Mike Reiger, the runner, was wrapped in a blanket and carried to a waiting ambulance.

"Look at his feet," Ray said. "He ran through melting tar and it looks like his feet are burned. He said he climbed the drain pipe to the roof and left his girlfriend in the room; apparently she decided to escape down the hallway. He wants us to look for her," Ray continued.

"Go ahead," Joe said, "but watch out for the entry teams."

"203, what's your location?" I queried.

"In the alley," Tim replied.

I met Tim coming my way and together we went back into the alley where he had spent his time as sector boss keeping an eye on the aerial ladder and two live-ins, Alvin Schroeder and Rich Klindtworth, who had dragged a heavy line to the roof of the Eagles building and were working the fire from there. The Eagles building was only 15 feet from the hotel, and they had erected a ladder bridge from one building to the other.

"Mike Reiger left his girlfriend and climbed to the roof and the snorkel rescued him. Even with the smoke detector alarming in the hallway, she figured she could get down the stairs," I informed Tim.

"Did she make it?" Tim asked.

"No, I don't think so. I was in front until they took Mike away in the ambulance. Tim," I said, "I'd like you to search the corridor when the fire eases up. I'll get a body bag to you."

Back in front of the hotel, I could see a hose line stretched through the doorway of the Latham Apartment building, which bordered the burning hotel on the south side. Jack Nash was at the operator's panel of 201. Ron had an entry team inside looking for extensions. Glancing back to the entrance to the hotel, I noticed Walt removing his mask. Hesitating for a moment while he wiped his forehead, Walt saw me and came my way.

"It's a mess upstairs. I left Dennis, Bob and Gayle on the landing." Following a coughing spell, he continued, "They'll be okay as long as the fire doesn't sneak in behind them. Ceilings are falling in both hallways."

"How's the air holding up?" I asked.

"Rural brought us some replacements. I'm going back to the Hall now and fill bottles."

For over five years Walt had been my mentor, and since Sarge had retired, he was a big asset to both me and the department. Walt was what I would call a pack rat; he was always hiding things. It was fun to see his reaction when he found someone using one of his supposedly hidden items. Upon recovering the item, a new hiding place was found.

With ceilings collapsing throughout the third floor, I was concerned about the welfare of Gayle and the entry team. Three times I tried to reach Gayle on his radio and not receiving a response I edged through the front entrance into the lobby area of the hotel. Directly in front of me a heavy line was winding its way to the upper level of the hotel. Separating the stairway and liquor establishment was a six foot corridor which led to a back exit door. Recalling my past inspection of the property, I crouched low to see if I could see the back exit door. At the back corner of the upper stairway I could just make out the doorway to the basement. The smoke was too heavy for me to see any further, and falling debris had blocked the door. Water cascaded from the upper floors. *With all the lines operating, it's hard to tell just where the water was coming from.*

I wasn't worried about the maintenance room in the basement; it only contained some tools and the boiler. Gayle had turned off the gas meter, so there wouldn't be any problem there. There was a shoe repair shop in the basement with an alley entrance and that could be a problem. *If the drain isn't plugged everything should be okay,* I thought. I put on my mask and started up the stairs to the second floor and met Gayle coming down. "How's it going?"

"Not worth a shit," Gayle replied in a voice muffled by his breathing apparatus mask. "Stuff is falling all over."

Just then Bob Possen, a live-in, came down the steps, with his warning bell ringing like an old dial phone. "I'm running out of air," he said, brushing by us.

Motioning Gayle closer I shouted, "Bring Dennis down to the second floor landing, he's up there by himself. When you get some time, have somebody check the basement for water damage."

Before I went back outside, I crawled up the steps to where Dennis was leaning back against the stairway wall spraying water with a big Santa Rosa nozzle. "The ceilings of both corridors are down and the inside rooms fell into the courtyard," Dennis said.

"Could you see anyone else operating?" I asked.

"The snorkel was working right over my head, and I could see spray at the north end of the street side corridor."

"I'm going up to take a look," I said.

As I climbed the steps to the third floor I heard a crash from above. When nothing fell down the steps, I continued crawling to the landing Dennis had vacated. Near the 3rd floor landing the fire was burning though the riser above the third step. *Can't stay here too long,* I said to myself. At the top of the steps a pile of debris prevented me from getting into the corridor area of the third floor. Retreating ever so carefully I returned to the second level and told Dennis: "The fire is eating through the step just behind where you were sitting. It must be burning under the staircase. I'll get a line on it—watch yourself."

Back on the street, I explained to Joe what was happening. He quickly put together a back-up team for Dennis and sent them inside.

An hour later the fire had begun to darken down and all but disappeared from view in the street, so I began climbing the Bangor ladder to the room of origin. Midway up the ladder I shouted to Gary Kurtz, "Is anyone working inside the building?"

He indicated both lines had been shut down, but Tim and Jerry Seibel, another volunteer, were inside looking for a victim.

I continued on into room 306 and illuminated the burn site with my flashlight. As I walked through the room I nearly stepped on a body hidden under debris near the bathroom door. Playing the beam over the bathroom and into room 304, it was plain to see this was the area of origin. I spent a few minutes looking over the scene and then stepped into the corridor through the doorway where Jesse had seen the fire. In front of me were piles of debris from the collapsed ceiling. The smoke was almost non-existent and my flashlight made it easier to climb over the debris in order to make my way to the corridor leading to the west. There wasn't much left of the west corridor; the majority of the inside rooms bordering the courtyard were gone except for a small portion where the hose line had managed to spray water. The floor looked pretty solid but still I tested it with every step.

I was halfway down what remained of the west bound corridor when I heard a crash. I turned to see Gayle picking himself up from the floor. "I don't think you should be up here alone," he said.

A few more steps brought me to the edge of a sloping floor which spilled into the void below. By holding onto an old steam radiator, I could see down into the burning courtyard of the hotel. No entry teams were in sight, so I radioed Joe and had him direct the snorkel stream into various portions of burning debris. I had been directing the hose stream for a few minutes when out of the corner of my eye I noticed Gayle approaching. "Get away from the edge," he warned.

Sensing the urgency in his voice, I started to back away from the sloping edge when suddenly the floor began collapsing and a crash sounded in the area below us. *No warning this time*, I thought. With one hand holding onto the radiator, I used the other to grab Gayle's outstretched hand. Once we were on firm footing Gayle said, "Holy crap, don't ever do that again." Suddenly the slanted portion of the floor gave way, dumping the radiator into the fire and debris 25 feet below. *That was as close a call as I ever wanted to have.*

I asked Gayle to take a crew into the second floor and close doors leading to the courtyard and see if he could find any victims. He replied, "Only if you get back outside."

"Thanks for keeping an eye on me," I said. Once outside I asked Joe how many victims had been recovered.

"I talked to Mel. He told me there were three still missing; that'll make six," Joe replied.

A flash of light caught my attention as Jack Zaleski, editor of the Daily Journal, snapped pictures. Later that morning I heard that Jack had spent the night interviewing witnesses and taking photos for that day's edition of the paper. *It's always good to keep the media on your side,* I thought; *they can do you a lot of good.*

The snorkel's 1000 gallon per minute nozzle had been placed on standby, and entry teams had proceeded into different levels of the building extinguishing fire in the remaining debris piles. On a shelf built into the Latham Building were two firemen placing dead pigeons in a garbage bag. It was silent testimony to the speed with which the fire had erupted.

A short while later Gayle radioed for a police officer, and Dallas Carlson, dressed in borrowed fire gear, went inside to photograph a victim reported to have her savings secured in a fanny pack attached to her body. After reviewing the scene and taking pictures, Dallas helped Gayle bring the victim down to a waiting hearse.

With only a minor amount of fire activity remaining, I directed the west entry team to check all the rooms and help Tim and Jerry locate any additional victims. Soon Tim and Jerry came down the alley carrying a body bag. "We've got the woman from the third floor," Tim said. "She was right outside the bedroom door." *That makes five,* I thought.

The snorkel and pumper 201 were busy securing their equipment and firemen were rolling hose when a voice at my shoulder said, "What do you think?" It was Detective Ken Feldner of the police department, wearing his ever-present gray/green fedora. Ken was well-respected in the community, and we had become good friends.

"Might know where it started," I replied.

"I put everything on hold for today," Ken said. "Oh, by the way, Dallas called and said there was nothing found on the victim he had accompanied to the mortuary. But, they were able to examine the party that jumped, and noticed cataracts. Dallas thought this might have some bearing on the situation, so he contacted the family. The daughter told Dallas that the victim's eyes were so bad, he could hardly distinguish day from night."

"Sounds a little exaggerated, but it explains why he couldn't see the ladder. Too bad. It was almost there."

"Just think what would have happened if you'd had a fire last week," Ken said.

Holy Crap, I thought. I'd forgotten about the State Firemen's Convention. *I can't begin to imagine what it would have been like to have three hundred firemen trying to help.* "I don't want to think about it," I said.

Ken and I continued to hash over what had taken place, and as different firemen made themselves available, Ken recorded what they had seen and done. After about 20 minutes, Jerome radioed that it was safe to investigate the scene, and Ken and I began working our way through the lobby and up the steps to the third floor. Ken was thorough; it seemed as though he took a picture every step of the way.

Moving some debris that had fallen since I had been upstairs earlier we managed to climb from the second to third floor by edging up the side of the stairway past the hole in the steps. "Here is where it gets interesting," I said. "The roof and ceiling areas have fallen into the corridor and by looking at what remains of the walls, you can see how the damage progresses down the hallway."

I was glad I had insisted Ken wear a pair of fire boots and coat. There were nails protruding not only from the debris on the floor, but from damaged plaster on the walls. Frequently I could hear Ken mumble, "Damn," as a nail snagged his boot.

"Look at the charring," I continued. "See how it changes in appearance; it looks like an alligator's backside."

"It seems to get worse as we go south," said Ken.

"I came through this area earlier to get a look at the fire in the courtyard and I noticed the door to 304 was gone. It was an old style six-panel door, probably made of oak. Under most conditions, fire would not destroy a door of that caliber in less than twenty minutes. It isn't a perfect science, but it helps figure things out."

Continuing down the hallway, we came to what was left of room 304's doorway and walked into what I felt was the area of origin. As I explained my thoughts regarding a mattress fire, I pointed to an empty water pitcher lying on the floor next to the bed. "You can see the bathroom door and frame are almost completely gone. The bathroom is accessed from both rooms, and the bathroom door to room 306 is open and still somewhat intact. When we go in there you'll see a clean spot on the carpet where Tim and Jerry removed the third victim's body. Tim said the doorknob was on the floor right next to her hand when they picked her up."

We followed the charring through the bathroom into the adjoining room, number 306, where it was apparent the fire had received oxygen from somewhere. As we went through the bathroom, Ken said, "There's a hole in the wall and the floor is open at the back of the bathtub." He took a number of pictures and followed me into 306, being careful not to step on the door knob. I hadn't mentioned it before, but this room seemed to have more damage than 304, and I mentioned this to Ken.

Listening to Ken helped me view it from a layman's standpoint. "What do you think of this?" I asked. "The mattress caught fire in 304, and thinking they had extinguished it with water from the pitcher, they moved into this room. They continued talking, smoking and drinking until someone hollered 'FIRE.' Remembering the mattress fire, the female opened the bathroom door and was overcome by smoke and heat, collapsing to the floor. The fire had already gotten a good start in 304 and was through the door into the hallway when something woke Jesse up and he was the one who hollered FIRE. Opening this bathroom door allowed the fire to get a fresh burst of oxygen, and assist burning out the rest of the door in 304 into the hallway."

I could see Ken concentrating on what I was saying, so I continued, "The male occupant broke out the window with that chair we saw in the street. The broken window added all kinds of oxygen and helped the fire eat away the doors on the bathroom and corridor. I'm not sure of the sequence of events, but I know the fire was through the door to the corridor from 304 because Jesse saw it, and you can read the speed in the charring. The draft assisted the fire up the hole in the bathroom wall and to the attic. It also helped the fire grow in this room, scared the subject and turned him into a victim."

"He jumped because he couldn't see the ladder?" asked Ken.

"We already know he had cataracts," I said. "Too bad; the ladder was almost at the window sill."

"I remember seeing the fire growing behind him," Ken said. "I don't know if I could have taken it much longer myself."

We reviewed in reverse everything we had discussed and arriving at the hallway were looking down the west corridor where I had been standing and Ken smiled, "I wouldn't want to be standing at the end of the hallway if the floor gave way."

"That's something I don't want repeated," I replied.

We traced the fire extension down the north-south corridor to a pile of debris at the junction of two corridors and the third floor landing. The sun was beginning to climb and now we could see how close the fire had come to burning completely through the landing and dropping Dennis into the fire. At the bottom of the steps we maneuvered around more debris until we could get into the bar area. Here we could see where the burning debris falling into the courtyard had spread the fire on lower levels including into the area where the stairway was located.

"Let's get some breakfast and compare notes," Ken said.

We were sitting at the rear of the Happy Hour Café eating breakfast, when through the back door came Deputy Fire Marshal Richard Radspinner. Tall and rangy, with severely chiseled features, he presented a very imposing figure. "You two have a funny way of inviting a person back to Devils Lake the week after the Firemen's Convention." Sitting on the edge of the booth, he asked, "Pretty tough night, Billy Boy?"

"Yes sir, it was real interesting," I replied.

"What happened?" he asked.

"I thought you could tell us," Ken said. "We've got our theory."

"I'll be back. Shouldn't take too long if I don't get sidetracked," Radspinner responded. "Don't release anything to the media; I'll do that."

About 45 minutes after he had left, Radspinner returned to review his findings. The waitress took his order, and he said, "I want you to tell me your interpretation, and then we can talk about the sequence of events."

Ken began reciting our version of the fire investigation, and from time to time I noticed Radspinner nodding his head in agreement. Ken finished the report by mentioning the party rescued from the roof of the hotel.

In response Radspinner said, "I noticed all the items you mentioned except for the drainpipe incident. The fire had to be tough on everybody, especially the firemen. They are to be commended and you can tell them that for me. It was handled well, but don't let that go to your head. Last night you experienced something no one ever wants. Too bad it turned out this way. Sprinklers would have saved some lives. Incidentally, I saw Mel Brodell moving booze from the back door of the hotel to his Corner Bar. He told me he was 'storing it for insurance purposes.' I bet he doesn't have liquor insurance, and he's probably going to sell it or pour it to the customers. In that place they probably won't know the difference. But mark my words, smoke got into those bottles and people will end up getting sick." From his pocket Radspinner pulled out a mini tape recorder and after adjusting the setting and volume played a segment of his interview with Mel. Ken and I listened as Radspinner explained the repercussions of what he might be doing, and the fact that the State Health Department was going to be notified.

Radspinner looked at me. "I was talking to your fire watch, Jim Moe, and he told me you still had another victim. I'd suggest you make some probe rods to get through the debris."

I left Radspinner and Ken and went to the fire hall to make a couple of probing rods. Gary Kurtz and Jerry Seibel were just finishing a cup of coffee and I beckoned to them to come back to the hotel with me. We made our way to the third floor and began searching the debris-laden hallway. We hadn't gone 10 feet when Gary Kurtz asked, "What does it feel like if you contact a body?"

"I would imagine it would be soft and spongy."

Gary looked at me and said, "I think I've found something."

We looked at each other and began removing debris, eventually uncovering the final victim. It was deathly quiet, broken only by a fireman saying 'The Lord's Prayer.'

CHAPTER 13

GUNFIRE AT THE

O. K. HARDWARE

It was a cold Monday evening in January 1978. The Webelos Scouts from Troop 31 and Rich Trenda, who shared scouting advisor duties with me, could be seen going into the City Fire Hall at 412 5ᵗʰ Street where they met once a week. Monday was my duty night and the time worked well for Rich and the Scouts.

Scout Secretary Robert Harveland, a freckle-faced high school sophomore and son of volunteer Gary Harveland, had just finished roll call when the fire phone rang.

"Fire Station, Oehlke."

"There's smoke coming from Bill's O. K. Hardware building."

"We might have a call, keep the Scouts busy," I told Rich.

"We'll work on the knots chapter," he replied.

I pressed the page button for the upstairs and when live-in Jim Moe answered, I said, "There might be a fire at Bill's O. K. Hardware. Get down here."

I put on my fire pants, grabbed my coat and helmet from the clothing rack, and started for the mini-pumper. The close quarters on the apparatus floor of the 1926 building which housed the fire department required that the mini-pumper be parked in front of the 65-foot snorkel. The smaller vehicle had to be moved in the event the snorkel was needed. Since each unit had their own door opener, opening and closing the overhead door was not a problem.

The trap door opened and Jim Moe slid to the apparatus floor; it was his duty night. "I got a call saying they saw smoke coming from the O. K. Hardware Building," I informed him. "They've only been closed for a half hour, so it's probably a false alarm." I threw my coat and helmet across the seat and climbed into the mini-pumper. As the overhead door opened, I drove out into the bitterly cold winter night.

The O. K. Hardware Store was only a half block east of the fire hall. The location was great for fire hall personnel as it was a convenient source of parts for day-to-day activities. Originally a Piggly Wiggly grocery store, the 60x125 foot cement block building had steel rafters and a pitch and gravel roof.

Smoke was seeping from the upper portion of the north wall. As I drove past the building I strained to see into the store, but the windows were already black from smoke. *Whoever called wasn't kidding*, I thought. "Fire Station—217."

"Go ahead."

"Sound the Plectrons, and turn the phone over to the Law Enforcement Center. Bring 201 to the parking lot on the west side of Bill's O. K."

"LEC," I radioed. "We've got a fire at Bill's O. K. Hardware; we'll need traffic control, public works and the ambulance."

"10-4; temperature is 10 degrees, wind is calm."

Tones alerting the volunteers had been silent for only a few moments when Jim came driving 201 through the intersection and into the parking lot of the hardware store. I could hear air hissing as the pumper approached and thought, *Shit, he forgot to disconnect the air connection at the station.* When the pumper got closer I could see a piece of the air hose protruding from the truck connection.

When he came to a stop Jim looked down from the cab and asked, "Why's it blowing air?"

"You forgot to disconnect the air hose." Reaching down I removed the broken fitting, stopping the unnecessary flow of air.

"I'll pull some hose; you hook up at the bank corner." (Ironically the bank now being referred to stood in the same spot as the Elks Building which had been destroyed by fire in 1969.) Climbing on the tailboard of the pumper I wrestled with the skid load, a packaged hose load used for quick attack, and finally dropped it to the ground. Dennis Olson came running across the street from the Youth Center Parking lot. "Go help 201," I shouted.

More vehicles began arriving and firemen were coming my way or heading to the fire hall where they kept their gear. "Grab that nozzle and work the fire," I shouted to two of the nearest firemen. As the men arrived at the fire hall, Rich Trenda and the troop of Scouts were eagerly waiting to assist them in any way they could.

"203—go to the south side by the back door. 204—set up on the north side and go to the roof." In moments the two units came into view and split from each other, indicating they had heard and understood my orders. Still more volunteers were arriving and in a short while, both units were set up and operational.

"217—LEC. Bill Sager (owner of store who had heard the fire siren), is on his way with the back door key."

"10-4. Thanks, LEC."

I was watching the hose straighten with water pressure when I heard a loud 'whoomph' and turned to see flying glass just miss the entry team as a large front window was blown out: the ammunition and gunpowder had begun exploding! The men ducked behind the block wall for safety. *That's all we need,* I thought. Dennis had left his assisting position at 201, and was working with the entry team at the front of the store. "Is everybody okay?" I shouted.

Each of them waved, and Dennis also held his backside, indicating he messed his shorts. *Damn! Humor comes from all directions.*

Satisfying its need for oxygen, the flame returned to the interior of the building, igniting and destroying anything combustible. From across the street someone hollered, "Ouch!" He was holding his cheek. *It looks like Ed Maley,* I said to myself. "Ambulance—217."

"Go ahead," said Earl Reed, manager of the ambulance service.

"Someone across the street got injured. Would you check him out? He's sitting on the curb by the bank."

"10-4. Ambulance clear."

The ammunition continued to explode as Earl, medical bag in hand, ran to where Ed Maley was sitting on the curb in front of the bank. Earl knelt in front of Ed and began examining his face. After a few moments, Earl suddenly jerked and looked over his shoulder. As he stood up, I realized he must have been hit, too. He glanced toward me. I couldn't help but smile as he shook his fist at me and then pointed to Ed's face and towards his own back. I just shrugged my shoulders and threw up my hands. What could I do, put out the fire? We're working on that as you're waving your fist at me.

While I had been watching Earl and Ed, Jerome had gathered a crew and begun hand jacking hose from 201 to 204. Tim's crew was pulling hose from 201 and dragging it to the south side of the building. Two firemen came around the corner of the building carrying the Quickie Saw from 204, and ducking low under the windows they hurried to the rear of the building. Police officers across the street were clearing the area of bystanders. They'd leave momentarily and return after the police had moved on. *They don't realize the danger they could be in,* I thought.

Two uncharged hose lines led from 201 to the Snorkel. Two charged lines led to the front and rear entry teams. The front entry team was flowing water, and the rear team was forcing entry through the rear door. The front team had split their heavy line into two attack lines, and was working them through the front entrance. That left one unused discharge on 201. *We'll keep 202 in reserve for the time being,* I thought.

Although I couldn't see the front team, the hose hadn't advanced, and the ammunition and aerosol cans kept exploding. *They just couldn't reach the opposite wall,* I thought.

"203—217."

"Go ahead," said Tim.

"How's your team doing?"

"They're working into the doorway but it's a mess. Can you stop that ammunition from exploding?"

"I'll see what we can do," I replied.

Coming from the west I saw Officer Dallas Carlson escorting Bill Sager to the scene. "Bring him over here," I shouted to Dallas.

"Did you notice anything unusual today?" I asked the store owner.

"We noticed a smoke smell all day."

I could hardly believe my ears! "Why didn't you call?"

"Remember a couple of times when we called you over, and the smell came from the incinerator at Super Valu? I figured it was the same thing, and didn't want to bother you. When it came time to lock up," Sager continued, "I turned on the night lights, locked the door, and went home for supper. I just blew it off. I'm sure sorry <u>now</u> that I didn't call."

"Why don't you have a seat in a patrol car and stay warm. We'll handle the fire, and when we get inside I'll be able to find you."

We'd been fighting the fire for 45 minutes when I heard 204 radio 203 and indicate they were going to ventilate the roof area. "Looks soft and spongy, but the tar isn't bubbling."

"Joe," Tim called, "don't let anyone on the roof."

A few minutes later I heard over my portable, "Oh shit, the roof collapsed."

"218—217."

"Go ahead."

"Get together with Walt and set up the monitor nozzle at the front entrance of the store. We've got to get water into the sporting goods area."

"10-4."

"Fire Station—218."

"Go ahead," replied Digger.

"Have the Scouts bring the monitor trailer over here behind the snorkel."

"They heard you, and they're on their way."

Rich Trenda and eight Scouts quickly appeared, wheeling the trailer into the hardware store parking lot. Gayle and Walt took over and struggled to position the monitor in front of the store, keeping their backs to the damaged windows and exploding ammunition. Gayle removed a hose line from the snorkel, and the front entry team hand jacked a hose from 201, connecting them to the monitor.

"I'm sure glad you put the monitor on a trailer, it's a lot easier to move," Gayle said to Walt.

"Had to," Walt replied. "It's too heavy to lug around on its own."

"Come here, Dennis," Walt said. Dennis Olson had been a volunteer for over two years, broad shouldered and easy going, he was rapidly gaining the respect of the old timers. As I listened, Walt explained to Dennis the intended use of the big nozzle. After a few minutes he stepped back and said, "It's all yours. Don't hurt anybody." Walt gave a 'thumbs up' signal to 201. The hoses filed with water and once it began rushing from the nozzle, Dennis appeared to relax.

"All right!" he exclaimed. Within about five minutes, the fire diminished and the smoke changed color. "See how far you can get into the building - I'll raise the nozzle," Dennis told the entry team.

Suddenly it got quiet. I looked at Walt, and saw the biggest smile you could imagine. The ammunition had stopped exploding!

"What do you think about attaching another hose to the monitor?" Walt asked.

"Sounds good to me. Tell Dennis and Gayle what you're planning."

Walt called Gayle on his portable: "218—220."

"Go ahead."

"I'm going to get a two-and-a-half inch line and attach it to the monitor."

"10-4, I'll be right there to help."

Moments later Walt and Gayle brought fittings from 201 and split the entry team's hose with a two-and-a-half inch wye. Reconnecting the entry team's lines allowed them to operate when the big nozzle was shut down. Walt stood and waved toward 201 and all the hoses filled with water. The big nozzle began moving water once again: *750 gallons a minute*, I thought. *That's a lot of water coming from one nozzle.*

Setting up the monitor was a good idea, and it wasn't long before control was called, and all I could hear was the rushing of water from the monitor nozzle striking debris inside the hardware store. Times had changed. I remembered when only four people on our department knew how to operate the snorkel, and the firemen wore painting masks for protection. All we ever practiced was climbing ladders and flowing water.

"217—Steve."

"Go ahead."

"We've got a pile of batteries and a lot of damage in back. I thought you might want to take a look."

"10-4, I'm on the way."

Hearing the radio activity, LaVern Bertsch came jogging from 201 and asked, "Can I go with you?"

"Sure, maybe we can both learn something."

We walked towards the rear of the building, examining the exterior before we went inside. Tim appeared to be standing guard near the open doorway. "Did you force the door?" I asked.

"Yeah, we used the saw." Suddenly I could picture Bill Sager's dismay when he saw the damaged door as I remembered the radio call stating he was on his way with a key.

LaVern and I moved past Tim into the debris-laden area where we met up with Steve. "This looks like it got pretty hot," he said.

Hearing the monitor nozzle moving around, LaVern said, "Joel (a probie) better not get careless with that stream." (A probie was a would-be volunteer, on probation.)

"I thought Dennis was operating the monitor."

"He was, but as I went by I saw him switch places with Joel."

LaVern and I started digging through the debris pile when suddenly Steve shouted, "The monitor's moving!"

"Gayle, get to that monitor, it's moving toward us," I radioed.

Moments later the flow of water ceased. "Sorry about that," radioed Gayle.

"Check with Walt," I continued. "Maybe we can wrap up some hose before it freezes."

The light from 204 shining through the hole in the roof did little to illuminate more than the pile below the hole. Tim left and returned with two large battery-powered floodlights. With the added lighting it was easy to see the spauling of the concrete floor, the burn pattern on the wall, and wire hanging from a warped roof rafter. According to the patterns it wasn't difficult to understand this was the area of origin. Now we had to find the point of origin.

"LaVern, would you go and get Bill Sager dressed in fire gear and bring him in here?" LaVern returned shortly with a subdued Bill Sager. I had to smile; he was outfitted from top to bottom in gear two sizes too large which only made him look more defeated.

"Sorry about the back door," I said. "What was in this area?"

"We had a big display of batteries and chargers here; I ran an extension cord over to a wall outlet above the ceiling."

I looked up at the hole in the roof and the adjoining steel rafters. "What do you think?" I asked LaVern.

"I'd like to get a look at that extension cord; maybe we can find something before it gets too cold and freezes."

LaVern and Steve brought in a ladder from the aerial and placed it up to the ceiling. As LaVern climbed, Steve held the bottom of the ladder. While LaVern worked from the ladder, I assessed my surroundings, and saw the entry teams putting out spot fires. It had gotten dark shortly after we received the fire call, and they had set up temporary lighting when the monitor operation was halted.

"217—219."

"Go ahead."

"We cleared a path to the sporting goods area. What do you want us to do?" asked Jerome.

"I'll bring Bill Sager to you. Take some pictures of the area, racks and display case, and help him secure and inventory the firearms."

"10-4." Jerome later told me there had been a fair amount of curiosity as to what was going to happen to the firearms. When he told them they were being turned over to the Alcohol, Tobacco and Firearms people, the curiosity disappeared.

Bill Sager and I walked around the building and as we came through the front entrance, I noticed the front entry team working toward the back of the store. Jerome was at the display counter taking pictures. We went to the display case and weapons rack to check for clean spots where items might have been removed. Not noticing anything out of the ordinary, I left Bill Sager with Jerome and Gayle and returned to the rear of the store. When I came through the back entry from the outside, LaVern looked down from a rafter and said, "This cord doesn't look good."

"What color is it?"

"I can't say for sure. Maybe I can find something over by the wall where it looks like it terminates in an outlet." LaVern climbed down from the rafter and he and Steve moved the ladder over to the north wall. Again LaVern climbed the ladder. *I hope this is the last time*, I thought; *things are icing up.*

Just then a generator started behind me and I turned to see Tim setting up a light stand. He adjusted the halogen light so it shined on the dirty black roof structure. This helped absorb the glare so it wouldn't shine in LaVern's eyes.

"There's exposed wood framing on the steel beams," LaVern said. "Above the debris pile is a 2x4 gone for what looks like eight or more feet to the north, and two of the steel beams are warped."

Concern showed on Steve's face as LaVern reached precariously for the cord. Clipping off a piece of cable, LaVern returned to a safer and more realistic position on the ladder, and Steve breathed a sigh of relief. "The cord looks like it might be orange," LaVern informed us. "I'll bring down a piece. Did you find any plug-ins?"

"No, not yet," I replied.

"The cord was orange," a voice behind me said. "I plugged in a couple of cheaters and some battery chargers, so I didn't need more extension cords."

Bill Sager was standing just inside the back doorway. "Did you check to see the amperage of the cord?" I asked.

"No," he replied, "but the chargers only draw a few amps."

LaVern came down the ladder with what appeared to be about 10 feet of the extension cord in his hand. "It looks like it was overloaded," he said.

As LaVern held the cord in the light, I could see holes in the jacket. "All we need now is verification," I said. "Help me find the cheaters and the end of the extension cord so we can wrap this up. Everyone's freezing!"

We were digging in the debris pile when Jerome came in the back door carrying the camera. LaVern explained what pictures he needed, and supported the ladder for Jerome as he climbed to take the photos.

I found two cheaters. "Here are the cheaters and there's wire attached to each side."

Bill Sager kept digging where I had recovered the cheaters and after a few minutes of careful searching said, "I found a battery charger." We found a clean spot and laid the cord, cheaters and battery charger out, and took more pictures.

I looked at Bill. "How many chargers did you have plugged in?"

He returned my gaze and replied, "Six."

Motioning toward the various items we had laid out on the floor, I explained: "Holes in the jacket of the cord, six battery chargers, and a couple of cheaters. Appears the cord was overloaded. I would say we've found the origin."

"If that's the case, why did the fire start in the roof?" Bill asked.

"The overheated extension cord burst in the ceiling and ignited the 2x4 holding the attachments for the suspending ceiling. That's why you smelled smoke. I bet the ceiling fell in and started the display on fire right after you shut the front door.

"Where's Probie?" I asked Jerome after I returned to the fire hall.

"I sent him over for Fire Watch until one o'clock."

"I hope the kid works out," I said. "I guess time will tell."

CHAPTER 14

ST. MARY'S ACADEMY—

END OF AN ERA

It was a bright, sunny school day in April of 1979 when the phone rang at fire department headquarters saying the upper floor of the St. Mary's Academy building was full of smoke. St. Mary's was a four-story Catholic High School located at 1125 7th Street, just east of Mercy Hospital. The school was only a small portion of the three-by-four block area. The remainder of the property contained Mercy Hospital, St. Mary's Convent, Lake Region Clinic, St. Joseph's Elementary School, The St. Mary's Knights football field, and 60 acres of cropland.

As 202 circled the school to the parking lot at the rear, I continued looking up at the third and fourth floor windows for signs of fire. When 202 came to a halt at the back entrance, the entry team donned breathing apparatus with intentions of advancing a hose line into the school building. Arriving volunteers attached 5-inch soft suction from the hydrant at 7th Street and 12th Avenue to snorkel 204, which was being positioned in the driveway to the east of the building. A large portion of the hose load from 202 had been off loaded and Dan Dosch was busy attaching the hose to a discharge on 204.

I noticed Dennis Olson looking up at the third and fourth floor windows. "What do you think?" I asked.

"Should be able to reach the fourth floor with the skid load," Dennis replied. The practice of estimating hose lay and the knowledge of the building's interior would prove valuable as the wye ended up in a satisfactory position on the second floor landing, giving the entry team more than enough hose to reach the attic and adjoining rooms.

I grabbed and donned the remaining breathing apparatus from 202 and followed Dennis and Dan into the school. "204," I radioed.

"Go ahead," replied Ray Eisenzimmer.

"Check the rooms on the third and fourth floors," I ordered. The three of us climbed the stairway and had just reached the third floor landing when Ray replied.

"217—Third floor looks good; fourth floor windows are black and smoke is seeping past the window casings."

Hearing a commotion, I turned to see a group of volunteers carrying forcible entry equipment and a hose line. "You guys follow us and drop off to check the third floor; we're going to the fourth," I shouted.

Above me Dan said, "Follow me, I know the way."

I was midway up the steps feeding hose when it stopped moving and I heard, "Dammit, I thought you knew where you were going!"

"I went to school here all my life; I know where we're goin'," another voice responded.

"You don't know shit, we're in a closet!"

"Find the door and get in the room," I shouted.

Now I was able to distinguish between the voices and heard Dennis order, "Give me the axe, I'll find a door." There was a 'thunk' as something heavy struck the floor.

"Watch out where you're throwing that damn thing!" Dennis exclaimed.

"I can't see shit, the smoke's too thick," Dan shouted. *Sounds like someone's a little frustrated*, I thought to myself.

I had to admit that fear sometimes promoted humor among firemen, and I was anxious to find out what else was transpiring among the team members. Removing a glove I felt each step and riser for any indication of heat and continued climbing to the fourth floor landing. I had just reached fourth floor when my radio squawked. "217—204. A window blew out on the fourth floor; lots of smoke, no flame."

"Don't turn on your nozzle, we've got an entry team coming in on your side," I warned. Trying to see through the smoke reminded me of that old saying, 'You could cut it with a knife.'

Back at the third floor level, someone shouted, "I found Sister Oliver's parakeet." *Holy shit, what now*, I thought.

Although I couldn't see what was happening down the hall, I could imagine the door to the classroom splintering as the sound of an axe rang down the hallway. *Why was the door locked?* I wondered.

For a moment the chopping stopped, and then I heard a lath and plaster ripping sound. The chopping sound began once again and looking down the steps I could see the smoke settling further below me. Suddenly the chopping ceased. "Move the hose!" Dennis shouted. I heard a grunting noise and felt the hose I had been resting on attempt to move.

I reached behind me to pass them more hose and the smoke that had been building below me lightened up and was moving upwards. *Must be going out the window.*

From the third floor level someone announced, "Looks good up here."

"Come here and back us up," I shouted. A few moments later three volunteers struggled past, dragging their hose.

"217—204," my radio squawked. "The smoke's really rolling out the window. Still don't see any flame."

"Sure is a narrow doorway," someone said.

As the smoke began to clear, I crouched low and made my way down the hall. I had just reached the opening when I heard, "How in the hell did the curtains catch fire?"

"I don't know," was the response. "The fire sure made a mess out of this classroom."

Visibility continued to improve as smoke rushed by me through the opening in the wall. *What the hell! Why didn't they open the door?*

"You guys work to the right," Dennis said, "we'll go north."

Upon hearing a distinctive sound I radioed, "204—217, what's with the glass breaking?"

"Someone broke out a window on the south side," Jim Meyers replied from the basket of 204. With the additional window removed it was only a few minutes before I was able to see desks in disarray and debris scattered all over the room.

"How's it lookin'?" I shouted into the room.

"I think we've got it," Dennis replied.

"Send some guys up to check the attic," I ordered.

Almost immediately a helmet-covered head appeared through the access hole followed by two others and the hose they had advanced into the room. As soon as the hose was free of the opening, I crawled into the classroom to better evaluate the situation. Just as I cleared the opening and was beginning to stand, I heard cheering from outside the school building. The smoke had cleared enough so that I could see Dennis Olson turn his head and say to his entry crew, "Do you think they're cheering because they'll be able to get back to class?"

"I don't think so," replied Dan.

"204—Take out another window," Dennis shouted to Jim in the basket of 204.

With a third window space open, it wasn't long before the only smoke remaining in the room was from smoldering debris that Dennis and Dan were attempting to extinguish. Except for an occasional spurt of water, the only other sound I heard was the footsteps of volunteers in the attic checking for fire extension.

As I examined the room, my gaze returned to the opening in the wall. I was about to comment on my discovery when Dennis said, "Dan, do you see where the door is?"

"Yes," Dan replied.

"You led us right by the door into the closet."

"I <u>thought</u> I knew where I was going," Dan said. In order to cover his butt, he continued, "<u>You</u> chopped the hole in the wall, and it's only two feet away from the doorway!"

"217—203. Looks good up here in the attic."

"Okay, we'll start wrapping up; leave someone in the building for a fire watch," I ordered.

Because school fires and fatalities are required to be reported to the Fire Marshal's office, I called Loydene and asked her to contact Bismarck for an investigator. Later that afternoon, Deputy Fire Marshal Radspinner arrived and together we climbed the stairs to the fourth floor of St. Mary's Academy. The first comment he made as we approached the classroom was, "I see you couldn't find the door!"

"Yeah, the smoke was pretty thick. One of the firemen thought he knew his way around, and led the entry team into a closet."

"I bet he'll have a hard time living that down," Radspinner replied. "Let him know it happens to the best."

We spent an hour going over the layout and damage to the classroom. "Somebody started the curtains on fire," Radspinner declared. "Work up your report and indicate suspicious origin."

This was the beginning of the end of St. Mary's Academy. A young man confessed to setting the fire after he was discovered setting another fire in a classroom of St. Joseph's Elementary School where high school students had been transferred for the rest of the school year.

The cheering we heard was from the students when Jerome Hoffart appeared at the 7th Street entrance carrying Sister Oliver's bird cage containing the parakeet named 'Tillie.'

A number of years later, Gary Stenson, who had been born and raised in Devils Lake, purchased the building and remodeled it into apartment units, and the facility was appropriately named 'Academy Park Apartments.'

CHAPTER 15

PICRIC ACID AND

ST. MARY'S ACADEMY

Following the closure of St. Mary's Academy after the fire in 1979, classroom chemicals, including a number of brown bottles containing Picric Acid, were inventoried and eventually moved to other educational facilities within the school district. The danger of handling this particular acid was spelled out in a notice I had recently received from the State Health Department. One of the specific concerns was the removal of the screw top lid. If encrusted with white crystals, the friction could result in an explosion, causing injury or death. I was not surprised when I received a call from Oliver Meer, St. Mary's Academy, requesting assistance in getting rid of their containers of Picric Acid. "Chief, is there someone I could contact in order to dispose of these chemicals?"

I had been dealing with explosives for a number of years, even instructing others on how to make and dispose of explosives. If situations arose, I would attempt to handle the materials myself, so as not to expose others to danger. Because of our involvement in explosives and hazardous materials, the care of the brown Picric Acid bottles became my responsibility until they were disposed of or turned over to another legal jurisdiction.

Discovery of the brown bottles and subsequent disposal of them introduced me to a lifelong friend Bill Byram, District Commander of the North Dakota State Highway Patrol. I had dialed up police headquarters, and was directed to the highway patrol office. The answering party said, "You've got to be kidding me!" when I explained my situation.

"We received a bulletin from headquarters," he said, "and it indicated there could be lots of Picric Acid in old chemistry classrooms. Are there any crystals showing?"

"Yep," I said, "lots of them; inside the jar and around the lid."

"What do you want to do?" he asked.

"I haven't the foggiest idea. I just want to get rid of it as soon as possible."

"I'll see what we can do," he replied, and hung up the phone.

I returned Mr. Meer's call and told him we were putting things together and we'd meet the next day.

The next day went by, and early on the morning of the third day, a Highway Patrol vehicle pulled up to the back door of the fire hall. As I watched out my office window, a tall and slightly graying officer stepped from the vehicle, came to the back door and knocked. "Come on in," I shouted.

"Hi, I'm Bill Byram," he said. "I understand you've got a little problem with some Picric Acid."

Taken back by his courtesy and professionalism, but recognizing the voice from two days before as the one on the phone at Highway Patrol headquarters, I hesitated for a moment before responding. "Yes, I told Mr. Meer to keep it secured at the school for the time being."

"The Training Academy in Bismarck said destroy it with gunfire," Bill replied.

Thinking of what to do this time of year with the frozen ground, I asked, "Could you drive out to the City Landfill with your car?"

"Sure, when should we try it?"

I called the school and made arrangements to conduct Mr. Meer and the jars of Picric Acid to the City Landfill site that same morning. The bottles had been placed in a padded cardboard box, and not completely understanding their hazardous potential, were carried cautiously to the Fire Department pickup and placed behind the driver's seat. It was approximately seven miles from the school to the entrance of the landfill where we were met by Greg Schwab, a heavy equipment operator, and Captain Byram.

"What's this crap about exploding some bottles?" Greg asked.

I got out of the truck. Breathing the fresh winter air cleared my senses, and reduced my headache. Turning to Bill Byram, I asked, "What are some of the side effects of Picric Acid?"

"I don't know; probably like dynamite," he replied.

"I never gave it a thought," I said. "I had that stuff behind my pickup seat. That's probably why I've got a helluva headache."

"Me, too," said Meer. "I feel a lot better since I got out of the pickup."

I turned my attention to Greg. "I want you to gouge out a spot in the clay pile with the loader, and we'll place these glass bottles on the ledge. The book says Picric Acid is dangerous."

"I can't believe those little bottles are a problem," Greg said. "Besides, that one is only half full. How many ounces in a bottle?"

"Six," I replied. "One bottle is crystallized and that means it's dangerous."

"I find that hard to believe," said Greg.

The heat radiating from the loader motor receded as Greg climbed into the cab, shifted gears and with a roar swiveled the tractor and made his way down the sloping road into the landfill area. Carefully positioning his equipment against a clay wall he began cutting a shelf with the edge of the loader bucket. In moments he had provided us a ledge about 20 feet long, and with a wave he backed away from the embankment while I drove down to the site with the bottles in the back of the pickup.

While I was placing the small 6 ounce bottles on the notch Greg had carved in the wall, Officer Byram had driven a couple hundred feet to the west and removed a large rifle case from the trunk of his patrol vehicle. I returned to the pickup and Oliver and I drove to a position above and to the rear of Bill Byram's patrol car.

Meanwhile Bill had finished assembling his rifle and was resting on a towel he had laid across the hood of his vehicle. He adjusted the scope on the rifle, swiveled away from the bottles, and fired at a branch at the opposite end of the embankment. The branch snapped in two and Bill waved and returned to aiming in the direction of the bottles.

I have always been suspicious of small explosives, especially when it is entirely new to me, but when the bullet struck that crystallized bottle all hell broke loose. I don't think my mouth fell open, but Bill turned back toward me with a look of wonderment on his face. To this day I'll not forget his expression. Next to me Oliver uttered, "Holy shit."

Off to the north of the embankment, Greg swung out from the cab of the loader, and wiped debris from the windshield. "Wow!" he shouted.

The hole in the frozen embankment made believers of us. My experience with explosives indicated four ounces of crystallized Picric Acid had the force of at least four sticks of dynamite. Amazingly, the other bottles of Picric Acid had remained intact, and Bill broke each of them with a single bullet from his rifle. None of them did more than shatter and disintegrate from the force of the bullet.

My friendship with Bill Byram grew as together we handled many other situations over the next few years. At his retirement dinner in 1992 I presented Bill a plaque with an empty brown Picric Acid bottle glued to it, and told the story of the landfill incident to the assembled 300 police officers. It had been an unforgettable moment for both of us.

CHAPTER 16

ARSON AT THE MAYER HOTEL

It was 3:00 a.m. Sunday morning, the beginning of Fire Prevention Week 1979, when Jerome radioed, "We have a fire at the Mayer Hotel!"

Pulling on my fire boots and pants, I reflected on my past relationship with the 50x140 foot, three-story brick building where I had grown up, and wondered where the fire might have started. As I pulled up in front of the hotel, Jerome Hoffart waved and shouted, "They think the fire is in the café basement."

"Hook up 201 to the VFW corner hydrant and run a line to the back door next to Goodman Electric and I'll go through the bar and unlock the door."

Grabbing the rest of my fire gear, I headed for the hotel entrance, snapping my coat buckles as I ran. Just inside the entrance, I met Police Officer Dallas Carlson, bar owner Perry Horner, and Bill Winnegge, one of the bartenders. "I can't find anybody upstairs," Dallas said.

"They lost the Burlington Northern contract, there hasn't been anybody up there since July," I replied.

Perry explained. "Bill and I were cleaning the bar when some guy came running up the basement stairs shouting 'Fire!' I don't mind telling you it scared the hell out of me!"

"I saw smoke coming from the kitchen doorway and called you," added Bill.

In the lobby, smoke was building down from the 12 foot ceiling, and over at the café entrance I noticed the door was moving. *It should have been locked this time of the day*, I thought. I pushed open the door and was greeted by heavy smoke and heat. My stomach churned, and I knew in my gut that this was going to be one hell of a day. "Is the back door locked?" I asked.

"Just from the bar, not to the outside," Bill replied.

"Is the safe locked?"

"Yep, we were just cleaning the floor," Perry said.

"You guys get out of here." Turning to Dallas I ordered, "Don't let anyone in."

"You got it," replied Dallas.

I could hear sirens indicating that the rest of the equipment was approaching. "204—217, set up on the north side of the hotel."

"This is 203, where do you want us to set up?"

"In the alley between the hotel and gas station," I answered.

"Will the hollow space hold the ladder?" Tim radioed. *Now I had something else to worry about.* During prohibition, bootleg liquor was hidden in a room under the alley behind the hotel, and the hollow space had never been filled in.

"Give it a try. Run your ladder up and bang on the doors again. Check the ground floor apartments last."

"202—If you can hear me, park in front of the bank."

"10-4," the driver replied.

To my left was the barber shop; on my right was the stairway to the second floor. A few feet further south was the stairway to the basement, and straight ahead was the entrance to the bar from the lobby. The bar was a large L-shaped room at the center of the hotel on the east side. As I entered the bar area my flashlight revealed chairs balanced on the tables. I cringed at the sight of more chairs resting on the bar top. I had cleaned this bar for years, but had always avoided putting chairs on top of the mahogany bar. I always took a certain amount of pride in the way the mahogany bar top gleamed following its once-a-year refinishing.

I made my way through the bar to the back door and opening it carefully, shined my beam to the right and saw smoke curling from beneath the kitchen door. Moving the beam to the left, I illuminated the fifty-five gallon barrels used for garbage. Further south down the corridor was the back door entrance to the hotel. Opening the door, I found Jack Nash and his entry crew getting ready to come inside. "The fire's in the kitchen," I said. Jack had brought an extra breathing apparatus and I shrugged into the harness as we moved down the hallway toward the kitchen door.

Shining my flashlight again toward the bottom of the door, it was apparent that the smoke had gotten dirtier, and the volume was increasing as it rolled out into the corridor. Behind me I could hear ringing as the entry team opened the valves on their air tanks. Jack and I had positioned ourselves on top of the freight elevator and he warned the others, "Here we go, pick up the slack." Cautiously I turned the door knob and was surprised to find I didn't need an axe to force our entrance. As I pushed the door inward my flashlight revealed heavy black smoke coming from the basement stairway. We dropped to our knees, and I moved to the side as Jack led his team down the stairs. Although Jack was only a few feet away, I could barely read the luminous letters on his coat as he disappeared in the murky darkness.

As the third member of the entry team disappeared into the smoke it seemed the heat level increased dramatically. *This is bullshit*, I said to myself, *nothing's worth their lives*. Although my voice was muffled by the mask of the breathing apparatus, when I shouted "Back out!" the entry team began returning up the stairs.

As the trio backed past me I heard, "Damn it's hot!"

"Hell of a way to start Fire Prevention Week."

I grabbed Jack as he passed and said, "Get out. We'll have to try another way."

Once outside, I left Jack with the entry team and hurried around to the front entrance of the hotel and grabbed a fresh air bottle from 'Old 202'. Walt Thiessen, the assistant chief, stood nearby. "Should I come with you?"

"Yep; put on a breathing apparatus."

Heavy smoke greeted us as we felt our way through the hotel lobby, and down the stairs into the basement meeting room. As we walked through the door, I felt Walt's hand add its weight to my air bottle. Feeling my way down the wall, I tried to recall the layout of the room in order not to get disoriented. To say it was dark was an understatement; our twelve volt hand lanterns couldn't penetrate the dirty brown smoke, they would only reflect against the surface. Not confronting any unusual obstacles, we arrived at the end of the meeting room and the set of double doors which, I recalled, would lead into the café basement. I opened the first of two doors and felt for the knob of the door leading into the café. I reached for Walt and indicated I wanted him to duck.

The sound of Walt's breathing increased as I pushed open the door and followed him through the opening. "Somebody built a wall!" he exclaimed.

Reaching past him, I felt a chicken-wire-covered wall to my left. *This wasn't here six months ago,* I thought. At the same time I noticed the temperature was increasing, "We'd better get out," I said. Quickly closing both doors, we felt our way out of the meeting room into the basement corridor.

Although the fire was on the other side of a 12 inch thick brick wall, the heat in the corridor was becoming noticeable as we walked south past what used to be my office and stopped at the first apartment. While Walt went to check for occupants, I swept the ceiling in the corridor with my gloved hand in an attempt to recover a Vanguard heat detector that I had placed a couple of years before.

I could hear Walt moving furniture in the apartment, and I was about to give up searching the ceiling when my glove brushed across the smooth round surface of the detector. I felt for the heat tab and could tell it was intact. *Hell of a thing; someone could die of smoke inhalation down here.* Pressing a tab to release the detector, I had just placed it in my pocket when Walt came stumbling out the door. "Nobody in here," he said.

A noise in the hallway drew my attention to a faint glow moving in our direction. Through the smoke Tim Kurtz's silver reflective fire gear suddenly became visible. "Did you check this apartment?" he asked

"Yep, thought we'd check the others on the way out. We tried to get into the basement of the kitchen."

"How'd it go?" Tim asked in a muffled voice.

"Couldn't find an opening; somebody built a wall," I replied.

"Hotter than hell and couldn't see," Walt interjected. "Too much smoke."

"We checked the other two apartments," Tim said. "They're both empty."

"Old Pete Mandy still live back there?" I asked.

"Nope, Pete moved to Minneapolis and is living with his son."

Together we returned to the street by the back stairway and gathered some firemen together for a briefing. Because of my familiarity with the hotel I determined that the best way to gain access to the fire was through the liquor storeroom in the basement. I chose two men to accompany me. "Walt, while I'm gone get some help and put the cellar nozzle through the floor of the kitchen. I'll take Dennis and Jim with me."

Back down into the basement, I led Dennis Olson and Jim Moe through the hallway. "Damn it's dark," I heard Jim say. After a few minutes of feeling our way down the corridor and through the laundry room, we arrived outside the door to the liquor storeroom. Dennis had brought an axe and used it to break the lock into the storage area. Feeling my way past the stored liquor, I led the way to the other side of the room.

"The fire is on the other side of this wall," I said. *How in the hell can they see where I'm reaching*, I thought. Taking a glove off, I placed my hand on the wall. *Doesn't feel like the fire is on the other side of the wall*, I thought. I pondered the basement layout and realized a bathroom separated the liquor room from the fire. Turning left I put my hand against the wall bordering the staircase Jack and his team had tried unsuccessfully to navigate. *Holy shit it's hot.* The heat was increasing and at the same time I realized what side of the firewall we were on. *Damn it's getting hot; it could come in behind us.*

"Let's get the hell out of here!" Jim exclaimed.

"Move some booze; maybe we can get to the other side," Dennis suggested.

Trying to remain calm I said, "It won't do any good; I forgot there's a room on the other side of this wall. Let's go back outside."

As we felt our way through the laundry room I was thinking about the area below the grill in the kitchen. For years there hadn't been any protection below the grill from grease drippings. In the early '70s Frank Schwab and I placed a layer of galvanized metal on the floor under the grill and up the wall behind it. When you were in the basement and looked up toward the grill area, you could see discoloration where the grease had soaked the floor. *That's got to be burning.* My thoughts were interrupted by Dennis when he said, "Put your hand on each other's tank so we don't get separated."

We had just found our way to ground level and were removing our air masks when there was a tremendous crash followed by a blast of hot air. Until some time later, we wouldn't know how close we had come to being victims of the arsonist, but our anxiety was apparent as we looked at each other and Dennis said, "Damn, that was close!"

Jerome came rushing around the corner of the building. "I'm glad to see you guys, the west side of the kitchen just collapsed."

Although I was thanking my lucky stars, I tried to appear nonchalant. "Probably the cast iron columns giving away. Have they got the cellar nozzle operating yet?" A cellar nozzle is a revolving sphere with nine, three-eighth inch holes that spray water in a circular pattern. Using one required cutting a hole in the floor and lowering it through the opening into the area below.

I could tell by the way they looked at each other that my casual response to the collapse had a marked effect. A few moments passed before Jerome said, "They just charged the hose." My eyes followed the line as it stretched like a sidewinder snake down the street past Dick Johnson and Gary Kurtz into the hotel. Dick looked up from loosening his mask straps as I approached and exclaimed; "It was close; we just got the nozzle through the hole and the damn floor collapsed!" Looking toward the obviously shaken Gary, he added, "'Num-Nuts' almost fell in the fire."

"Did you leave the nozzle running?" I asked.

Gary reached down and felt the hose leading into the café. "Feels like its running, but I don't really give a shit."

The fire had been reported at 3:00 a.m., and it was mid-morning when I noticed Detective Joe Weisbeck and City Attorney Louie Jorgenson approaching from across the street. Joe stood about 5'8", broad shouldered, with a pock-marked face. Louie was over 6' tall, thinning blond hair, and a ready smile. "Find anything yet?" Joe asked.

Joe's first big assignment, I thought. "Nope," I replied. "Looks like it started in the café basement." They were quite a pair; neither one carried a note pad or tape recorder.

"I got a call from a guy in Fargo saying someone was going to start a fire in a hotel in Devils Lake; looks like they did," said Joe.

"How in the hell did he know?" I asked.

"Something happened in Jamestown during the night, I guess." Joe said. "The Jamestown Police were watching for a vehicle coming from the north and picked it up at the edge of town."

Quite often I wonder why firemen resent police officers and vice versa. It must hinge on who has the most dangerous job, and the amount of time they spend doing their duties. Occasionally, as a volunteer, I had felt the same way. Now, as Chief of the department, I realize they are just doing their job as best they can, and it's important both departments work together to achieve a mutual goal. It's times like this when the firemen see me conversing with Joe and Louie that help correct any misunderstandings. I looked at Joe, and replied with what I hoped was sincerity, "Congratulations; mighty good police work." *I hope the guys see this,* I thought, as I reached out and shook Joe's hand.

"We can thank our lucky stars," Louie said, "but we've got a long way to go."

"It'll make my part of the job easier," I replied, "looking for the point of origin."

"I'd like to go on an investigation with you sometime," Joe said.

I'd noticed the twinkle in the eyes of that normally somber face and replied, "Anytime; I'll let you know what's going on and you can decide."

As Joe and Louie left to do their job, I noticed some of the firemen looking my direction. *Maybe this'll break the ice,* I thought.

It was sad watching the building that had been my home and place of business for over thirty years go up in smoke. I couldn't help but think about some of the memories that were being lost in the burning structure.

The collapsed portion of the kitchen ceiling created an opening that was allowing most of smoke in the lower portion of the hotel to vent out to the atmosphere. If a fire is discovered early and is ventilated immediately, it is usually contained to that area. The fire in the café basement had been gaining in intensity prior to emergency services notification. Not being ventilated until sometime later when the roof collapsed, it had found outlets for its wrath in various cavities within the hotel structure. The fire had become elusive; manpower was stretched thin as they searched with their ungloved hands for the various places it may be hiding. Some of these fires traveled 25 feet horizontally, burning 4x4 foot holes through the floor before being discovered. Upon reaching the attic (cockloft), fire spread throughout the 7000 square feet of open space burning away spider webs and destroying some of the structure on the north end.

Hose lines had been advanced into the second and third floors from the aerial ladder on the south end of the building. At the opposite end of the building the snorkel had illuminated the scene until daylight, and now was providing water from its bucket outlet to entry teams on both floors. On the sidewalk between the snorkel and the outside café entrance a fireman was spraying water upwards through the window of room 226 on the second floor in an effort to keep the window casing from burning. In front of the nozzle man someone had propped open the door to the Honker café. The door was equipped with an emergency alarm that continued to squeal unless turned off with a special key. *That's got to be unnerving,* I thought, *especially to the guys on the snorkel.*

"Turn the damn thing off," someone said.

"You need a key to shut it off," Ray Eisenzimmer had explained more than once.

I just happened to be rounding the corner of the hotel when I heard Cliff Ludwig shout, "I've got the goddamn key." Cliff removed an axe from its holder on the side of the snorkel and walked toward the steel exit door. He was an imposing figure. Broad and muscular, he had once played football for the Devils Lake Satans. Following high school graduation he had attended Vo Tech School and now was a lineman for Otter Tail Power Company. I had known Cliff for years, and envied his attitude and ability to work with high voltage electricity. When it came to emergencies he had a no-nonsense approach.

"Oh shit," someone said as Cliff raised the axe and brought it down on the alarming device.

"Don't baby it," Ray shouted.

Cliff looked at me and seeing only a smile, turned back to the door, raised the axe above his helmeted head and brought it down with a resounding crash. It moved a little, but not enough to shut the damn thing off. Again the axe was raised, this time high above his head, and when it struck, the push bar parts flew everywhere. There was silence. Smiling he reached down and picked up the pieces and threw them through the café entrance. Some of the firemen who had witnessed the destruction applauded. Cliff turned and smiled. "Thank you," he said.

Although the venting of smoke through the kitchen collapse and other openings on the second and third floors allowed some of the firemen, because of what they were doing, to remove their breathing apparatus, we would need more air. Our cascade system and pump were stationary; Walt had returned to the station to begin the refilling process.

Outside the front door of the hotel were two firemen dressed in full gear, wearing breathing apparatus, and holding their helmets and air masks in their hands. They were part of the recovery team. *I hoped we wouldn't need them.*

I glanced through the main hotel doorway and saw that the smoke had for the most part disappeared. A hose led up the lobby steps to where a fireman was hanging over the edge of the stairway wall spraying water into the kitchen basement. "I'm going in," I said to the recovery team.

Looking through the smoke past the broken floor joists into the café basement, I could just make out the top of the big Vulcan grill shining through the burning debris. *Holy crap,* I thought, *Jerome wasn't shittin' me when he said the roof had caved in.* Below us, fire caused by burning grease and methane gas, billowed out from the main sewer line.

"How long have you been here?" I asked.

"About an hour," the fireman replied.

I reached for the nozzle and said, "Go out and have some breakfast. Tell Jerome to send someone else in to take the nozzle." A short while later Gary Harveland came up the steps and relieved me of the nozzle.

Outside once again, I went to the rear of the snorkel and used the intercom to talk with the platform operator. The fireman that had been on the sidewalk when Cliff destroyed the alarm had placed a ladder against the fire escape and dragged his hose through a third floor window. Firemen were visible in other rooms of the third floor removing sections of ceiling material and exposing areas where the fire had traveled horizontally. Jerry Seibel was in room 326 using a Halligan tool to rip apart sections of burning window molding and throw it to the ground. Jim Meyers had unreeled the booster hose from the snorkel and was wetting down the material as it landed on the sidewalk. Occasionally, short bursts of water would stream out over the snorkel crew, adding its spray to the lightly falling rain.

I hadn't been outside for long when I heard a shout, "Man down, Harveland fell into the fire!" Rushing around the corner to the hotel side, I imagined I saw the steel door frame flex as the recovery team rushed inside to rescue Gary. *What the hell is going to happen next?* I wondered.

Other firemen heard the cry of distress and entered the hotel to assist the recovery team, and within moments they all returned with Gary Harveland being escorted between them.

"The wall gave way in front of him," Larry Locken explained when he reached my side. "He was holding onto the hose, and flame was coming from that damn sewer pipe just below him when we pulled him out. I sent him to the ambulance to get checked out."

"We've had enough of this crap," I said. "We're going to flood the basement." I radioed Charlie Grafsgaard, water department foreman. "Have we got enough water to flood the hotel basement?" My portable radio was silent as Charlie pondered the water necessary to flood the 50x140 foot cellar.

"Tower is full; pumps in Warwick are running; go ahead," he replied.

"218—We're going to flood the basement. 203—How's it looking?"

"We've been putting out fires between floor joists and we're making some headway. What do you think about ventilating the roof above the fire?" Tim asked.

"Go ahead; take a cellar nozzle with you," I replied.

Looking over the scene, I noticed firemen resting against the wall of Ramsey Bank, eating lunch from Styrofoam containers. The fire line was marked in yellow tape, and police officers were either dozing in their patrol cars or eating a sandwich. I was about to turn my attention back to the scene, when I saw my brother Dave approaching. "How's it going?"

"I don't mind telling you it's been the shits. I think we've got it pretty much under control, but we've had some close calls, and I decided to flood the basement."

"Where did it start?" David asked.

"I was told someone set the fire in the basement."

"217—303, I'm going to bring the 6-inch pump up to pump out the basement when you're done," Charlie radioed.

"Put it in back by the basement stairway," I replied.

"I've been delivering meals for Kenny Koehn from County Kitchen," David continued. He's sent up 128 so far. Do you need more?"

I could see the sadness in Dave's eyes as he stood looking at the building that he had called home for eighteen years. "We've already been here for almost twelve hours; I hope we don't need supper."

As David turned to leave he said, "Mary left cookies on the winter cover over the back stairway." Before he left, he looked up once again to where the firemen were working and with a catch in his voice said, "I sure hope it gets rebuilt."

"218—Set up the monitor and let's flood the basement."

To the side I noticed Gary Harveland heading toward the outside bar entrance. "How are you feeling?" I called.

"A little sore, but I'll get over it," he replied, and with a wave of his hand walked to where firemen were working inside the bar area.

It was 3:00 p.m., and with the fire controlled, Ron Vetsch and I climbed the stairs to check the damage. We began by taking some pictures from the second floor toward where the air handling equipment and roof had fallen into the kitchen. Completing our survey of the second floor, we moved to the third floor and Ron continued trying door knobs. Occasionally he would find a locked door and force it with an axe. I'd look through the room and then we'd move on to the next room. Toward the end of the corridor I saw a hole someone had chopped in the middle of the floor and was about to mention it to Ron when he stopped swinging. "What's wrong?" I asked.

"I lost the friggin' axe," he said. As if to further emphasize his statement, he turned and offered his empty gloved hands.

I was usually against swearing, but occasionally could be heard muttering expletives myself. My primary concern was being overheard by outsiders via the radio system when we were on the fire ground. This was not one of those times, and I looked at Ron in disbelief. "You lost the friggin' axe?"

With a smile he replied, "Yes, I lost the friggin' axe; it went through the door into the room."

Ron and I finished checking rooms and were on the roof looking down at the fire ground activity. At the southeast corner of the hotel the water department's 6-inch pump was backed into place at the head of the basement steps. Charlie and some of the black-clothed firemen were unrolling the limp 5-inch discharge hose.

"It's about time it quit raining," Ron said.

The rain that had fallen most of the day hadn't amounted to much and I had paid very little attention to it, except for one time when I entered the bar area and slipped on the tile floor. I credited that instance to water from an entry team. They had been in the bar fighting fire that had come up through the floor in the area where Dennis, Jim and I had been checking the liquor storage room.

"219—Check the water level in the basement and give me a call," I directed.

"217—204, we've finished checking for extensions, everything looks good. We're going to flood the basement."

"217—219, the water is rising fast, there's hardly any smoke."

I thought of a way to check the level and asked, "Can you get to the café basement through the meeting room?"

"Nope," Jerome replied, "water is too deep."

An hour went by before I heard Charlie calling on the radio. "Looks like the basement is full."

"When it gets to the top of the stairs, start pumping and we'll shut down," I replied.

A while later Ron and I climbed down from our vantage point on the roof, and I glanced toward the street where the pump was spewing a large stream of water through the discharge hose and down the gutter toward the catch basin. Ever attentive to the goings on around him, Charlie looked up from his position next to the pump and waved. I gave Charlie a 'thumbs up' signal as I crawled in through the second floor fire escape window. "Looks good," I said to no one in particular.

The fire scene was finally secured at 6:00 p.m., sixteen hours after we had received the call. *I'll set up a fire watch; plenty of time tomorrow to begin an investigation,* I thought.

INVESTIGATION:

As I drove toward the hotel the next morning I contemplated what had been presented by Joe and Louie. The street next to the hotel had been blocked off with bright yellow fire line tape stretched between barricades. I climbed out of the pickup and sat on the tailgate, pulling on my boots and reviewing the last thirty-six hours. From inside the hotel lobby entrance came a police officer delegated to securing the scene until we were done with our investigation.

"How did it go last night?" I asked.

"Pretty quiet," he responded.

"I'll be starting in the café basement if you need to find me."

Grabbing a hand lantern, I went down the lobby stairs, through the meeting room to the café basement where Walt and I had discovered the chicken wire covered wall. Without the smoke my lantern was able to identify the brick foundation wall on the opposite side of the basement. At the very end of the new wall was enough room for me to slide through into the basement of the café where the fire had started. *If that wall hadn't been there,* I thought, *fighting this fire might have been a piece of cake.*

I shined my light toward the basement steps we'd first tried to navigate with Jack's crew, and saw all kinds of debris scattered from one side to the other. It was going to be another long day.

I adjusted the lantern beam to flood, and the increased illumination exposed the water and debris line as it had floated upwards. Moving the beam revealed where the fire had proceeded south in the direction of the bar, where it had eaten a hole through the floor and burned into the bar area. On the floor directly below the café dishwasher, and next to the bathroom walls were the remains of three 30-gallon cardboard barrels. Further examination determined the barrels were full of receipts. Charring and destruction led upwards from this area and proceeded across the basement to the area which had been under the Vulcan grill. The holes burned through the floor helped me understand how the fire had gone upwards and spread out through the upper floors.

I was digging through debris when I heard someone clearing his throat. Good old Jack Zaleski, editor of the Journal, was preparing to take a picture.

From the top of the basement stairs came a new voice. "What the hell is going on down there; I thought the electricity was turned off." Footsteps coming down the stairs eventually brought the lanky figure of Fire Marshal Richard Radspinner to the base of the steps, where he sat down and, resting on one elbow asked, "Find anything yet?"

"No," I replied. "But I did find the area of origin."

"Show me." I showed him what I had found while Jack took some pictures.

"Pretty good," Radspinner said. "Here let me help you." And with that he entered the area and in a short time explained how the fire started.

"When the call came to the Law Enforcement Center from Fargo that there was going to be a hotel fire in Devils Lake, they asked the caller how he knew that, and he said, "I was at the bus stop in Jamestown having something to eat. A guy got off the bus and came over and sat down across from me. He asked me if I wanted to make some money by taking him to Devils Lake. I told him no, I was tired and had to get back to Fargo. He mentioned he was going to set a fire in a hotel for a buddy of his.

"The caller took his time driving back to Fargo and by the time he phoned, the fire was already going," said Radspinner. "Now, it gets interesting.

"It seems that this guy from the bus leaves the booth and goes and sits with a young couple on the other side of the room. Before the caller had finished eating, he saw the three of them leave the café together. He asked dispatch to let him talk to the Police Chief, but they told him he was on the scene of a hotel fire and couldn't be reached. The guy apologized for not calling sooner, gave his name and telephone number and hung up.

"The other dispatcher radioed the chief and relayed what she had found out. He had her contact the Jamestown Police and watch for a car coming from the north. When he got back to the Center he talked to the informant in Fargo about what had been said. Shortly after he hung up a call came from Jamestown saying officers had stopped a car with three individuals inside, coming from the north."

"Why didn't you come up to the scene?" I asked.

Radspinner went on with his narrative. "When I called state radio, they told me that the people from Jamestown were locked up at the Law Enforcement Center. I spent a couple of hours questioning them. The young couple was innocent; they just wanted to make a few bucks. Pat McMahon was a different story; although the couple supported his story as best they could.

"McMahon told me he had brought rope with him in his suitcase, but he had to stop and get some kerosene before they left Jamestown. They pulled up to the hotel here in Devils Lake. Pat got his stuff out, unlocked the front door, and went into the hotel through the café and downstairs to the basement. Three barrels of old receipts where Pat was to set the fire had been placed in the basement directly below the dishwasher."

Radspinner continued, "Pat's buddy tried to get a professional arsonist from the State of Washington to do the job a few months earlier, but he wouldn't because there were people living in the hotel. Pat told me he needed money and used to work with the owner. He found out from the Washington arsonist how to start the fire, and figured he could help his buddy and make a few bucks at the same time. His buddy told McMahon nobody lived in the hotel anymore.

"Then he explained how he laid rope in the barrels and soaked them with kerosene, and then pushed the rope up through a hole next to dishwasher drain pipe. The arsonist told him that when the dishwasher needed hot water, it would ignite the burners and start the rope on fire, leading down to the barrels. McMahon said he went upstairs, arranged the rope and turned on the hot water faucet for the dishwasher.

"The cute part of this whole mess is the fire originally was intentional, but turned out to be accidentally ignited," Radspinner said.

"You're shitting me," Jack muttered. Radspinner had not noticed Jack still standing in the shadows. Looking at him and then back to me I nodded, indicating it was okay, and he continued with his story.

"No, I'm not," Radspinner said, "Pat set up everything like he was taught by the arsonist in Seattle. But as he left the basement with the rest of his rope and the empty kerosene containers, he threw a cigarette into one of the barrels. When the three of them left town, they took a wrong turn and headed east. When they realized their mistake and were returning to Devils Lake, Pat had sobered up enough to have second thoughts about what he had done and asked to be taken back to the hotel.

138

"Smelling something burning, he hurried down the steps and turned on the lights in the meeting room, to discover the room was filling with smoke. Scared, he forgot what his buddy had said about there not being anybody living in the hotel, and he ran down the basement hallway shouting 'Fire!' Not realizing there was a back door leading out of the basement he ran back down the hallway and up the steps to the lobby, all the time shouting 'Fire!' I spent some time this morning with the guys cleaning the bar and they identified McMahon from the photos I took of him in Jamestown. Incidentally, I had a little visit with Joe before I came over here. He said he and Louie were heading over to visit the owner and would be over to take you up on your offer of teaching him the best methods of fire investigation. I was upstairs looking it over before I came down here; wonder where they're at."

Radspinner had just finished talking when we heard a noise coming from upstairs. I shouted, "Look out, you'll fall through the floor!"

At the head of the steps appeared Detective Joe Weisbeck and City Attorney Lewis 'Louie' Jorgenson. "You'll never believe what happened," said Joe.

"Anything is possible," I replied.

"Hey Radspinner, how you doing?" greeted Louie.

"Not bad, everything considered. Did you find out who Pat's buddy was? He wouldn't tell me."

"I've got something that will definitely make your day," Joe said.

"Louie and I went to Earl Pederson's (building owner) office this morning. We visited with Perry Horner and his bartender yesterday afternoon and checked their stories and identification of the suspect. We told Earl that we felt that someone who was knowledgeable of the building had marked each key on a ring we found, telling what the key was for. On Earl's desk was a legal pad and Louie reached for it and said, "The cardboard tags identifying the keys looks like this kind of backing."

"Good old Louie turned the pad over and, guess what?" Joe said.

"It's hard to believe," Louie interrupted, "but that was the same pad that the tags were cut from!"

"We even found a green marking pen he probably used to mark the tags that identified the keys," Joe added. "He turned over his phone records when we asked and they verified what McMahon had said. There was a telephone number that I wired to the Seattle Police Department, probably belonged to the arsonist that tried to teach Pat."

I looked at Joe, Louie, and finally Radspinner. I don't think the deputy fire marshal had any idea what Joe and Louie had been going to say. All Radspinner could say, was "Holy crap, there's a dumb shit born every minute."

"Where's Earl now?" I asked.

"Locked up in the slammer while Louie works up charges," Joe said. "Hard to believe he was once our Municipal Judge."

"Yeah," Louie said, "and McMahon was once the City Attorney and had worked with Earl."

"Where did you find the keys?" I asked.

"The sheriff got an anonymous call saying there were some items in the ditch just south of town, and when he got there he found some rope, a couple of Hilex jugs and a ring of keys," Joe replied.

Jack was taking notes when Joe said, "Not so fast, Jack. You'll have to wait until everyone is charged before you write anything."

"It will be my pleasure. I'll hold the presses until charges are filed. This will be one hell of a story: a former Municipal Judge and City Attorney charged with arson. I might even print a special edition."

"I don't have any trouble with that," said Louie. "I have already talked to the judge and he is waiting for the complaints. He'll have the hearing as soon as we finish typing them up."

Joe looked at me. "The judge would like a list of expenses for fighting this fire as soon as you can get it to him."

EPILOGUE:

Both McMahon and Pederson were sent to prison.

McMahon pleaded guilty and began serving his sentence immediately.

Earl Pederson had a court trial and after a 90-minute deliberation was found guilty. The trial was chaired by William Neuman, Rugby, and juried by taxpayers from Bottineau County, June 8, 1980.

The Mayer Hotel was demolished by Strong's Excavating during the summer of 1980, and shortly thereafter, Third Avenue (bar side) was vacated and Ramsey Bank expanded over the vacated property and further west along 4th Street.

CHAPTER 17

NORTHERN SEED AND FEED—

TOXIC CHEMICALS

Northern Seed and Feed was a seed and fertilizer establishment located on the northeast corner of the intersection of College Drive and 6th Street in Devils Lake. The property included a retail store and office, two 15,000 bushel elevators, and two rather large 15,000 gallon tanks containing liquid fertilizer. Some of the retail items included grass and treated grain seed and various types of dry fertilizer. You could either pick up your material, or have it delivered for a price. It was a family run business and well respected throughout the Lake Region.

A building inspection had been completed the previous day by the Fire Department. The major concern was bare wiring on an air compressor in the basement of the elevator attached to the office area.

Jerome Hoffart and I were reviewing inspection reports Friday morning March 17, 1981, when the phone rang. "There's a fire at Northern Seed and Feed," the caller said.

As we left the station we could see smoke rising above the tree tops to the west. When I arrived, Brad Smith and his secretary were busy handing records out the office door to waiting hands. Flames were climbing the elevator wall, and heavy black smoke was high above the structure obscuring the sky. I called the LEC for assistance, and along with the arriving fire equipment and volunteers, police officers began rerouting traffic. Earl Reed parked an ambulance across the street in the Dakota Implement parking lot.

Once equipment was positioned and two entry teams were working, I was able to visit with elevator manager Brad Smith. "What's that dripping from the truck?"

"It's seed treatment," he said. "Tetrachloronitrobenzene (TCNB)."

"Is it toxic?" I asked.

"Yes," he replied, "you need to wear a mask, goggles and gloves when handling the chemical."

"What's the truck doing inside the elevator?"

"Customer's kid ordered too much," Brad replied. "He was going to call this morning and let us know how much he really needed. I didn't want to unload and reload, so I had the driver park the truck in the elevator. Do you think the truck started the fire?" Brad asked.

"I'm not sure; when did you notice the fire?" I asked.

"I didn't. Janice, my secretary, saw smoke coming from a vent in the office."

"Did you get a chance to read the inspection report from yesterday?"

"I reviewed the report with your guys; it mentioned bare wires by the compressor. Do you think that had anything to do with the fire?" Brad asked.

"I doubt if we'll ever know for sure."

Brad's description of the dripping chemical was a health risk we couldn't chance. "Kirk," I called. "See if you can hook a chain onto that truck and maybe we can drag it out." In moments he returned from the snorkel dragging a heavy log chain. He shouted to the entry team, and they directed their stream in front of him as he attempted to hook onto the burning vehicle. Flames from both the elevator pit and the truck body were rolling around him as he inched his way under the bed of the truck. *We've got to get the truck out before the tank splits.* Just then Kirk reappeared dragging excess chain. Don Nakken maneuvered his truck around the hoses and backed up to where Kirk was standing. As the delivery truck was pulled from the elevator, there were explosions of fire as fumes coming from the gas fill pipe were ignited. Immediately the entry team directed their hose stream on and into the truck as they worked to extinguish the fire.

"What do you want <u>me</u> to do?"

Turning, I was surprised by the gaunt face of friend and volunteer firefighter Kent Peterson. Caught off guard, I blurted, "What the hell are you doing here?"

"This'll probably be my last fire, and I wanted to be with the guys one more time," he replied. Months before Kent had declared, "Cancer has gotten a hold of me, and there isn't anything the doctors can do." He continued to attend meetings and training sessions, and an occasional emergency.

I tried to hide my emotions, but failed as I looked into his eyes and said, "Take some tarps and cover the sewer manholes. When the guys from the Street Department get here, have them dump some sand to hold the tarps in place. Then check in with 'Bear.'"

Everywhere he went that morning, Kent was put to work doing something useful by his fellow firefighters. Every move he made was monitored by his friends, and more than once I watched firemen stop to inquire how he was doing. With a smile on his face, he would respond, "Great, just great."

Dragging the delivery truck from the elevator allowed the fire to grow and climb with a vengeance toward the top (head house) of the elevator. I withdrew the entry team and moved the snorkel into a position between the two elevators. Water from the elevated platform acted like a sprinkler system as the stream was directed through the head house window. The upward movement of the fire was slowed, but the horizontal activity into the other parts of the elevator increased.

One of the areas the fire was impinging upon was the office wall. On the office side of the wall, an entry crew cooled the wall providing protection to Brad and his secretary as they removed the remaining records. When they had finished, Gayle Hovdeness came to my side and asked permission to withdraw the crew.

"We can't hold much longer," he said.

"Don't let the fire get into the office," I ordered.

"It's getting damn hot in there," he countered.

"Just keep the wall cool, we need the office."

"You're shittin' me!" he exclaimed.

"Just get in there and hold that wall."

"Okay, we'll try, but you better get me some help."

It took a whole lot of trust on Gayle's part to return to the office area, but that is what fire fighting is about. With a wave of his hand, Gayle directed the entry crew back into the office.

"203," I called.

"Go ahead," Tim replied.

"Take the monitor and wash the office wall through the ramp door; I don't want to lose the office." While Tim and his crew were connecting the monitor nozzle, I looked into the ramp area and saw paint burning on the office wall. *Gayle wasn't kidding*, I thought.

"Okay, send us some water," I heard Tim radio.

Within moments the monitor was spraying 750 gallons per minute into the ramp area and onto the office wall and into the pit below. Above the ramp door fire glowed as it ate its way through the tin covering. Julie Nelson, street foreman, was directing his crew as they piled sand on the tarps Kent had placed over the manhole covers. We were flowing over 2000 gallons of water a minute, and it wasn't long before we were able to control the fire and save the office.

Prior to the seed treatment barrels being taken to the city landfill, Kirk discovered all the barrels had bulged from the heat, but only two had split allowing liquid to escape.

With the help of a fork lift from Dakota Implement, the barrels were loaded on two vehicles. First, the damaged barrels were covered with more sand. Both vehicles were then driven to the landfill and off loaded in different areas; the damaged barrels to a remote part of the landfill, and the remaining barrels located for easy pickup by the chemical supplier.

During the activity the unknown contents of two 15,000 gallon tanks at the rear of the property were viewed as a possible problem. There were no chemical symbols on the tanks, and Brad was nowhere to be found. In the meantime, Earl Reed had been on the phone to Chem-Trec, doing his best to gather information on the liquid. Earl had been on the phone for hours, when he was finally directed to contact the Extension Office at North Dakota State University in Fargo. Following a short discussion, it was determined the liquid was an acid, and used for adjusting the PH level in the soil. Neither the acid nor the TCNB was a concern once it was in the soil, but handling the raw material could cause a period of strange behavior, much like that of an individual who has had too much to drink.

Bright and early the next morning, a truck displaying chemical placards followed Kirk and me to the landfill, where we assisted in loading the barrels. When I say assisted, I should say Kirk and I assisted each other while the driver stood and watched. After the tenth barrel, we were getting tired and one of the barrels started to slip toward Kirk.

"Give us some help, you lazy bastard," Kirk shouted.

"No friggin' way," the driver replied.

I should have realized the driver knew more than Kirk and I did about the potential hazard when handling the barrels, but my concern for the moment was getting the job done. With a mighty heave we managed to hoist the final barrel into the back of the truck.

Back at the station, Kirk and I drank a cup of coffee while the duty man went to lunch. I was taking notes for the fire report as we conversed about the chemical incident, when I noticed my handwriting was nothing more than scratches on the pad. Although I could see clearly, I couldn't control my hands worth a darn. I looked toward Kirk, and noticed his coffee cup tipping in his hand.

"Look out, the coffee's hot!" I exclaimed.

"Huh?" Kirk replied.

"Are you feeling kind of funny?" I asked.

"No, I was just thinking about the fire," he answered.

About that time Officer Johnson came into the office. "Could you change the bulb on my light bar?" he asked. Minor maintenance of police vehicles had become the responsibility of some members of the paid staff of the fire department. It wasn't unusual to be interrupted from your own chores to help out the police department. Officer Johnson's request was minor in nature and usually took no more than five minutes to complete.

"Sure," Kirk said. Getting up from his chair he went to the workbench for a screwdriver and beacon bulb. Even though Kirk had said he felt okay, I kept an eye on him as he worked on the light bar.

Sometime later, after a couple of cups of coffee, I was feeling better and Harry was returning from his third trip to the urinal when Kirk came through the back door. "The son of a bitch is done!" he exclaimed. I had explained to Harry what I thought was bothering both of us, and with a smile he looked at me and then Kirk. "Thank you," he said as he headed out the door.

The clock read 2:30 p.m., and Kirk was sitting in the chair Harry had vacated, leaning back with his eyes shut, snoring peacefully. *He's got to be tired,* I thought, *it took him an hour to change the bulb.*

Five months later Mary and I were visiting with the now bedridden Kent and his wife Marcy at their home on 8th Avenue, when we heard a heavy-handed knock on the front door. As she opened the door, Marcy was greeted by aerial 203's Captain Tim Kurtz, dressed in fire gear and followed by the members of the ladder crew to which Kent belonged. At that very moment red and blue lights began flashing up and down the street.

Kent smiled and struggled to gain a sitting position on his bed. Jerry Seibel opened the curtains and Tim reached out and gently adjusted Kent so he could look out at the activity taking place in the street.

Beside each of the fire apparatus, I could see their crews facing the house. Tim signaled with his free hand and a resounding, "We'll miss you," was heard throughout the neighborhood.

As Kent sat with Tim holding him, the falling snowflakes were illuminated by the multitude of red and blue flashing lights, creating a scene of unbelievable beauty against an already white landscape. Kent indicated to Tim that he wanted to lie down once again. I watched as Tim slowly lowered Kent to the bed and stood back looking down at the smiling face.

"We're going to miss you," Tim said.

"I'm going to miss you guys," Kent replied.

As the remainder of the aerial crew filed into the front room to say their last goodbyes, one by one they removed their helmets and gloves and gently grasped the outstretched hand in a final farewell.

As the last member of the aerial crew closed outside door, I heard Kent say, "We'll get together again someday."

CHAPTER 18

AQUARIUMS AT STROMQUIST

I had gone to the fire hall on that Tuesday evening in 1984 to get materials for instructing a class at the Rural Fire Department. It was a little early for class and I had decided to take the Mini-Pumper and water some newly planted trees along College Drive, when I received a radio call indicating smoke coming from Doug David's mobile home in Stromquist Addition. With siren screaming I raced to Stromquist Addition, and the area of the call.

Al Schroeder and Bud Crowell were waiting when I rounded the corner, and they immediately grabbed and donned the only two breathing apparatus on the little fire truck. As I climbed from the cab I glanced toward the pump panel and saw that the water level gauge was registering near empty. "Pull a line to the doorway," I shouted.

Arriving volunteers pulled hose from the hose bed and proceeded to connect the mini-pumper to the hydrant down the street. *Oh-oh, there's a yellow top on the fire hydrant, we've got to be careful; can't supply more than two light lines,* I thought. A yellow top on a hydrant indicated a limited amount of water available. Too much pump suction could collapse the water main, and there was only one water line feeding all of Stromquist Addition.

Bud was leaning against the door to the entry shed, and Al was using a Halligan tool to pry open the locked door. Ducking low, they opened the door and were greeted by a rush of smoke. Through the smoke I could see the glow of flames.

The rattle of aerial 203's ladders could be heard over the fire ground noise as it came to a halt on the Avenue side of the mobile home. From somewhere beyond was the distinctive sound of 202 as it approached the scene.

"217—219. No problem in the water heater room. We turned off the gas and electricity." Dennis Olson had climbed to the roof, knocked the rain cap off of the furnace vent, and was looking down the chimney. After a moment he turned and gave me a 'thumbs up'. *I wonder what made Dennis think the furnace would be running in the middle of June,* I thought to myself.

Down the street, 202 had pulled up next to a hydrant and was in the process of connecting its soft suction. Concerned about collapsing the main I ordered the pumper, "Bring your unit up behind the aerial, and work from your water tank." Shortly after a line was advanced from 202, members of the recovery team were positioning themselves at the rear entrance to the mobile home. *One thing about a mobile home, I can see three sides just by moving a little,* I thought to myself. A number of arriving firemen donned breathing apparatus and were waiting to spell Al and Bud; Gayle had volunteers relieve the police officers who were controlling traffic. *They won't be happy doing the police officer's job,* I thought, *but it'll keep them busy.*

Emergencies always draw bystanders and this evening was no exception. Although we had been on the scene for only a short period of time, vehicles had followed the fire trucks from uptown and the entire surrounding neighborhood seemed to be in attendance. "Has anyone seen the owner?" I inquired of the onlookers.

"He left for the movie about 20 minutes ago," someone answered.

Ben Johnson was looking my way. "I was in the yard when he and his buddy left. Doug said they were going to the show."

"LEC—217, contact the Lake Theatre. Tell Doug David to return home."

While visiting with Ben I had my back to the mobile home, but a sudden look of horror on his face prompted me to turn around. Smoke was rolling out every corner of the mobile home. "They're ventilating," I said.

"I thought it blew up!" Ben exclaimed. *From all appearances it does look like it went all to hell,* I thought to myself.

Ron had driven 201 to the scene without using lights and siren, and eased it next to the mini-pumper. *Good thinking, he'll be able to switch if something happens to the mini-pumper.*

By this time a second line had been advanced into the mobile home. The smoke was thinning when Bud appeared at the door and motioned me to the bottom of the steps. "We didn't find anybody home, but you won't believe what we think happened," Bud said.

Very little smoke remained in the mobile home as I entered through the front door. Opposite the doorway I counted six large aquariums. Maneuvering through fallen debris into the kitchen, I counted six more, a total of 12. Toward the rear of the home, the ladder crew was moving furniture and checking for fire extension. Bud pointed toward the floor behind an aquarium. "We think this is where it started," he said, indicating an orange colored extension cord.

There were numerous burn holes in the orange jacket. "Just like O. K. Hardware," I said. "Why do people insist on using those lightweight cords?"

"Probably because they're cheap," Al replied. "Looks like each aquarium had two heaters and two pumps; some tanks have lights attached to the back."

"How much load on the cord?" I asked.

While Al was trying to determine the exact amperage in each of the units, I followed the orange cord to an area behind another aquarium and found two splitters feeding the other units. "How much of a load are you figuring?" I asked.

"About three and a half amps per aquarium," Al replied.

I reached down and clipped off a length of the orange cord. Spitting on my glove I rubbed a black smudge, and was able to read the number 18.

"Too much load," I said. "I hope he had insurance."

A commotion outside caught our attention and Bud went to the front door. "Chief," Bud called, "Doug just drove up. Should I bring him in?"

Doug came through the front door rubbing tear streaked cheeks. Sadly he looked over the various aquariums, the majority of their inhabitants floating belly up and the remainder in obvious distress. "Did you save anything?" he asked.

"No. The fire killed everything and made a mess out of your home. What were you going to do with all these fish?" I asked.

"I was raising stock, to sell. I hadn't even gotten around to insuring them. I can't understand it; I just left home a half-hour ago."

"We can estimate the smoke and fire damage to the trailer, but I need to know the cost of this whole setup."

"Just a minute," Doug replied. He went to his smoke-covered desk and opened a large payroll style checkbook. "The whole setup, including the fish, comes to $9,348.64. I just put everything together this afternoon.

Holding up the severed extension cord, I said, "It's only rated for 3 or 4 amps, and you connected over 36 amps of appliances."

Once again tears began streaming down his cheeks, "I didn't know," he replied, as he turned and made his way out of the trailer.

Al got the camera and went through the home taking pictures of the various locations for the fire report. I started down the hallway and saw Bill Eisenzimmer coming my way. When he saw me, he raised his finger to his lips indicating silence. Motioning toward a closed bedroom door, Bill hooked his finger into the door pull, and quietly slid the door open to reveal Tim Kurtz reading a Playboy magazine by the dim glare of his hand light. "Glad we've got accountability," Bill said, "or we might have left Tim here when we went back to the hall."

Tim looked up smiling. Pointing toward an inflatable doll standing in the corner he replied, "I always thought the little guy was gay; I guess I was wrong."

I looked at the one we had taken to calling Bear and smiling said, "Things aren't always the way they seem, are they?"

CHAPTER 19

MISSILE SITE:

SMOKE IN THE SILO

In the fall of 1975 the Anti-Ballistic Missile System (ABM) was made fully operational in the northeast region of North Dakota. Mutual aid agreements between the United States Air Force and the responsible jurisdictions became part of some departments' operational procedure. A number of missile sites were located close to Devils Lake, and within the responding area of the Rural Fire Department. In the event the Rural Department was unable to respond, a reciprocal agreement allowed the City Department to take its place.

Late in the fall of 1979 I received a call from Rural Fire Chief Pete Hanson. "We just received a call. 'Juliet 7' has smoke in the control room."

"You're primary, Pete—you should go," I replied.

"I'd rather not," Pete said. "You know more about the setup than I do."

"Okay, but you owe us one. Call dispatch and tell them we're on the way."

I thought back to the fall of 1963, when the Morrison-Knutson Construction firm received the contract for constructing the silos to house Anti-Ballistic Missiles. For over a year the third floor of the Mayer Hotel had been home to the senior staff of the corporation. Visiting with them revealed a number of things about the missile sites, but no classified information. Because they were staying at the hotel, and I was managing the business for my mom, I was considered knowledgeable about the details of the construction. As untruths go on the scale of 1 to 10, *this situation has to be a twelve,* I thought to myself.

I paged upstairs for a ride-along and Gary Johnson responded by sliding down the fire pole to the apparatus floor. "What's up?" he asked.

"We got a call from Rural saying there's smoke in the control room of 'Juliet 7'."

"Isn't that an ABM site?" Gary asked.

"Sure is; you don't have to go if you don't want to."

"Count me in. Let's ask Alvin if he wants to go, too," Gary remarked.

Alvin was at home and agreed to meet us at a gas station. Before we left the hall, Gary took a few moments to make sure all the testing tools were operational. Grabbing the Geiger counter and fresh batteries, he climbed into the passenger's side of the mini-pumper. On our way to rendezvous with Alvin, Gary changed all eight "D" cells and tested the counter. Removing three radiation dosimeters from his pocket, he reached over and clipped one onto my radio pocket.

I didn't want to call any attention to ourselves as we drove through town, so I kept the lights and siren turned off, and obeyed the traffic signals. It was suppertime and traffic was light, and it wasn't long before we saw Alvin's pickup.

"Juliet 7 is about a mile south of Rohrville Elevator, isn't it?" Alvin asked.

We all agreed on the location, and I was watching for deer crossing the road in front of the mini-pumper when Gary said, "I can see flashing lights."

"Could be the sheriff," I replied. As we got closer it became apparent that it was a highway patrol vehicle and stepping from the vehicle was Trooper Jerry Buchli. I rolled down my window as we approached and asked, "What are you doing out in the middle of nowhere?"

"I'm supposed to point the direction to Juliet 7," he replied.

"Do you want to go with us?" I asked.

"No thanks. I'll get back on patrol."

Turning south I drove about 500 feet down the gravel road, where I was stopped by a military policeman. "May I see your identification please?" he asked. He stepped back into the darkness as we dug through our fire gear to reach our billfolds. Each of us handed him our driver's license and after comparing pictures, he waved us on.

"He didn't smile," Gary said.

"No shit," Alvin replied.

Arriving at the access gate to the missile site, we were required to go through the identification process once again. Once through the gate and past more guards we were stopped by a short, stocky Gunnery Sergeant. "I think we're okay," he said. "Sensors indicated a bad fan motor on the control panel." At the sound of a helicopter approaching, Gunny said, "It's the Officer of the Day coming to check our security; he'll probably bring the operations officer because of the alarm."

In moments the ground outside the fence was illuminated by a powerful landing light. The blades continued revolving as the helicopter settled on a landing pad outside the fence. Two uniformed figures climbed down, and crouching low made their way to the MP's at the gate. I watched them in my rear view mirror as they produced identification, returned the MP's salute, and came toward the fire truck.

The officer in the lead had the bars of a Captain in the Air Force and was followed by a 2nd Lieutenant. My first inclination was to step from the truck and shake his hand. Gary was reaching for the door handle when Gunny said, "Don't get out of the truck."

Returning the Gunny's salute, the Captain asked, "What have we got going, Gunny?"

"It appears we have a burned out fan motor behind the control panel in the control room, sir." *There was no nonchalant attitude here,* I noticed.

"Thank you for responding," the Captain said as he shook my hand and looked in the cab at Gary and Alvin. "Would you like to go down into the control room and check it out with me?"

When the ABM sites were being constructed during the 60's and 70's, I had the opportunity to go through one of the sites. Since Gary and Alvin hadn't had that chance, I introduced them to the Captain and Gunny. Together they went down the ramp to the control room. The Lieutenant and I stayed on the surface, and 20 minutes later they returned to the fire truck.

"Lieutenant, did you write down their names?" the Captain asked.

"Yes, sir," he replied.

I shook hands with the Captain and Lieutenant. Grasping my hand, Gunny smiled and winked. "Thanks," he said.

As I backed through the gate, an MP stopped us and said, "We'll direct you until you can get turned and headed toward the highway. Leave your headlight beams on low. On the sides of the road, you'll see black out lights on a number of security vehicles."

Making my final turn to align the truck with the gravel road, I heard the distinctive sound of the helicopter taking off. In moments the flashing red strobe could be seen moving rapidly toward the northeast and the missile site control complex.

"There's one," Alvin said, pointing to the east of the missile site fence, as he spotted a security vehicle.

"There's two more," Gary said, pointing to the left. "Holy shit, there's a machine gun!" he exclaimed.

"Just remember," I said, "you're not to talk about what you saw inside or outside of this site."

It was a quiet ride back to the fire hall. Knowing the curiosity Alvin always displayed, I wondered what answers, if any, the Captain gave to his questions.

CHAPTER 20

ARSONIST AMONG US

Studies have proven and statistics show that oftentimes when a suspicious fire occurs or arson is suspected, the first place to look is at the owner of the property. Financial difficulties cause people to do desperate acts, as was the case with the Mayer Hotel fire in 1979. However, arson fires are occasionally caused by people you would least suspect—firemen themselves. While departments have difficulty accepting that this situation could be occurring in their own circle, such was the case in Devils Lake in 1982.

Early one evening in September 1982 a caller said, "Smoke is seeping into the dining area of the Ranch. It looks like it might be coming from upstairs."

A premier supper club, "The Ranch" was just a short drive south of Devils Lake on Highway 20. Originally a large livestock barn built into the hillside, it was remodeled in the 1950's turning the lower level into an on and off sale liquor establishment. A kitchen and dining area able to seat 50 customers was constructed on the second floor. During the late 1970's, a two level addition and a larger kitchen were added to the south end of the structure.

Reviewing items such as weather, distance to hydrants, manpower, etc., had become second nature after seven years as Fire Chief. As I turned into the parking lot of The Ranch, I planned what we would be doing.

There were about three dozen vehicles in the parking lot, but no fire truck. *Must be at the top of the hill.* Some charring was visible under the fluorescent sign that advertised "The Ranch" to passersby.

At the top of the hill firemen were getting ready to enter through the west door which led to the kitchen and dining area. Each had donned breathing apparatus, and were getting attack lines ready; another fireman was connecting the pumper to a hydrant. "Don't bring in the hose yet. I'll give you a call," I said.

Hurrying inside, the first thing I saw was a step ladder leading through a hatch into the attic. At the bottom of the ladder was one of the helpers from the kitchen. "What's going on?" I asked.

"A fireman climbed into the attic," he replied.

"Since it was Alvin Schroeder's duty night, I figured he was the one up there. What's your name?" I asked the young man.

"Robert Harveland."

The name was certainly familiar; maybe he was related to Gary. Gary Harveland was a volunteer with our department and his family attended the same church as my family did. "Thanks for holding the ladder, Robert; I'm going to check out the dining area."

"The customers won't leave," he said.

"Maybe they won't have to." I headed toward the dining area as other firemen came through the back door. "Keep an eye on Alvin," I said. "He's in the attic."

The 30-foot long corridor contained doorways which led to restrooms, and the boiler room. At the far end of the corridor was a fire door which led into the dining area. I was about to enter the dining room when I heard a commotion behind me. Gayle Hovdeness was having words with someone I couldn't see. "Hold it down," I said, retracing my steps.

Robert had one foot on the ladder, and glaring at Gayle, said to me, "You told me to keep an eye on Alvin."

"I meant for the firemen to keep an eye on Alvin," I said.

"Excuse me," Gayle said, as he shouldered Robert out of the way. Looking toward Kirk, Gayle ordered, "Go up and check on Alvin." Robert slowly removed his foot from the ladder, but his hand remained on the beam.

Moments later Kirk returned to the opening. "Alvin found the problem. I need a pair of side cutters."

"Do you need a hose line?"

"No, it's just hot ballast," he replied.

A few minutes went by and Kirk reappeared. "Here take this," he said, handing down the problem ballast. Reaching past Gayle, Robert grabbed the transformer from Kirk's outstretched hand. I could tell by the look on his face that the skinny redhead was no match for its weight and heat. "Damn, that's hot!" Robert exclaimed, dropping the ballast.

I couldn't help but notice the smile on Gayle's face as he picked up the transformer with a gloved hand. "Serves you right," he said as he headed out the door.

Later, Alvin reported "I didn't see any smoke when I got there, but I did see a burn mark below the letter 'h' on the outside sign, so I climbed into the attic and found a fluorescent ballast smoking.

"What's the scoop on the redhead?" I asked.

"I just know he works in the kitchen. He helped me move the ladder. He mentioned he had just moved here from Wahpeton and wanted to be a fireman. His uncle told him he had to have a job before the membership committee would consider him for probation."

"Who's his uncle?" I asked.

"Gary Harveland," Alvin replied.

I wasn't surprised by this information. "What else did he say?"

"He asked me why I was going into the attic."

"What'd you tell him?"

"Nothing, I heard a truck siren about that time so I told him to hold the ladder and I climbed up to get a look in the attic. I told him I'd talk to him when we were done."

"Did you get a chance to talk to him later?"

"No, he was talking to Jerome when I came down."

"We can always use more help," I said. "Maybe he'd move in upstairs. Tell Jerome I want to see him."

"What's up?" Jerome asked, as he came into my office.

"Who was the skinny redhead at The Ranch?"

"Gary's nephew," Jerome replied.

Over Jerome's shoulder I could see Gary Harveland removing his fire coat. "Gary, what do you know about Robert?" I questioned.

"He's a good kid. His dad Arnold is my brother. He's had a tough life," Gary continued. "Mother's gone, dad's been in prison. He's been staying with his sister and her husband."

"We've got some empty beds in the dormitory; do you think he'd be interested in becoming a live-in?"

"You'll have to ask him," Gary replied. "I'm sure he'd like to, as long as it didn't interfere with his job."

"I'll get a background check on him."

A few days later, a call from the Wahpeton Police Department indicated Robert Harveland didn't have a record. I called Robert and asked if he was interested in moving into the fire hall. "Thanks a lot," he said. "I'll come up and see you this afternoon."

A few weeks later Alvin, Jerome and I were filling extinguishers when we heard footsteps on the basement stairs. Officer Dallas Carlson appeared in the doorway and said, "Someone tried to burn a trailer at Greater Dakota Homes Trailer Sales."

"What do you mean, tried to?" I asked.

"It's something Stan found this morning in one of the mobile homes," Dallas replied.

Motioning toward Alvin I said, "We'll meet you out there just as soon as we're done with these extinguishers. Give us half an hour."

When we arrived at the trailer sales, I found Dallas visiting with Stan Orness, the owner of the mobile home sales business. "What time did you make the rounds last night?" I inquired.

"About 9:30," Dallas replied. "I sure didn't notice anything unusual."

"I found the mess this morning," Stan interjected, as he led us behind the office to a large, 12x70 mobile home. The street side of the structure didn't show any signs of fire, but when Stan opened the door we were accosted by the all too familiar sight and smell of dirty black soot covering everything. "To the right down the hall," Stan said.

As I walked down the hall, I couldn't help but notice the oak woodwork. *Pretty expensive unit,* I thought.

The beam from Alvin's flashlight revealed the heat line from the fire tapering toward an open doorway. Hesitating at the doorway, he motioned and said, "Look at that." My eyes followed the light as it swept over what was left of a double bed, and settled on the ceiling light fixture. It was a three-bulb affair, and each of the bulbs was sagging downwards. Past experience had proven that an intact bulb would melt, aiming toward the area of origin, so it might just be the clue we needed to determine the cause of the fire.

The double bed below the light fixture had burned and melted the foam mattress and box spring. *Must be treated with fire retardant,* I thought. Alvin dropped to his knees and began sifting through a blob of melted foam on the floor directly below the light fixture. "What have we got here!" he exclaimed, uncovering the remains of a matchbook imbedded in the sticky foam below the bed. *Looks like someone has it in for Stan,* I thought.

Alvin began taking pictures, and I stepped outside to where Stan and Officer Carlson were standing. "Is someone upset with you?" I asked, looking at Stan.

"Not that I know; what makes you ask?"

"The fire in the bedroom was set," I replied.

"How do you know?" Carlson asked.

"There was a matchbook in the foam from the mattress."

"I better get hold of Detective Ziegler," Officer Carlson replied.

Shaking his head, Stan asked, "Why would someone do that?"

Officer Carlson had been talking on his portable radio and in a few minutes Police Chief Chris Mathieson and Detective Don Ziegler drove up in an unmarked police car. I shook Chris's hand. "It looks like someone tried to burn one of Stan's mobile homes," I said.

"What makes you think that?" Don asked.

"The trailer had sheet rocked walls which kept the fire in the bedroom where Alvin found the evidence that it had been deliberately set."

"OLD PEAVEY"—SECOND AVENUE NORTH

The 28th of November began as a normal Sunday in the City of Devils Lake, when Gayle radioed informing me of the possibility of fire in the elevator on North 2nd Avenue. "I recognized the caller; I'm going to turn on the sirens," he said.

A fire in a grain elevator required special considerations: flooding the dumping pit, removal of contents, and most importantly the possibility of dust explosions. To my surprise the fire was not in the big elevator, but in an unused 20,000 bushel grain elevator just east of the main elevator. Because I'm naturally curious and there was no reasonable explanation for the elevator to be burning, I contacted the Law Enforcement Center. "Page up Don and Chris, and send them my way."

Gayle had hooked pumper 202 to a hydrant on 2nd Avenue and 8th Street. A police officer pulled up next to me and I directed him to block off College Drive so the larger hydrant could be used.

If I was concerned about the lack of manpower on a Sunday morning, it was forgotten as fire equipment and manpower began arriving. Volunteers came from all directions in various stages of clothing. It wasn't long before they were dressed in fire gear and pouring water on and inside the burning structure. *Training pays*, I thought. I was watching the operation when LaVern came my way asking, "What's in the tank?"

Tucked into a corner of the structure was a ten thousand gallon storage tank. "I'm not sure, but it could be a chemical; keep it cool," I advised.

"Billy," a voice called. Police Chief Chris Mathieson came striding my way. Over his shoulder I could see Detective Don Ziegler, who was looking over the crowd.

"Chris, I'm concerned."

"Do you think someone is setting fires?" he asked.

"This elevator hasn't been used for years; there's no gas or electricity," I said. "There's no reason it should be on fire."

"We'll check out the crowd and take some pictures," Chris said.

Scanning the group of gathered bystanders, I spotted Cass Besse, elevator manager, looking my way. Motioning him over I asked, "What's in the barrel on the west side?"

"Nothing to worry about, it had molasses in it."

"Molasses?" I questioned.

"Yep, it was used to make cattle feed. The elevator hasn't been used in ten years," Cass replied.

"217—LEC." Recognizing the voice of the dispatcher, I said, "Go ahead, Carol."

"There is a gentleman here from Grand Forks Fire Equipment. He heard about the elevator fire and brought in a couple of cases of helmets for the firemen."

"Send him this way," I replied, "I ordered them a month ago."

As I turned my attention back to the task at hand I saw Fr. Gerald Buscher heading my way. Father Gerald had been our Chaplin for five years and made it a point to put in an appearance when there was a fire.

"I thought you'd be preaching this morning," I said.

"I'm between masses," he responded with a smile. After I updated Father Gerald on the situation, he left to walk among the firemen, and lend moral support where he could.

A short time later a pickup arrived with two large boxes filled with new helmets. Stepping from the pickup dressed in military fatigues was Tim Brooks, a salesman for Grand Forks Fire Equipment. "We heard about the fire at Camp. I told the Captain about the helmets, and he told me to 'get them to you right away'." About the time Tim pulled up, I noticed Father Gerald leaving the scene. He stopped at the intersection, turned toward the elevator, and gave the Sign of the Cross. With a wave he continued walking back to St. Joe's. *Quite a guy!*

"217—219, what's in the boxes?"

"New helmets; hand them out."

A sudden 'Whoosh' drew my attention back to the burning elevator as a fireman was thrown to the ground in a cloud of dust. For a brief moment, flame followed the dust out over his head. As I started for the fallen man he got to his feet and waved. *It appears grain dust is still explosive even after 10 years,* I thought.

It was three o'clock in afternoon and with the majority of the fire extinguished, most of the equipment had been returned to the fire hall, except for the mini-pumper. A team of firemen headed by Kevin Hassett was extinguishing random fires using a hose connected to the hydrant which 202 had vacated at 2nd Avenue and 8th Street. I finished wrapping caution tape around the area and went to where I could observe LaVern and Alvin doing their investigation. The fact that there had been no gas or electrical hookups to the elevator, and LaVern had found an open door behind the molasses barrel indicated they should begin their search inside the structure.

Strong's Excavating had been contacted and their backhoe was being utilized to assist in the search for clues as to the cause of the fire. The bucket of the backhoe would dump a load of rubble in front of Alvin, and as he began to dig through the debris, LaVern would direct the operator to grab another load for him to search. Human senses are necessary tools when searching for the cause of a fire, but this day they were utilizing another valuable tool, the flammable liquids detector—a 'sniffer' which could detect the presence of an accelerant in the debris. As LaVern continued directing the operator toward another area of the burned-out building, Alvin waved and shouted, "Turn off the backhoe."

"Did you find what you're looking for?"

LaVern held up his hand, palm out, silencing Dave.

I watched Alvin sweep the sniffer over some pieces of charred wood he had recovered. Even from 30 feet away, the piercing sound of the alarm on the detector indicated a possible flammable liquid. As soon as the alarm sounded, LaVern motioned for me to come to where he and Alvin were working. Signaling Dave, LaVern indicated the need to widen out the suspect area. Without taking his eyes from the suspect area, Alvin handed a number of pieces of burned wood to LaVern; LaVern put some of the items in a bag and handed them to me.

Identifying a member of the hose team, LaVern called, "Kevin! Get me an old helmet, and fill it with water." In moments Kevin returned with a discarded helmet and filled it with water from the fire hose nozzle. Crawling through the debris, he managed to hand the helmet to LaVern with most of the water intact. LaVern explained: "I'm going to drop a piece of charcoal from the burn area into the water and see if we get an oily film." An oil film could indicate an accelerant was used to start the fire.

The testing LaVern and Alvin did from two areas proved the possibility of petroleum products in the debris. Quantities were removed from each area, marked and placed in a container and sealed. The next morning, the Highway Patrol transported the containers to the State Crime Laboratory in Bismarck. *Seems like a lot of work, but if we do it right, it will please Aaron, and we'll get the results quicker.*

I left Kevin and his attack team manning their hose line and returned to the fire hall to do my paperwork. As I came through the back door I found Alvin and LaVern visiting with some of the firemen. Gesturing toward the office, LaVern said, "Let's talk."

The three of us sat down in my office and LaVerne began his explanation. "There appeared to be fires set by each of two elevator boots," LaVern said. (The boots contained cups made of tin that carried grain in chutes from the pit under the driveway to the top of elevator, where it would be distributed to various storage bins. The floor and chutes were constructed of wood.) *If a fire started on the floor or in the boot, it would follow the dust up to the top of the elevator, and we'd be screwed when it came to putting it out, because there was no operable sprinkler system,* I thought.

Looking at Alvin I asked, "What do you think?"

"I agree with Vern," Alvin replied. "A door was forced open on the west side behind the tank of molasses, and somebody got inside and set fires."

"Did you notice anyone special in the crowd?"

"No," they said in unison. "We were too busy," LaVern offered.

"Do you think this ties in to the other fires we've had?"

"Do you mean both The Ranch and the mobile home?" Alvin asked.

"Yes," I replied.

"I don't think someone set The Ranch."

"What's that about the mobile home?" LaVern asked. Alvin explained what he had investigated at Stan's mobile homes sales, and apologized for not letting LaVern in on the investigation.

"That fire was two miles away from the elevator," LaVern said. "What makes you think they might be connected?"

"I'm just saying they were both set on the inside, out of sight," I replied. *Better let Chris and Don know what we're thinking.*

Out on the apparatus floor Robert was getting instructions from Tim Kurtz. *Tim will point him in the right direction,* I thought, *he couldn't learn from anybody better.*

SEVEN-UP AND TESTER'S GARAGE

On Monday morning, November 29, we received a phone call from
Aaron Rash, Director of the North Dakota State Health Department,

saying he had received our package. After answering a few questions, I was told our materials, when submitted, would be expedited. Results would be phoned immediately, followed by a written report.

The rest of the day was spent doing tours with youngsters and Sparky, our resident Dalmatian mascot. The afternoon's group spent over an hour asking questions and searching the basement at 412 5th Street for Homer the Rat. Homer was a figment of my imagination, and the search for this mysterious creature was often the highlight of a field trip to the fire hall. On occasion, Sparky would get involved and help the children search for the invisible rodent.

Just after supper Jerome called asking me to meet him at Mike Tester's house.

Alvin was back by the garage and LaVern was parking across the street when I pulled up. "Jerome called. What's up?" LaVern asked.

"I haven't the foggiest idea," I replied.

The front door to the house opened and Mike Tester appeared. "Come on back to the garage."

As we walked back to the garage, I could see Alvin pointing and Jerome taking pictures. "What did you find?" I asked.

"Looks like somebody's setting fires around town," Mike interjected. *Sounds like the word is out.*

"What happened over here?" Alvin asked.

"Somebody backed into my garage last year and made a hole," Mike said.

On the alley side of the garage was a hole about two feet above the sill plate. It was about 12x6 inches with charring showing at the top of the opening. When I shined my flashlight through the opening, I could see wet and charred newspaper and cardboard from a 7-Up container lying on the floor inside the garage. "Did you get pictures of both sides?"

"Yes," Jerome replied, "I shot a roll."

About that time, Detective Ziegler arrived. When he pulled up adjacent to us, Alvin asked, "What are you doing here?"

"I got paged from the LEC," Don replied.

"How in the hell did they get the word? Did you call the Law Enforcement Center?" I asked Mike.

"No," he replied, "only the fire hall."

Don asked the LEC to switch the conversation to 'scramble' and spoke into his radio. "Did you get the name of the reporting party?" he asked.

"No," Loydene replied. "But the caller was male. He said 'There's a fire at 7-Up and 407-5ᵗʰ Street South'. Unit 9 put out a fire in a dumpster at 7-up. He didn't notice anything at 407, so he went to the fire hall to get his extinguisher refilled."

"Unit 9," Don radioed. "Come to the alley behind 407-5ᵗʰ Street South."

A short while later Unit 9 (Pete Belgarde) pulled into the alley and rolling down his window asked, "What's happening?"

"Where did you use your extinguisher?" I asked.

"7-Up dumpster," Pete replied. Looking toward the garage he observed. "Looks like you needed it."

"No, I just wanted to know how long ago you were at the dumpster."

"Fifteen minutes or so; you can check with dispatch," Pete replied.

Don asked Mike, "When did you notice this fire?"

"Quarter after six," Mike replied. "I came home for supper and saw smoke coming from the garage, and dumped water from the birdbath on the fire."

My watch read 6:40. "Close enough," I said, thinking about the time and distance between the two fires.

Alvin continued digging into the charred wood with his jackknife, penetrating just a little. "Not much depth," he commented.

"Bag the paper and cardboard; I'll try and get a fingerprint," Don said.

"Who's got the duty tonight?" LaVern asked.

"I do," Jerome said.

"Have you had unusual fires on your shift?" LaVern asked.

"No, nothing I can think of. The weird ones happen to Gayle," he replied.

"Maybe someone is upset with one of us," I said.

"Or upset with Don," Alvin replied, gesturing toward Ziegler.

Looking at Pete, I asked, "Did you see any charring on the garage when you drove by?"

"No charring and no smoke," Pete replied.

I wonder if someone was watching from inside the garage, I thought to myself.

PEAVEY ELEVATOR/SHEYENNE GRAIN

The next few days went by fast with many things to finish before the end of the year report. Aaron Rash called on the 2nd of December. "There are petroleum distillates in the charcoal, but it could be related to vehicles in the elevator driveway." *Aaron's report left too many openings, he wants me to think it out.*

It was the holiday season and parties were scheduled for almost every night and each weekend. With the unexplained fires we'd been having, I was concerned about the stress being imposed on the firemen and their families.

Late in the evening of December 4th, a fire was reported at the Sheyenne Feed and Grain Storage Elevator in the Fairmont Creamery complex at 7th Avenue and 1st Street. The elevator, storage elevator and coal bins were only a part of the total complex. The remainder consisted of a four-story brick building bordering the Great Northern railroad tracks, and a 200x50 foot structure originally used for processing milk and cheese products. At the time of the elevator fire, George Fredricks had a wholesale minnow operation in the east 50 feet of this building. To the west was a large area filled with rolls of carpet and padding. The remainder of the building contained frames in which honey production was being stored prior to processing. A set of stairs from this area led up to a 20x30 foot addition which had been constructed years after the original building.

Before the siren on the Memorial Building had quit its donkey bray, I had driven to the fire hall with intentions of moving the mini-pumper. I opened the door to the station and was startled by the appearance of Robert Harveland, dressed in fire gear. Recovering my composure I said, "Get in the mini-pumper."

I went around to the driver's side, climbed in and pressed the door opener. The door began rising, hesitated, and stopped. *What the hell?* I started to reach for the button again when I noticed Robert pushing the button on the wall. The door continued to rise as Robert climbed in the truck. "I opened the door for you," he said. I considered chewing him out for challenging my intelligence, but instead said, "Thank you."

The serious look on his face turned to a smile and he replied, "You're welcome."

It was six blocks to the hydrant on 1st Street where Gayle had begun hooking up and a number of firemen were already on the scene dragging two-and-a-half inch lines toward the elevator. Flames were already show-ing in the head house windows at the top of the elevator. As we slowed to a halt, Robert climbed from the cab to help, and with the door open the loud sound of the snorkel siren heralded its approach. In my rear view mir-ror, I saw the snorkel turning past 201 to follow me into the compound. I moved to the left and out of the way as the driver made a wide swing and began backing the snorkel into a defensive position on the north side of the elevator. Fire was now coming from the roof of the head house.

"204—hook up two hose lines to your truck, and attach a line from your truck to the other storage elevator sprinkler system."

There was little wasted motion as arriving firemen readied themselves for a defensive attack. It showed they had been paying attention and had worked hard at training sessions. I could see red pagers on the belts of the firemen as they changed into their fire gear. *That's what I call dedication.*

From the north, 202 turned into the compound. "202," I radioed. "Hook up to the hydrant by Armour's fuel tanks. Hand jack a couple of hoses, and get some manpower to the east ramp door; drag a third line to the track side for 203."

The siren and rattle of ladders drew my attention once again to the 1st Street intersection where 203 appeared heading my direction. "203—take the alley and go around to the track side of the elevator and help stretch the hose from 202 to your location. 201—drag a line into the west drive-way," I ordered. *That leaves two additional lines.*

Sometime later fire began showing through the metal skin on the el-evator, and I warned of the possibility of collapse. Wooden elevators were usually 25,000 to 30,000 bushels in size, based on whether the lamination began with 2x6's or 2x8's. Laid flat like log cabin construction, the planks were interlocked at the corners and secured with 20 penny nails. This procedure was used as the elevator moved upward until the final portion was completed using 2x4's. The complete elevator was then covered with a skin of sheet metal. The size of the elevator was determined by the height of the structure and number of storage bins involved. I wasn't concerned about the collapse of the elevator to the inside area because of the water being directed on it, but the trackside could fall and block train traffic. Considering that possibility, I decided to drive around to the south side where 203 was operating.

Fires always bring bystanders and an elevator fire, no matter what size, draws onlookers from all around a region. The respect the community had for their fire department was evident as I approached the intersection to turn onto 5th Avenue South. Not wanting to draw attention to my movement I hadn't turned on the emergency lights of the mini-pumper, but traffic passing by saw me coming and stopped. Some of the vehicles had occupants that I recognized as living at least 10 miles from Devils Lake. It was great to see the waves and thumbs up as I drove by. *I've go to tell the guys,* I thought, as the gestures brought tears to my eyes.

Once on the south side of the underpass I could see flashing emergency lights from an approaching vehicle. Slowing as it came abreast of the mini-pumper, Pete Hanson, the Rural Fire Chief shouted, "Where do you want us?" By the number of blue lights stopping behind the big pumper, I could tell he had a formidable crew of rural firemen with him.

"Keep an eye on downwind embers," I shouted. "Send your extra help to the fire ground."

"You got it," Pete replied. Putting the truck in gear he moved toward 1st Street with his entourage behind him. Each pickup had two or three trained firemen in the front seat, and each waved or gave the thumbs up salute as they passed.

After the last blue-lighted pickup passed, I signaled left and traffic once again halted as I crossed to the open area on the south side of the tracks. Fifty feet in front of me was the well driller's dynamite storage locker! Estimating the distance from the burning structure I decided the dynamite wasn't in any danger. To the east 203 straddled a set of tracks flowing water into the upper portion of the elevator. Two firemen were locked into position on the ladder, supporting the hose which led up to the silver-clothed fireman at the top of the ladder. *Damn Tim,* I thought, *he's got to learn to delegate.*

An area below Tim had eaten through the tin cover and the opening exposed fire burning inside the elevator. As I watched the ladder crew's activity from across the tracks, I thought about the Empire Builder on its way through town. *There's no way to bypass the elevator from the east,* I thought, *the yardmaster is going to be pissed.* I looked at my watch as I contemplated the train's schedule and decided there was time to notify the depot in Grand Forks, 90 miles to the east of Devils Lake. I radioed the LEC and asked them to contact the railroad for rerouting the Empire Builder to the New Rockford leg, allowing the train to travel 40 miles south of our location. Shortly after, a police car pulled up and Chief Mathieson climbed out with a portable radio in his hand. "Billy," Chris said, "what the hell is going on?"

"I wish I knew. Right now I'm concerned about the elevator falling across the tracks, and how much dynamite is in that locker," I said pointing toward the wooden structure.

"I heard about the train; what's this about dynamite?" Chris asked.

"I guess we could move it, but I'm not too concerned."

"I'm concerned," Chris said. "Who in the hell does it belong to?"

"Holbeck's Well Drilling. Grace Holbeck lives on 2nd Street."

"I'm going over and ask her to get it moved," Chris said.

"217—LEC."

"Go ahead."

"The yard master in Grand Forks is upset about rerouting. But he changed his tune when I told him the elevator might fall onto the tracks. He asked when it might be open, and I told him to contact you tomorrow."

"LEC, would you have the sheriff go down the tracks and make sure no train comes this way?"

"Will do," Lynette replied.

I was watching the operation across the tracks when the big ladder began to shudder. The portion of the elevator the ladder was resting on fell into the burning elevator, leaving the ladder without support. The sudden movement caused the nozzle spray to shoot upwards, driving a reaction force down the aerial to the firemen below. Tim shouted, "I'm coming down," and began a cautious descent to the ground.

Hearing a noise behind me I turned to see Les Anderson and his hired man Eddie 'the dynamite man' Kraft backing in with a flat bed truck. "Doesn't look good," Les said.

"No, it doesn't," I replied.

Eddie had a sinister smile on his face. "What's the smile for?" I asked.

"I was thinking about the hole it would make if the dynamite exploded," he replied.

"If what exploded?" a voice asked.

Officer Carlson and Detective Ziegler came up beside us. Indicating the wooden shed, Les said, "We were just talking about the dynamite in the locker." The amazed look on their faces when they understood what might be in that locker was priceless. They both looked toward the locker, and Ed shouted, "BOOM!"

For all of us, Ziegler said it best: "Someone ought to string you up by your balls."

"Don't worry," Ed said, "the blasting caps aren't in the locker." Scratching his head and smiling he said, "Or are they?" Taking a ring of keys from his pocket Eddie unlocked the door to reveal a storage shed full of dynamite.

"How many cases have we got?" Les asked.

Ed retrieved a clipboard from inside the storage shed and scratched some numbers on a piece of paper. "About two hundred cases of quarter pound sticks."

"How many sticks in a case?" Dallas asked.

"One hundred quarter pound sticks, but no blasting caps," Ed replied smiling.

Les and Ed began loading dynamite on the flat bed and I crossed the tracks to where the ladder crew was having a discussion. Just as I got within hearing I heard Rick Mikkelson say, "You're the Captain, you don't belong on the ladder."

"Okay, you go up there," Tim responded, pointing at Bill Eisenzimmer. I watched as the big ladder was repositioned, and Bill headed up the ladder followed by Jim Koble and Rick Mikkelson. In moments the nozzle was once again spraying into what remained of the elevator.

Driving down the right-of-way for the railroad tracks, I was able to cross over at 8th Avenue and drive back to the scene by way of the alley between the tracks and 1st Street. When I got to the end of the alley, I looked over the crowd of onlookers. Most of the people I recognized and they acknowledged my presence. Tom Waltos, an insurance adjuster, who lived across the street from the elevator, came over to where I was parked.

"See anything unusual?" I asked.

"No, I just heard a siren and then looked out the window. What's going on?"

Knowing I could trust Tom to keep his mouth shut, I replied, "Keep an eye on the crowd."

Walking to where Officer Carlson was standing I asked, "Find anyone interesting?"

"I stopped Ron Vetsch from kicking the hell out of a young bystander," Dallas replied.

"What do you mean?"

"Ron had seen him at a number of fires and thought he had something to do with them," Dallas said.

"That's the last thing we need."

"I got the kid's identification," Dallas continued, "and had the LEC check him out. He was working before and during some of the fires, so I really don't think he had anything to do with them. I turned the information over to Ziegler."

"217—Fire Station."

"Go ahead, Joe," I replied.

"Duane Bye called. There's fifteen thousand bushels of canola in the elevator, and the phone system was disconnected years ago."

"What's that about?" Dallas asked.

"The fire alarm dialer in the elevator is connected to the phone line," I replied. "No phone, no alarm. This elevator didn't have an outside alarm horn." Watching the fire ground activity caused me to consider: *Maybe we could have stopped the fire if the alarm had been connected.*

A short while later, Assistant Chief Thiessen came my way to review the progress the men were making. "Everything looks pretty good," Walter said. "I checked with Pete and he's got guys checking downwind for floating embers, but more of the track side wall is giving way toward the tracks. Not much more we can do, unless you want me to set up the monitor nozzle."

"Sounds good," I said. "I put the hitch on the mini-pumper. It's parked over there in the alley."

It was 4 a.m. when all the hoses except for two were shut down and equipment began returning to the fire station. These lines led to where the fire watches were stationed on both the north and south side of the smoldering elevator. The south side of the elevator had not fallen onto the tracks, but needed to be removed before vibration of a passing train would cause it to drop. The proper use of the snorkel, ladder and monitor nozzle, along with individual hose streams, kept a fair amount of the interior structure intact. Analyzing the remaining structure, I thought, *looks like we'll have enough left for an investigation.*

Sitting in my office the following Monday morning looking out over the apparatus floor, I wondered who would benefit from all the fires we had been having. *Maybe it wasn't set. Hope the salvage people get here soon.* The back door opened and Chris rounded the corner followed by Dallas. "I didn't see anything significant," Dallas said, as he handed me a package of photos he had taken Saturday night.

I thumbed through the pictures while Chris and Dallas poured themselves a cup of coffee. I laid the pictures on my desk and after selecting two, handed them to Chris and Dallas. "Do you see anything unusual?"

"No." Chris looked toward Dallas. "Do you see anything?"

"No," Dallas replied. "Just a fireman at the top of the ramp," Dallas replied.

"Do you see a hose?" I asked.

"No," they replied.

"Do you recognize the fireman?" I asked.

"He's too far away," Dallas said. Just then the phone rang. "This is Justin Mayberry from Northwest Salvage; we'll be in Devils Lake early tomorrow."

"Great," I replied. "Have you assisted in the investigation of many elevator fires?"

"We've been involved in a few."

"The salvage people will be here tomorrow and we'll search the elevator," I told Chris and Dallas.

After finishing their coffee they left and I returned my thoughts to completing the paperwork in regard to the elevator fire. The back door opened and I hid my notes as Robert Harveland appeared in my office doorway. He was dressed in a bright yellow, short elastic waist jacket advertising Agsco Crop Chemicals. "Nice jacket," I said.

"Got it from my brother-in-law," Robert replied. "He gets a new one every spring when he orders chemicals."

"Does he have a big farm?" I asked.

"Thousands of acres by Wahpeton," Robert replied. "He's married to my sister."

Trying not to smile at Robert's response, I looked down toward the floor and noticed what looked like new tennis shoes. Seeing my downward gaze, Robert said, "I got new shoes at Kmart last night, too."

"Nice," I said.

After Robert left I turned my attention to finding an Arson Investigation book my wife had given to me for Christmas a number of years before.

It was a thick book, and hard to misplace with its maroon cover. Giving up the search, I returned to studying the pictures Dallas had brought. *I wish I could figure out who's standing on the ramp.* A number of years earlier, the City Attorney had recommended putting a problem to rest for a day or two before reviewing it again. "You'll have a better chance of solving the problem," he said. The advice was meant to temper me from saying something I'd later regret. With this thought in mind, I put the pictures back into the envelope and was just placing them in my desk drawer, when I heard, "What's with the pictures?"

Once more Robert was standing in the doorway. "Just pictures of the fire," I replied.

"Oh," he said. "I'm going to work."

Once Robert was out the front door, I retrieved the pictures from the drawer. I separated the pictures of the lone fireman standing on the ramp, and clipped them together with a note addressed to Don Ziegler. This time I placed the envelope in the safe.

As it was a regular scout meeting night, I called families and canceled meetings for the rest of the year, claiming the holiday season as an excuse. I then called each of the paid men and volunteer truck captains and asked them to be my guests at the fire hall at 7:00 p.m. They started coming in early and by 6:45 they were all upstairs in the meeting room.

"We've got to do something," I said, starting the meeting. "The fires always seem to happen on a Saturday night. I want you to divide up the surveillance responsibility of Lake Region Grain, Peavey, and Northern Seed and Feed on Friday and Saturday nights until daylight."

I heard someone climbing the stairs and quit talking. Robert's red head appeared above the railing and without hesitating he asked, "What's happening?"

"We're putting together a plan for keeping an eye on the city." *I wonder what kind of hours he keeps.* Without comment he turned and continued on into the dormitory.

The conversation turned to manning the different complexes and who would be involved in the roving patrol. It was decided that at least three individuals would occupy each elevator all night long, and they would transport themselves to the area with only one vehicle and park at least a block away. "Chris asked that you don't bring guns with you," I cautioned.

The first laughter I had heard in weeks came when Kirk said, "What he doesn't know won't hurt him."

We were discussing the scheduling for the coming weeks when the phone rang. It was Dick Johnson. "Where in the hell have you been?" I asked.

"I put smoke detection in the corridor between the Duke's and Royal Lanes. Is it okay to tie into the alarm board at the fire hall?"

I was glad to hear that he had taken the initiative to protect his property, and told him so. Filling him in on our plan of surveillance, I ordered, "Stop in tomorrow and get your assignment." I hung up the phone and turned to face the group once again. "I'll talk to the elevator managers and get keys to the buildings."

The following morning I met with Chris, Dallas and Don, and discussed the procedure we had planned for the coming weekends. "Why are the fires always happening on the weekend?" Don asked.

"I was thinking more along the line of whose duty night it might be," I replied.

"Whose duty night has it been?" Chris asked.

"At first it looked like Gayle's duty night, but we've had calls on other duty nights. I'm not sure what to think. I'd like to ride around with one of your people this weekend."

FIRE HALL REVISITED
"I'll have Pete pick you up in the buck wagon."

Early Tuesday afternoon LaVern and I were digging through debris from the north side of the elevator. Each time the backhoe reached into the structure LaVern and I would direct its movement into an area we wanted to examine. After an hour enough debris had been removed to allow us to examine the elevator floor. Justin shut down the backhoe and climbed over to where we were searching. Using a rake, he began removing debris from the area of the elevator boots.

In moments the area by the first boot was uncovered. Charring was evident at the top portion of the access hole to the chute. "Someone set a fire," Justin said. "It climbed the dust to the head house." Investigation of the two remaining areas indicated the same thing. "I've seen a number of set elevator fires; this one is pretty well preserved. Your guys made one helluva stop." *I was wondering about his expertise as he was only twenty-four years old, and then Justin said,* "All they needed was a rag; the dust carried the fire up the boot. I'm sure you won't find any evidence."

A chance meeting with would-be informant Rich Gooby later that week caused me to re-think what I was trying to deny. A sick feeling came over my stomach as he suggested, "Look among your own."

Later that evening I was reviewing the assignments for the three structures when a horn sounded at the back of the fire hall. Slouched down in the driver's seat of a big LTD Ford two-door with a cowboy hat pulled down over his forehead was Pete Belgarde. I climbed into the passenger's seat. "Where did you get the machine?"

"Drug enforcement," Pete replied. "Here, take this hat, pull it down and you'll look like one of the boys." As we drove the uptown district, we were passed by roving patrols of both officers and volunteers. That first night, no one knew what we were driving, and we heard volunteers call the LEC for identification of our license plate. The next day I talked to members of the roving patrols, and all were surprised to hear it was Pete and me in the LTD.

Friday night had been quiet, and Saturday night was also uneventful and we put over 200 miles on the LTD before Pete dropped me off at the fire hall. Instead of going home, I slept in my office chair until daybreak, when I was awakened by pounding on the back door. I unlocked the door to reveal Robert Harveland. "Larry Hesser got inside the elevator without us knowing, and scared the hell out of us. Kirk almost shot him!"

Just what we need, I thought.

I called Sheriff-elect, Perry Horner. "I told him not to sneak around the elevators without someone knowing he was there," Perry said.

"He damn near got himself shot."

The week of December 12th proved to be quiet and day-to-day inspections were curtailed as businesses were busy with the oncoming Christmas holiday. Scheduling the elevator watch was completed, and Pete Belgarde and I were to work roving patrol both nights. It was cold outside, and there weren't many people out walking around. We had met Jerry Johnson in the Mercy Hospital parking lot, where he was keeping an eye on someone walking along the Soo Line railroad tracks. "He started out over by Sunset Trailer Court, and he's only got a jacket on."

"Keep an eye on him," I said. "Don't let him freeze to death."

Pete and I made a number of observations ourselves but nothing as unusual as what Jerry had seen. Once again the weekend offered very little activity and no clues as to who might be causing the rash of fires. We began to doubt our theories. Pete dropped me off about 4:00 a.m.

"How did it go?" Gayle asked. Following an update of the evening's activities, I headed home for a decent night's sleep.

On Monday morning a call from Chris brought me to the railroad siding next to Lake Region Grain on North College Drive. As I approached 10th Street, I could see Chris standing between a boxcar and the elevator. Ray Young, elevator manager, was standing in the doorway of the elevator. "Ray found something that had been slid under the door," Chris said.

Lying on the wooden floor of the elevator was the burned remains of what looked like hand towels. "I didn't see them when I checked last night; maybe I missed them," Ray said.

"Same stuff in the box car; someone tried to burn it, too," Chris added.

As I was taking pictures, a patrol car stopped to see what was going on. Chris called for a couple of evidence bags, and carefully separating the materials, he sealed the bags and handed me one. Imagining 'what might have been' is a wasted effort, but I couldn't get the thought out of my mind that even as my men were inside a building—protecting it—someone was daring enough to try and start it on fire. *What was I missing?*

When I returned to the fire hall, I placed the bag in a cardboard box, and locked it in an upstairs filing cabinet. I scheduled another meeting for 7 o'clock that evening.

It was well before 7:00 p.m. when a call from Jerome indicated everyone was upstairs waiting. All eyes were on me as I entered the meeting room. The concern I felt for those guys at that moment was unbelievable. *What's next?* I crossed the room to the inspector's office and retrieved the bag Chris had given me. I handed the bag to the first man and after a quick look, he passed it on. Everyone was silent until it arrived in the hands of Kirk Klemetsrud. "What's with the paper towels?" he asked.

"They were set on fire and slipped under the loading dock door of Lake Region Grain and into a boxcar on the siding."

"Jesus," Kirk said, "that's in full view of College Drive."

"When were they found?" Ron Vetsch asked.

"This morning," I said.

"Could it have been done when we were in the elevator?" Ron questioned.

"Yes."

For a moment they looked at each other, and Jerome asked, "Now what?"

"Christmas is coming; I don't want you away from your families, I'll think of something."

"Bullshit," Kirk replied. "We're in this together." They nodded their heads in acknowledgement, giving me a vote of confidence.

"I'll go on the radio with a message asking people to keep their eyes open," I said.

"What about putting something in the Journal?" Tim asked.

"Whoever is doing this has got a set of balls," Ron said.

"You ain't a shittin'," Kirk added, and for emphasis stated again: "And in full view of College Drive."

THE FAIRMONT CREAMERY

The week passed quickly and Harvey traded duty nights so Gayle could be home with his family on Christmas Eve. I was at my brother's home on 6th Street for our annual family Christmas get-together.

"217—Fire Station," my portable squawked.

"Go ahead, Harv," I replied.

"Tom Waltos called. He was walking his dog near the old creamery building, and smelled smoke. There's no one in the station, I'll leave it unmanned."

I shrugged into my parka and headed out the door. "I'm on my way to the hall," I radioed. "I'll bring 202 to the scene." At the hall, I changed into my fire gear and opened the door of pumper 202 to find Robert sitting in the passenger seat. "I thought there wasn't anyone in the fire hall when Harvey left," I said.

"Harvey told me to go to Gary's for supper and bring him back something. I just came in the door when he left."

Busy getting the truck into motion, I chose not to respond and sensing my silence as disapproval he said, "I should have stayed in and made something to eat."

"That's why I got you guys the ham in the fridge," I said.

"Oh," Robert said, "I thought it was Gayle's."

"He traded duty nights with Harvey so he could be home with his family," I said.

As I drove south on 6th Avenue, I spotted 201 coming north toward me with his flasher signaling a right turn. *Poor bastard missed the corner*, I thought to myself.

I followed 201 into the compound and turned 202 over to Don Nakken with orders to place it in reserve. Harvey traded places with Jack Nash, and he, Jim Nelson and Jim Moe donned breathing apparatus. Jack dropped the skid load from the back of the pumper and drove to the only hydrant at the east end of the complex. Harvey forced the door and the two Jims began advancing the hose into the flaming interior of the office portion of the creamery building. Lyle Johnson had shrugged into a breathing apparatus and took Harvey's place on the hose.

As the team forced their way into the building, the flames subsided and smoke color changed from black to gray. In moments the flame they had extinguished returned, and shortly after, Lyle Johnson came scrambling through the doorway and landed in a puddle. Steam was coming from his bunker gear as he laid face down in the water. Grabbing him by the coat collar, Cliff Ludwig and I pulled him away from the doorway.

"I'm taking a line inside," Ron Vetsch shouted.

"Stay out of the building." I looked around and spotted Mayor Dennis Riggin approaching. *That's all I need*, I thought to myself, "Dennis, let's take a walk."

We walked out of earshot of the working firemen and discussed the situation as I understood it. At one point I almost divulged the names of suspects I had on the list in my billfold. Instead I dwelled on the fact that the fire in the creamery building wasn't near as bad as it looked, and Lyle made it seem worse than it really was.

Moments later Lyle came over to where Dennis and I were talking and said, "It's really hot in there." I looked at Dennis and noticed a smile forming, *probably at Lyle's speedy recovery.*

"You're well-liked Lyle; but you've got to get your shit together. One of these days you're going to get hurt and no one is going to believe you," I said.

"Tell the guys to be careful," Dennis said and walked away.

While visiting with Dennis, I managed to keep an eye on Ron's hose line as it advanced into the creamery building. In moments frames of wax and honey were being passed outside. Some of the wax continued to burn, and a relay had been formed to pass the frames to a pile in the center of the parking area where Tim's ladder crew washed them before setting them to the side.

Carl Lange, a neighbor, had brought coffee for the firemen and I was watching the various activities when a voice remarked, "It looked like smoke was coming from the center of the building." The voice belonged to Tom Waltos, the reporting party.

"Did you see anything?" I asked.

"Not a thing," Tom replied. "My neighbor said to tell you he heard you talking on the radio Saturday morning about flammable material left in the open, and went out to take the gas tank out of his boat, and it was gone."

"When's the last time he saw it?"

"I don't know," Tom replied, "he just said to tell you."

Not long after Tom left, Ed and Helen Senger approached and asked, "Have you been upstairs?"

"What's upstairs?" I asked.

"Antiques, you name it," Ed replied. "Chairs, dressers, tables."

Cliff had returned to operating the snorkel and illuminating the scene. "Can you get into the addition on the roof over the office?" I asked over the intercom.

"No," he replied, "I looked it over a while ago, and there's no outside access."

I motioned to Ed. "Come with me. I want you to show me where the steps are."

As he started to point out the location of the stairway, a rush of smoke came through the doorway. Beating a hasty retreat, Ed shouted: "The steps are just east of the office."

That 20x30 foot room can hold a lot of antiques, I thought to myself. "Give me your breathing apparatus," I said to Harvey.

"Let's go," Dennis Olson said. Together we felt our way through heavy smoke toward the aforementioned stairway. I could hear hose streams operating on what later turned out to be fire in carpet and foam padding belonging to Keating's Furniture. All around us were the muffled voices of ladder men tearing down cork ceiling tile. I followed Dennis upward into the unbelievably hot atmosphere. His hesitation was evident when he reached the top and I heard a crash as he forced open the door. "Wow," Dennis said. Looking past Dennis's fire boots, I caught a glimpse of furniture stacked to the ceiling. I had been right: That was a lot of antiques.

"Doesn't look like the fire got up here," Dennis said.

Not waiting for me to answer he slammed the door shut forcing me back down the steps. Once outside, we removed our masks, and Dennis explained what we had done and told the Sengers: "Everything looks good."

I could see a questioning look on Helen's face and reassured her, "Dennis knows antiques and understands your concern. As soon as we can we'll take you upstairs."

Even with added hose lines, it took over an hour before Walt was satisfied with the extinguishment and told me the fire was out. During this time the remainder of the honey frames had been removed from the office, and some of the fire-damaged rolls of carpet and padding were carried out into the parking area of the complex.

"Larry Duhamel called. His fuel tank is missing."

Deputy Sheriff Jerry Idland and Dallas Carlson were standing behind me.

"One of the guys said there's a gas tank in that entrance shed," I said, pointing toward what remained of the wooden frame shed attached to the creamery.

Jerry was an example of a true professional in the way he dressed. Neat as a pin; trousers and shirt creased, boots shined. One thing I noticed about Jerry is that if he needed to get dirty he would. After pointing him in the right direction, I watched him climb over debris and through the entry shed. In moments he came from inside the building carrying a five gallon outboard motor fuel tank. "We'll take this back to the center and dust it for prints, if that's all right with you."

Dallas noticed me surveying the bystanders and said, "We'll go around and take it up the alley to the car."

Wrap-up was called and before Tim's crew secured the property for the insurance adjusters, he had the Sengers escorted upstairs to check on their antiques. He later said, "They were really excited when they saw everything intact."

Considering the number of items upstairs, I replied, "I'll bet they were."

I spent some time looking over the scene, and realizing the night was almost shot, returned to the fire hall to take a shower. There was only one light illuminating the apparatus floor, but it was easy to tell by the shine on the concrete and the full hose rack that preparations had been completed in anticipation of the next emergency. Even though I could hear a lot of noise coming from the second floor, I decided to go up and take a shower.

Upstairs in the meeting room, I found a couple of firemen visiting, eating sandwiches and drinking coffee. *Someone has been gracious*, I thought. They waved, acknowledging my presence as I walked across the carpeted floor. Opening the door into the kitchen, I froze when I heard Robert say to Jerry Seibel: "Have some of the ham I bought. Make a sandwich; Harv and I can't eat it all." He looked me straight in the eye and said, "I'll make you a sandwich if you want."

THE GARAGE

On Tuesday morning Sheriff's Deputy Harry Johnson came into the fire hall carrying an extinguisher. "Jerry told me to bring it here to get it refilled."

As I reached for the extinguisher, Harry pulled it away and said, "Before I forget, I've got something to tell you. I was patrolling the uptown business district when I saw someone throw something into a dumpster by the Eagles Club. When the guy saw me, he took off running west down the alley. By the time I got to the end of the alley there was no one in sight. I went through the next alley, and when I returned I found the dumpster on fire and used my extinguisher to put out."

It was a short explanation but he really got my attention. "Did you notice what he was wearing?"

"A short yellow jacket; boy could he run."

"Any writing on the back?" I asked.

"No, I don't think so, but he was a blur. Incidentally, Jerry said to tell you that they didn't find any distinguishable fingerprints on the fuel can."

It was another quiet week, with New Year's Eve passing without so much as a phone call. I had just finished watching the Rose Bowl when my radio indicated a garage fire at 208 7th Street. I drove to the fire hall with my red light flashing. Once again I found Robert sitting in the passenger's seat of a pumper truck. Climbing into the driver's seat I asked him why he didn't go out on 201. "I was waiting for you," he replied.

It was only two blocks to Curt Rekkedahl's garage fire, and instead of going all out, I took my time and watched Robert out of the corner of my eye. There wasn't a notable change as we left the fire hall, but when we turned onto 4th Avenue and could see the fire equipment and personnel just ahead of us, he started squirming. It was then I noticed he was wear hip boots. "Where are your yellow trousers?" I asked, referring to the turnout gear issued to all firemen.

"There in the washer. I just got around to washing them after the last fire," Robert replied.

Stopping at the Masonic Temple, I ordered Robert, "Help Jack hook up to the fire hydrant." He climbed from the truck cab and slammed the door. I watched the operation for a short time, made sure the ambulance was in attendance, and radioed Walt that I was returning to the station.

After I returned 202 to the station, I went into the office and played back the tape of the fire call. As I was listening to the tape, a police car pulled up to the back of the station and I heard a knock at the back door. I opened the door to find Officer Rich Tewes of the Devils Lake Police Department.

"Earl Reed is sitting on a garbage can covering a shoe print. I'd like to have you come down and take a look at it."

Could it be possible? I thought. "Hold on Rich, I'll be right with you."

I charged upstairs through the meeting room and kitchen into the dormitory. Scanning the room to make sure I was alone, my gaze settled on the bed in the northwest corner. Moving quickly before being discovered, I picked up a pair of sneakers from the floor and checked the tread pattern. I was not surprised to discover they were wet. Setting them down, I opened a dresser drawer and found a pair of yellow chore gloves. They were damp, and smelled of fuel oil. Carefully placing them back in the drawer, I checked the clothes washer and found Robert's yellow trousers damp from the wash cycle. I removed them from the washer and examined them for telltale signs, of what I wasn't sure. Not noticing anything special, I placed them back in the washer and returned to the apparatus floor and told Rich I'd meet him at the location of the fire.

"Earl's behind the Masonic Temple," Rich said, and headed for his patrol car.

As I followed Rich out the back door I noticed a brick protruding from the rain gutter on the addition to the fire hall. Naturally curious, and not having seen anything there in the past, I waited as Rich drove away and reached up to recover—my Arson Investigation book! I ran my hand further along the gutter and discovered a flashlight and a pair of yellow chore gloves similar to those in Robert's dresser drawer. I quickly replaced the items where I had found them and called the Law Enforcement Center to make sure they had their fire phone in service as I was returning to the scene of the garage fire. Carrying the burden of what I had just discovered and afraid of what I might find in the next few moments, I parked the pickup and walked around the corner of the Temple to find Earl sitting on an upturned garbage can, just as Rich had said.

"It's about time, I almost got run over. The firemen used an MDU truck to pull the car from the garage and damn near hit me," Earl complained. If the situation weren't so serious I might have laughed.

Rich met me as I approached the can and he and Earl carefully picked it up to reveal a foot print. "Rich," I said, "take some good pictures of that footprint. Give Ziegler a call and meet me at the cop shop."

I got Perry Horner's attention. "Get Robert and some hose and let's go back to the fire hall." In a few minutes, wet hose was dumped into the pickup and the three of us drove to the front of the fire hall. When Robert went inside to open the overhead door, I quietly said to Perry, "Come to my office when I tell Robert to put slats in between the hoses."

After we had unrolled the pieces of hose and flipped them onto the hose rack, I instructed Robert on the proper spacing of the slats between the horizontal lengths. "I'll get a fresh pot of coffee started." Turning toward Perry, I said, "Let's go and talk about your swearing-in ceremony, I'm sure Robert can handle the slats." Robert looked away to do the spacing of slats, and I was able to signal Perry to keep his mouth shut.

As Perry followed me to my office I said, "Follow my lead in case Robert comes this way. I want you to know I suspect Robert of starting fires, but the only proof we've got is a tennis shoe print at the scene of the garage. I know there are guys on this department that would love to do him in after all the misery he has caused. I wouldn't blame them. Hell, I'd even help them."

"What if you're wrong?" Perry asked.

"Believe me, I'm right. Who'd miss the little weasel? Tewes is waiting for us at the Center."

I'm not sure what prompted me, but I signaled Perry and he responded by saying, "Why don't you and Robert come down to the Center and see my office."

Suddenly Robert appeared in the doorway, and said, "I'm done with the hose; what else have you got for me to do?"

"Would you like to go down and see my new office?" Perry asked.

I almost fell from my chair when he responded, "Sure, sounds good to me."

We climbed into the pickup with Robert sitting by choice between Perry and myself. The El Camino was crowded this time, as I did my best to not associate myself physically with Robert.

Arriving at the center, I noticed the Police Department office area was open just as Perry said, "I have to get a key for my office. I won't be sworn in until tomorrow, so I haven't any keys."

We followed Perry down an inner hallway to a lighted office, Robert strolling behind him in a nonchalant manner. Seated at a desk in the room were Officers Rich Tewes and Don Ziegler. "Robert," I said, "these gentlemen would like to speak to you."

Immediately Robert froze in place, and glared at the officers. "Robert," Ziegler said, "please sit down." Robert continued glaring at the officers as he sat down. Perry and I backed from the office, closing the door behind us.

I followed Perry to his office. Perry picked up a phone and asked the switchboard to landline the Wahpeton Police department. Able to hear only one side of the conversation, I had to wait for a few minutes until Perry replaced the phone in its cradle.

"When they first called to check on Robert," he said, "they only talked to the receptionist who brought up Robert's name on the computer. The detective on duty tonight was familiar with Robert and the family and was very interested in what I had to say. This summer, the Wahpeton Fire Department found Robert standing next to his brother-in-law's burning T-Bird. He was also operating a combine and truck while harvesting, and three field fires started for no apparent reason. The last time he was dumping grain in the elevator, they discovered a fire in the pit area. Luckily they extinguished it before it got out of hand. It looks like you got your man." There was no elation in Perry's statement. That skinny redhead had lived at the fire hall and done plenty of damage to the community.

A half hour passed and Ziegler came into the observation room where we were waiting. "He won't talk to us. I'm going to call Merle." Merle Henke was the local Crime Bureau Agent. He lived just outside Devils Lake on a hobby farm. His dress code and disarming appearance caught many people off guard.

Perry and I poured a cup of all night coffee. It was close to midnight when Merle walked in the door. He had reviewed past fires and Perry told him about his phone call with Detective Johnson of the Wahpeton Police Department. Picking up the phone Merle paged for Robert to be brought to his 'office'. With a wink at us he went around the corner to the interrogation room.

Merle was sitting at the table reading a book when Robert was escorted into the room. We had the sound system turned on and could hear their exchange. "Robert," Merle said, extending his hand, "I'm Merle, have a chair. Would you like a pop?"

"Sure," Robert said.

Merle looked toward Tewes waiting at the door and said, "Get us a pop, and leave us alone."

Merle put down his book, leaned back, and rested his cowboy boots on the table.

Moments later, with pop in hand, Robert leaned back, and rested his hip boots on his end of the table, and casually took a sip of pop.

I told Perry to turn off the speaker and he and I sat and reminisced about the years we had known each other. Pitcher Park, the fire in the Mayer Hotel, his service as a police officer and now his election to Sheriff of Ramsey County. We would occasionally glance toward Merle and Robert, keeping an eye on the activity in the interrogation room, and after about forty-five minutes Merle got up from his chair and reached out and shook Robert's hand. Motioning for Robert to stay seated, he left the room and came to where we were. "He's a little remorseful, but he wouldn't admit to anything except being involved in the garage fire. He said someone was with him and started that fire. I noticed his hip boots and asked him where his regular fire pants were. He said they were in the wash. He hasn't got a girl, and he got a glazed look in his eyes when we talked about one of his old girlfriends. I'm sure he had something to do with all the fires."

As Merle started to leave, he turned and said, "By the way, Robert doesn't like police uniforms and hates Gayle for shoving and laughing at him at The Ranch."

A short while later Robert was brought into the booking area for fingerprinting. The head jailer brought him to where Perry and I were standing, and looking at the floor he said, "I'm sorry."

Robert was taken from the booking area into the bathroom facilities, where his clothes were taken from him and he was directed to take a shower. Deputy Harry Johnson came into the booking area to keep an eye on Robert so Perry and I could exam his clothing. After the jailer had finished searching Robert's clothing, he placed the items on the counter. "He won't need these."

"Let me see his underwear," I said.

Examining his jockey shorts I could see wet spots where he had ejaculated. "You're shittin' me," Perry said, when he saw where I was pointing.

I called Jack Zaleski at the Journal early the next morning and told him what had happened. Jack immediately understood the possible repercussions. Because of his concern, the story of Robert was tucked away on the bottom of page three. For that I will be eternally grateful.

There was elation in the voices of all the firemen when I called them Monday morning. Many wanted questions answered but I told them I would speak to the group at a meeting that night at 7:00.

Monday was a busy work day. Questions were called in from various newspapers. These I referred to Jack. Firemen who never came to the hall except for meetings and training sessions appeared at various times asking if the coffee pot was on. As I was the only person aware of what had happened, I was hard pressed not to tell my closest friends: Jerome, Walt, Gayle and Harvey.

It was 7:00 p.m. when I climbed the steps to face the firemen. There was a sign hanging on the wall: **NO FIRES UNTIL THE MEETING IS OVER!!!**

I had spent over an hour reviewing my notes, and when I opened them and looked up to face the group, I said a little prayer. Closing the folder, I began telling the story of Robert and the fires. I finished with his confession to Merle Henke, and what we had found in his shorts. Just as I completed my explanation, I heard the back door close followed by footsteps on the stairs leading to the second floor. At the beginning of the meeting I had mentally checked off all the firemen on the roster. There were even some old timers. *No one was missing.* I was curious as to who would be coming up the stairs.

Appearing above the railing as Robert had once done when we had another meeting was Chief Deputy Fire Marshal Richard Radspinner. "May I speak to the group?" he inquired softly. Many of the firemen had heard of Richard, but had never met or seen him. At 6' 2" he was an imposing figure, but almost comical with that little pork pie hat.

Accepting my silence as permission, he began. "I heard by the grapevine what happened up here, and I felt I had to drive up and talk to you." Richard began with a short morale-building speech and concluded with the information that a big percentage of arsonists are sexually motivated, and it isn't unusual to find a fireman setting fires for various reasons.

When he finished, he thanked the group and added, "I have never been invited to your supper on meeting nights, and I would be delighted to join you some evening." There was a resounding round of applause and he left the way he had come. I later found that Richard had driven three and one half hours from Bismarck for a five minute speech, and was returning home that evening. *Quite a guy.* I thought. *He taught me a lot.*

An expedited hearing took place a few days later and Robert pled guilty to being an accomplice at the garage fire and was sentenced to serve time at the State Penitentiary in Bismarck. Following his incarceration, things quieted down substantially, but a year and half later, I received a call from Robert.

"I'm up for parole in a month," he said.

"What are you going to do when you get out?"

"I'm going to come back to Devils Lake and kill my dad."

Somewhat taken back, I hesitated and asked, "Why would you want to do that?"

"He told me he was in the penitentiary for bad checks, but he lied. It was for something much worse." *That blew my mind. I knew I had to be careful with any more questions.*

"What gave you that idea?" I asked.

My psychologist is the same one Dad had."

"Where does your dad live now?" I asked.

"In Devils Lake at SkyView Apartments on the second floor."

"It's too bad you feel that way," I replied, not knowing what else to say.

Robert changed the subject and a short time later hung up the phone. I immediately called the Fire Marshal's office and was able to get the address for the parole board. I sent them a letter alerting them to the conversation I had just had with Robert. Needless to say, his parole was revoked for six more months.

A period of time had gone by when Curt Fogel, a Deputy with the Fire Marshal's Office, stopped by on his way home to Lakota. We were reviewing an investigation he'd recently done when the phone rang.

"Hi, this is Robert." I motioned for Curt to share the telephone.

"Hey, Robert, how's it going?"

"I'm working at Offut Farms in Moorhead."

"How long have you been there?"

"These are great people, and they have a good looking daughter," he said, avoiding my question.

"What brings you to the phone?"

"I'm going to drive a truck to Cando to pick up seed potatoes."

"Why don't you stop in and see us when you come this way. You could park your truck in that area across from the fire hall."

There was a noticeable hesitation and then he said, "No, I don't think so. I caused you guys enough trouble when I lived there."

"What makes you say that?"

"Nothing special. I just wanted to say 'hi', and let you know what I was doing. Oh, by the way, I've got a girl, real good looker. See you around sometime."

With that he hung up the phone and left Curt and I staring at each other.

That afternoon, I called the Fire Chief in Moorhead and told him about Robert's background. I could tell by the conversation that he was having a hard time believing me, but thanked me for the information. Two weeks later Moorhead had fires in a car, house and bowling alley, all unexplained. *I tried to tell them . . .*

CHAPTER 21

REFLECTIONS IN THE MIRROR

During the late 70's and early 80's the number of emergency calls averaged one every day-and-a-half. I had asked repeatedly for another fireman to teach Fire Prevention and educate the public. One morning during coffee, Fire Commissioner Balzer Kurtz offered his support of an additional fireman if I would cease working nights at the fire hall. Once an agreement was reached with other commissioners, Balzer suggested I look around the community for someone who would fit the bill and be accepted by others in the department. When I presented the name of Harvey Bartholme to his friends at the fire hall and the City Commission, Harvey got the overwhelming support needed, and thus began his fulfillment of a lifelong dream of helping his community.

With the addition of Harvey, I no longer worked nights. Projects I had previously worked on during these duty nights now had to be done during the day, and early morning was always best for these activities. Harvey was at the radio station recording Public Safety Announcements and I was just pulling on my coveralls to begin working on some traffic controllers when the phone rang.

"Fire Station, Oehlke."

"There's a fire in the house next door, I live at 909-3rd Street," the caller said.

"Where's the fire?" I asked.

"She said it's upstairs."

"Is everyone out of the house?"

"Oh boy, are they ever!" he exclaimed.

I paged Walt. "I'm responding to a house fire in the 900 block of 3rd Street. Turn on the sirens." I threw my coat and helmet in the pumper cab and was just starting the engine when the passenger door jerked open and Dick Johnson climbed in. "What's goin' on?" he asked.

"Something about a house fire on 3rd Street," I replied.

The distance from the fire hall to the scene was only six blocks, but a crowd had already gathered as we came to a stop in front of house number 911. The siren located near Prairie View Elementary School was winding down as Dick and I climbed from the cab. A voice offered, "My son started the fire in a bedroom upstairs."

As I turned I saw a young lady coming toward the pumper carrying a youngster. I couldn't help but notice that she was barefoot and dressed in a long overcoat. "He was playing with a lighter that belongs to my boyfriend." The saying *cute as a bug's ear* came to mind as she talked. Smiling, I asked, "Where's your boyfriend?"

She looked toward the ground and said, "I don't know where he went. He ran out of the house when I shouted fire."

"He left you and the kid alone?" I asked.

"Yes," she replied.

Police Officer Dallas Carlson had just arrived. "Is 'so-and-so' your boyfriend?" he asked, referring to an individual suspected by the police as a possible drug dealer.

"Yes," she replied.

"Did he take anything with him?" Dallas asked. Since their conversation didn't concern me, I moved away and busied myself donning a breathing apparatus. Two volunteers were dragging a hose to a nearby hydrant, and Dick was unrolling hose for entry into the burning home. Firemen were arriving on the scene, most without gear. Signaling Jack Nash, I shouted, "Take over the pump, I'm going inside."

Watching Dick, it had dawned on me that he was new on the department, and needed to be monitored closely. From behind me I heard Harvey say, "I'm right behind you." *Now I've got two to worry about,* I thought.

The hose began filling with water as I ushered the two of them through the door and up the steps. Despite the seriousness of the situation, I smiled as I realized the three of us were crowded together on the landing between floors. Through the smoke, I could just barely make out what appeared to be fire in a room on the upper floor just to the south of the stairway. Dick adjusted the nozzle spray and directed it through the open doorway. After a few short bursts of water the glowing remained. Rather than place Harvey in harm's way, I began pushing past. "What's wrong; where you going?" he asked.

"Stay here," I said, "I'm going to ventilate the smoke." I crawled up the remaining steps to the 2ⁿᵈ floor, crouched low and searched for a window. Behind me Dick shouted, "Pull the hose." I hadn't made it five feet before I heard, "Wait for us."

Looking back I said, "Try to move in on the fire."

Just to the north of the area of origin I could see the dingy white of bathroom fixtures, and decided it was too close to the fire to open a window for ventilation. I continued crawling feeling for a door or window. Old style construction in this area involved narrow two-story single family, wood frame construction, and based upon that experience I crawled further north until I felt a bedroom door. Reaching up, I twisted the door handle and pushed it open. Just before smoke filled the room, I looked up to see a double bed, dresser, etc. In the northwest corner was an old style carved wood wardrobe. Part of a double hung window that I had been looking for showed from behind the wardrobe and I crawled in that direction after swinging a leg under the bed to check for victims. I grabbed the corner of the wardrobe, put my foot against the wall and pulled, exposing a double window. Unable to push up the lower half of the window, I figured the two halves were locked together. As the smoke got heavier, the temperature increased. I decided not to wait any longer. *Better smoke than water damage*, I thought as I pulled myself upward into the heated atmosphere. Feeling for the latch of the windows, I twisted it open and pulled on the lift handle of the window. Once, twice, I pulled. Deciding glass damage versus more home destruction from fire was the lesser of two evils, I turned and backed into the glass pane using my air tank for a ram. The heat of the fire had been just noticeable until I broke the window. Suddenly, smoke rushed out through the window, bringing the heat of the fire to where I was standing. I dropped to a crouch as the smoke thinned and visibility improved near the floor. I removed a glove and reached up with my hand to feel the heat level. *It's too hot*, I thought to myself. A moment later I removed my helmet and grasping it by the chin strap swung it in a wide arc with intentions of breaking the upper level glass. *I sure wouldn't approve of one of the firemen taking off his helmet*, I thought. Shattered glass fell on my wool face mask, and out the window. Glancing at the ceiling, I could actually watch the smoke rush out through the upper portion of the window.

Quickly sweeping loose glass from the lower portion, I put my helmet back on and stuck my head out through the lower opening. The fact that the fire was burning behind me didn't bother, as it seemed to be isolated in one room at the head of the steps. I must have looked like quite a sight, hanging out the window with smoke rolling over my head, and shouting in a muffled voice, "Look out for falling glass!"

"Put water on the fire," I heard Harvey shout.

"I am, Dammit," Dick responded.

Back in the corridor I noticed everything was covered in oily black soot. *This is not good,* I thought to myself, *it looks like plastic soot.* We had just recently been warned about the hazards of plastic burning, and that information, if not heeded, could bring life-threatening results.

A voice shouted up the steps, "Is everything okay up there?"

"Give us some more hose," Harvey shouted through his mask. Moments later I heard the clumping thunder of booted feet of someone climbing the stairs and dragging a section of hose.

I watched from the opposite end of the corridor as firemen crawled toward the room where we had discovered the fire. Once inside a fireman said, "God Dammit, you could have hollered that all you had going was a mattress fire!" *Harvey and Dick are catching hell now,* I thought, *they won't forget.*

It was quiet for a moment and as I was moving to make my presence known fireman were asking, "Where's the Chief?"

I heard muffled laughter and more than one, "Holy shit," and "Hot damn," uttered from inside the bedroom before Harvey replied, "He's down the hall venting smoke."

"You didn't keep track of him?"

"Can't follow him everywhere," Dick replied, "he's all over the place."

Six firemen were standing in a semi-circle around a burned-out mattress. Against the far wall was an old style dresser with a large tilting mirror rising from the back. The smoke had almost cleared out of the room, and I could see the mattress reflection in the mirror. I almost asked, "What's so funny?" when it dawned on me that they had been spraying the reflection in the mirror rather than the burning mattress.

From below I could hear volunteers examining other parts of the house. At the bottom of the steps, I approached Assistant Chief Walt Thiessen and explained to him what I had seen. "Doesn't surprise me, they've got to learn to <u>think</u>." he said. *That's a great idea,* I thought. I don't think Walter realized until months later that he had provided a key word that I would insist be included in all our training sessions and class teachings for other departments.

Back outside, I saw Officer Carlson visiting with the blonde's boyfriend. Holding a bag containing green leaves at shoulder height, he asked, "Is this yours?" *Hot damn,* I noticed, *it's full of marijuana leaves.*

"No. That don't belong to me," the man replied.

The grin on Dallas's face indicated to me that he knew the bag of grass was his. "If it's not yours," Dallas said, "I'll have to burn it up; we can't have this getting into the wrong hands."

"Where did you find it?"

Distaste showed on Dallas's face, and he said, "Right where you dropped it when you ran out of the house." The man moved away, not wanting to incur more wrath from Dallas.

"I'm the one who called in the fire," said a voice.

"How long had she been living here?" Dallas asked, gesturing toward the fire structure.

"She and that guy had been renting the house for six months and I noticed people coming over at all times of the day and night. I don't think the guy had a job."

"Did you ever see something like this," Dallas said, holding up the plastic bag.

"Nope, but when people came over, they weren't in the house very long."

I almost choked when he said, "She and the kid didn't have any clothes on when they came to my house. She told me she was in the bathtub when the kid came in and told her there was a fire in the bedroom.

"Thanks for the information," Dallas replied, "we'll be in touch."

As we turned to walk away, the neighbor exclaimed, "Praise the Lord."

"What the hell was that for?" I asked Dallas.

"He's an itinerant preacher and she ran next door without clothes on. I bet he got his eyes full."

Then for the benefit of those watching, Dallas raised the bag into the air and shouted, "I'm going to burn it." Her boyfriend was still standing on the boulevard. *What a worthless piece of shit,* I thought to myself.

CHAPTER 22

INVESTIGATIONS AT THE FORT

For many years members of the City Fire Department were asked to investigate fire incidents on the Fort Totten Indian Reservation 10 miles south of Devils Lake. Some situations were traumatic, others humorous, and still others were political in nature. I did my best to respect the American Indian culture, which made it easier to deal with various situations. I made new friends during the investigations, and eventually I was allowed to participate without requiring an escort. I was always careful not to abuse the privilege and felt honored to be accepted. Toward the end of the 20th Century the community voted to change the tribe's name, and Spirit Lake Nation was chosen for its relation to stories of the past.

In June 1975, I performed my first investigation on reservation property. It was a house fire, eight miles south of Devils Lake on Highway 20. Because of jurisdictional policy, I had to be invited by the responding fire department, in this case the Devils Lake Rural Fire Department. I was invited and accompanied by Clair L. 'Shorty' Young, Assistant Chief.

Despite the fact that the Rural Fire Department headquarters was eight miles from the scene of the fire, the four year old, three-bedroom, one-story house appeared to be intact as we drove into the yard. "Helluva stop," I said to Shorty. As I examined the outside of the home, I noticed minor fire extension through the kitchen window on the east side of the house. "Who are the volunteers in this area?"

"There's a half dozen in the south district," Shorty replied, "Lambert Kraft is the Captain."

About that time a pickup pulled into the yard and a short, slightly built individual got out and came our way. "Here's Lambert now," said Shorty.

"I thought I'd come over and see what's going on," Lambert said, shaking my hand. "I farm just down the road."

"You're just in time; we're going to check out the house," Shorty said.

Most of the area around the house was bare of grass. Fowl of all sorts—chicken, geese and ducks were evident everywhere. I noticed Shorty and Lambert had moved to the north side of the doorway allowing me to enter ahead of them. Approaching the doorway from the south, I was immediately repulsed by the smell of dead meat. Twenty-eight years later I still hadn't managed to find a smell to equal that nauseating odor. As Shorty and Lambert stood there, I realized their courtesy was not only to allow me to go through the door first, but to keep the smell from permeating their clothing. On the ground next to the door was a pile of chicken guts, turning black and crawling with maggots. I began gagging and that set off a chain reaction involving Shorty and Lambert. Hurriedly I opened the door and literally welcomed the smell of charred wood. Shorty and Lambert continued to gag as they came through the door, slamming it closed behind them.

"Phewee," said Lambert, "that almost made me puke."

The house had what many would describe as the lived-in look: cereal bowls on the table, dishes in the sink, beds unmade, and a TV set in the corner. Everything was covered with a combination of soot and the yellow powder. "We got the call early this morning; looks like they were cooking. When I got the pager call, I came up the road and the family was standing in front of the house with the door wide open. Fire was coming out the window on the opposite side of the house. I grabbed my extinguisher, and emptied it through the doorway. The fire truck got here, and we cleaned up some of the mess," Lambert explained.

"I was at the hall, so it only took about ten minutes for me to get here with the truck," Shorty added.

I had been training officer for the rural fire department for a couple of years. Except for the yearly social event, the 'SMOKER' (cards, dice and roulette wheel), I never saw any of the south crew at training sessions. At that moment I hesitated praising what Lambert and Shorty had done, but in reality, it couldn't have gone much better. I turned toward the two of them and repeated my earlier observation, "You guys did a helluva job." After a moment I added, "There are a couple of things I've been mentioning at training sessions for the past year: Don't disturb any more than you have to when you put out the fire, and getting here with the truck in one piece is better than driving into a ditch and killing yourself." *You have to be careful when talking to farmers,* I thought, *they're used to working on their own.*

I took pictures of the living room before going into the cooking area and was reviewing the fire scene when Lambert said, "The fire was going up the wall right here and out the window when I shot the extinguisher." In the next breath he asked, "What nights do they have drill at the hall?"

"Monday at seven," Shorty replied.

Curious as to a hot smell coming from the kitchen area, I removed some of the debris and exposed a glowing burner plate. "Did you turn off the stove?" I asked Shorty.

"Didn't have to, it was off when I came in the kitchen," he replied.

Carefully removing debris, I began exposing a red hot electric burner. In the tray below the burner coil was a puddle of metal.

"Did you talk to the family?" I asked Lambert.

"Yeah," Lambert said, "they'd been cooking stew."

"I was here too," Shorty interrupted, "but I didn't want to ask them what kind." Apparently Shorty had heard the story about fattening up dogs for a holiday feed. Years before when I was working on the water line into Devils Lake from Warwick, I had asked my friend Bob Touch whether or not the story was true. With a smile he said, "Dig a little deeper, puppy on the bottom."

Returning to the task at hand, I instructed Shorty, "Pull the breaker; I don't think the switch works."

Shorty went to the furnace room and returned carrying the fuse block for the stove.

As the burner cooled down, I was able to remove the control panel from the back of the oven and lay it on the kitchen table. We removed the switch and found the contacts frozen. "That explains why the burner didn't shut off," I said to Lambert.

"I understand the switch keeping the burner hot, but why did the fire start?" Shorty asked.

"The melted aluminum radiated heat to the cupboards, and they caught fire. Damn lucky the family woke up and was able to use the phone."

SADNESS AT FORT TOTTEN

The Devils Lake Sioux Tribe on the Fort Totten Indian Reservation was governed by federal laws and codes, and it was not unusual for the governing jurisdiction to request a recognized investigator to assist when an unusual situation warranted. I was observing training at the tower facility on Highway 2 when I received a radio call from Special Agent Chuck Trottier of the Reservation Police Department. "217—Could you come out to Crow Hill?" he asked.

Knowing an explanation would not be transmitted over the radio waves, I agreed to be there in about a half hour. Sometimes when Chuck called, it was because there were fatalities. *I hope this isn't going to be one of those times,* I thought.

Seeing Harvey rappelling from the fourth floor of the training tower, I took the tag line from the rope handler and guided him to the ground. "Chuck called from the Fort. Do you want to go along?" I asked.

"Sure do," he replied, removing his rescue belt.

Harvey Bartholme was the Fire Prevention Officer for the Devils Lake Fire Department and worked with various day care providers and school teachers on the reservation, so I depended on his directions to get us to Crow Hill. We had just driven past the community of Fort Totten on Highway 57 when Harvey said, "Turn here." As we came to a stop in the parking lot of the main housing complex, I noticed Chuck Trottier standing next to a Police Department 4-wheel drive vehicle. As Chuck strode our way, I glanced into his 4-wheeler and failed to see any passengers. Past experience had shown me that the lack of a passenger usually indicated we were investigating a fatality. "God, don't it let it be children," I said out loud.

Chuck stood a little taller than six feet and weighed about 220 pounds. Except for his slight red complexion he didn't appear to be American Indian. His face was rough and pockmarked, his hair close cropped and tonight he wore his signature beige coveralls. *He is one mean looking dude,* I thought to myself.

"How's it going?" Chuck asked.

"We were rappelling at the tower," Harvey replied.

"You mean you got that old man up in the tower?" Chuck asked, pointing at me.

"You'd be surprised," I said. "Now why did you get us out here?"

"I'm not sure what happened. Dispatch called and I got here just as the fire truck pulled up. I could see flame and smoke through the front door. When the firemen went inside, it only took a moment before they had the fire out. They ventilated the smoke and I went inside and made sure nothing got moved around," Chuck replied. Looking me in the eye, he said, "There were some fatalities."

Most often children were the fatalities; Harvey assumed this was again the case when he asked, "Where were the parents?"

After working with Chuck for years, I could usually tell by the look in his eyes when an emergency involved children. *As tough as the old bastard looks,* I thought, *he's just a big softy when it comes to kids.*

"They weren't here. It probably wouldn't have made any difference," he replied. Chuck was remembering some situations where neighbors had reported fires and occupants in the house didn't realize something was happening in another part of the house until it was too late to rescue anyone.

Chuck and I waited as Harvey walked around the exterior of the single family dwelling taking pictures. Everett Comer and some of the firemen from Fort Totten Fire Department were standing off to the side, and Chuck waved them over.

The Fort Totten Fire Department had many changes over the years. One stalwart fireman remained and did his best to educate others in the hazards of firefighting, and that was Everett. A slender and slightly built individual he stood about 5' 8" and weighed about 150 pounds when wet. A family man and dedicated fireman, you could always depend on Everett and his crew doing their best to bring an emergency to a successful conclusion.

Everett led half a dozen firemen to our side, reached for my hand and introduced his crew. "What do ya think?" he asked.

"According to Chuck, you made a helluva stop," I said.

"We didn't touch anything; it wasn't much of a fire to put out. I don't think we used 250 gallons of water," he replied, smiling at the compliment.

Hearing a vehicle approach I turned to see John Burke, driving a hearse, pull into a space away from our vehicles. In the passenger's seat was John's assistant Miles Carpenter. I waved in recognition and thought to myself, *We don't need to see the meat wagon.*

Harvey looked toward the hearse, and without hesitating he picked up a hand light and ventured through the doorway into the house. I started to follow, when suddenly he came back out and leaned against the house wall. "Give me a minute," he said.

Fearing the worst, I steeled myself and entered the doorway Harvey had just exited. Just inside was a body, small in size, I would guess about ten years of age, reaching in a direction relative to a crib in the middle of the room. *Harvey must have spotted the crib when he came in the door,* I thought.

"Oh, sweet Jesus!" I muttered.

Behind me Harvey cautioned, "Don't look in the crib."

"I've got to." Peering over the railing into the soot-blackened crib, I didn't notice any thing until I looked toward the opposite end of the mattress. Undressed except for a diaper was the soot-covered form of a body about the size of a football. The inside of the open mouth was black with soot. As I rolled the form to the side, I saw the white outline of the body. A gurgle came from inside as I returned the body to its original position. I did my best to shield my emotions, but when I turned back toward Harvey, I could see the tears running down his cheeks, and I cried too. "Why did they leave them alone?" Harvey muttered.

"Parents leave their children alone a lot out here," said Chuck, who had come in behind us. "I'm sorry we didn't get them out of here before you came."

"Me, too," I replied.

Harvey began the investigation by taking pictures of the room and its location in relation to the rest of the house, finishing the roll of film with pictures of the youngsters.

While Harvey was taking pictures I spent time looking over the heat lines and outlets. Everywhere I looked, the floor was littered with comic books. Although the walls were blackened by the soot, my flashlight had no trouble following the heat line to a doorway in the southwest corner of the living room. Through the doorway was a bedroom, small by most standards, but typical of the housing units on the reservation. Comic books were scattered throughout the room, and on top of the bed was a variety of magazines with a floor lamp lying in the middle of the pile. I could see a hole in the mattress below the bulb radiating from the center like a bomb crater.

With camera in hand Harvey stepped into the crowded bedroom followed by Chuck Trottier.

"I want you to look around the room and tell me what you see," I said.

Before Harvey could respond, Chuck asked, "What's that lamp doing in the middle of the bed?"

Harvey didn't respond immediately, but continued examining the room before he focused on the bed. He motioned Chuck to stand aside and went back into the living room. The beam of his hand light reflected off the door casing as he worked his way back into the bedroom. "Do you suppose someone was reading comics and the only light they had was the floor lamp?" he asked.

"Take some pictures of the pile, and we'll move everything so we can get the bulbs out of the light fixture above the bed," I instructed.

Harvey loaded a fresh roll of film and took pictures of the four walls, bed, comics and lamp. Before leaving the room he took pictures of the doorway and heat line, and returned to the living room where he finished the roll of film. Exposing the remaining portions of the film might seem wasteful, but experience had proven that courts and investigators don't appreciate blank spots on rolls of film.

Chuck and I gathered some of the reading material from the top of the bed, and those I could identify were written down. Carefully removing the lamp, I checked the top of the bulb for wattage and maker. We moved the bed for access to the ceiling light, and Chuck asked Everett to bring in a ladder.

When Everett handed me the glass reflector, the first thing I noticed was the dust buildup inside the dish. "Sure is a lot of dust on these bulbs," he said, as he handed them down to Chuck. As Everett removed the last of three light bulbs, he jarred the light fixture and it dislodged from its ceiling anchor. "These are really brittle wires."

"What's it say on the light fixture?" Harvey asked.

"Use 60 watt light bulbs only," Everett replied.

"Look at this," Chuck said, holding out a bulb to Harvey.

"100 watt bulbs; that explains the brittle wires."

"Take the 100 watters to a neighbor's house and see if they work," I said to Chuck, "and let's take the bulb out of the floor lamp and see what kind of switch is holding it."

Harvey began unscrewing the bulb and said, "It says three stage: 100, 200 and 300 watt." Handing the bulb to me, he carefully removed the socket and cut the cord leading to it. He handed me the socket and said, "I'll be right back." In a moment I could see his flashlight beam shining on the door jamb as he came back into the bedroom. In his hand was a voltage meter. "Shine your light in the socket."

Turning the meter to ohms he placed the prongs on the casing for the bulb and touched each one of the switch contacts. I watched the needle jump when he placed a probe on position number two. Trying the switch on different positions determined what filament(s) had been illuminated in the light bulb. Harvey looked at the base of the bulb, tested his probes and placed them on the individual circuits of the bulb. Satisfied with what he was seeing, he put the three stage bulb in the socket and tried the switch once again. "I can feel the position the switch was in," he said. "Must have been the 200 watt filament."

Chuck returned and handed me the 100 watt light bulbs. "None of them work," he said.

I looked over the bedroom and stepped to the door casing so I could observe both the living room and bedroom by turning my head. "Harvey, what do you think of this?" I asked. "With what you have found and with Chuck and Everett's help, we can safely say this fire was accidental. It was almost dark outside when we got here, the floor lamp was being used to illuminate reading material. By the looks of the child in the crib, it could have been crying. I would guess the youngster on the floor was reading on the bed, and had the lamp lying on the bed so she didn't disturb the baby with its glow."

"Makes sense to me," replied Harvey. "When the fire started the youngster probably got excited and headed for the front door, opened it, and came back to get the baby. The rush of air caused heat and smoke to build and overcome her. Doesn't appear to be any clean spots except where she was laying. I guess we'll never know," he said.

"Parents will never learn," Everett said.

"We'll send you a written report in the morning. Give one to Everett will you?" I said looking toward Chuck.

"Thank you," Chuck said.

Exiting through the front door, I encountered John and Mike dressed in coveralls and rubber gloves bringing in a body bag. I looked at John and nodding toward the bag Mike was carrying ordered, "Use two."

SADNESS AT TOKIO

In the middle of the afternoon one sunny day in May, I received a call from Marley Becker, owner of the grocery store at Tokio, North Dakota. A small community on the Fort Totten Indian Reservation, it was located just west of Highway 20, 11 miles south of Devils Lake.

"Bill," Marley said, "Chuck Trottier wants you to come out to Tokio."

"What's up?" I asked.

"There was a fire at the housing complex by the railroad tracks. Chuck wants you to find out how it started. Someone used a garden hose to put out the fire."

It wouldn't be long before I thanked my lucky stars for saying, "Tell Chuck it'll be a little while before I can get there."

My partner on this investigation was LaVern Bertsch. I had been working with LaVern for a number of years on various investigations within the community. He was a fire department volunteer and manager of the body shop at Marketplace Motors. Short and blocky, firm in his convictions, he did not respond verbally without thoroughly reviewing the situation. This worked well in both auto repair and fire investigations.

We made small talk as we drove toward Tokio. The drive took only 20 minutes, but it had been at least an hour since Marley had called the station. Turning off the pavement onto a gravel road leading to our destination, I could see a long black vehicle approaching from the west. At the same time LaVern muttered, "Oh, shit, not again."

"At least they got out of here before we arrived," I said. "Maybe it didn't have anything to do with our call."

"We could be so lucky," LaVern replied.

Nothing was said between us as I drove the last mile to the housing complex and pulled into the yard on the west side of Chuck's 4-wheel drive Blazer. Parked about 50 feet east of Chuck's vehicle was a Fort Totten Housing pickup loaded with gardening equipment. In that yard were two young men planting a tree, and around the foundation of the house were newly-planted shrubs. "Looks like Housing is doing some yard work," I said to LaVern.

Motioning toward the fire structure LaVern said, "That must be the garden hose they used."

On the north side of the house, a garden hose and nozzle were lying in the dirt just below a charred window. There was little grass, so it was easy to see where the hose led to an outside spigot on the neighbor's home.

"I'll take some pictures," said LaVern.

As LaVern left the pickup, Chuck came around the west side of the house leading a male subject by his trouser belt. The subject's hands were behind him, and there was a bloody bandage on his right forearm. *He probably tried to give Chuck some grief,* I thought.

When Chuck got to his 4-wheeler, he opened the back door and physically hoisted the handcuffed subject into the caged rear area. Then he reached in and secured the two ends of the seat belt across the party's lap, stepped back and closed the door. "What's going on?" I asked.

"The son of a bitch bailed out of his bedroom window. I found him hiding in the weeds and bleeding all over the place. He smells like a brewery, and he landed in horseshit," Chuck replied.

"Look's like he's moving pretty good."

"We'll see. He said he didn't have anything to do with the fire."

"How'd he get the bloody arm?"

"He didn't have enough sense to clean the glass from the broken window, and he cut himself when he jumped." Chuck was a tough and thorough interrogator, but if this guy stuck to his story as Chuck 'ran him through the wringer,' he had to be telling the truth.

LaVern had completed his circumference of the house and was finishing with pictures of the garden hose and burned window casing when he said to me, "Glass is lying all over the yard." I walked to where LaVern was standing and could see sunlight glistening from various pieces of window glass. Picking up a piece, I noticed there was smoke on only one side.

"We put the fire out with a garden hose." Turning toward the voice, I saw one of the Housing Maintenance employees approaching.

"What happened?" I asked.

"We were planting shrubs when we heard glass breaking and saw flames coming through the opening. I dragged the hose over to the house and put the nozzle through the window."

From somewhere to the west I heard a siren, and in moments a bright green fire truck came over the hill about a mile away.

"Oh shit," said Chuck, "I forgot to call Everett."

The downhill slope seemed to increase its speed and moments later the truck pulled into the parking lot. As the truck came to a halt, I could hear the swish of air as Everett engaged the parking brake. Climbing down from the cab, he said, "Better late than never. Where's the fire."

"The boys from Housing Authority took care of the fire for you," I replied with a smile.

Everett saw the garden hose behind LaVern. "You've got to be kidding me!" he exclaimed.

"Nope," Chuck interjected, "they used a garden hose to put the fire out."

"Was anybody in the house?" Everett asked.

"Five people," Chuck replied.

Until that moment I had forgotten about the hearse we had seen. I had only seen the subject Chuck had hoisted into his vehicle.

"The house is still standing," Everett remarked.

"Fire was in one room," Chuck said. "There were three people in that room; two others were in other parts of the house. Gesturing toward his vehicle, he said, "I've got one dude that jumped through a window; he'd been drinking. The other one is passed out on the living room couch. I was at Marley's store when I got the radio call from the Housing guys."

Gesturing toward the maintenance personnel Chuck said, "These boys work fast. The fire was out and the smoke detector in the living room was still squealing. When I went inside to unplug it, I noticed the one dude sleeping on the couch below the detector. I just let him lie."

As LaVern and I went around to the south side of the house, Chuck and Everett fell into step behind us. Rounding the corner, Chuck indicated the window his subject had broken with his body. Examining the window glass and the ground below the opening I saw what appeared to be blood. I said, "Looks like Chuck wasn't bullshitting." Further east was the front door to the home. The door was wide open and the pungent smell of wood smoke hung in the air. The door opened into the living room portion of the home, and lying on the couch was the individual totally unaware of what had happened.

"I can't take this crap any longer," Chuck said as he headed for the kitchen. He searched the cabinets to no avail, but finding a pot in the oven, he filled it with water and returned to the living room, dumping the contents on the sleeping subject.

With a sputter, the startled man exclaimed "What the hell!" As he attempted to clear his mind, you could see the fear in his eyes when he recognized Chuck Trottier towering over him.

Chuck reached down and grabbed the subject by the shirt front and physically lifting him to a standing position with one big fist said, "You're coming with me," and with that, Chuck tippy-toed him out the front door.

Dirty black footprints on the carpet led to a room in the west side of the home. LaVern took a couple of pictures of the footprints and our boots, and we walked down the hall toward the bedroom. I followed the footprints through the doorway, being careful where I stepped to avoid destroying what evidence we might find. Everything in the bedroom was covered with a black shiny film, except for three white images visible on the sheetrock wall next to the burned out window. *My God*, I thought, *they were children*.

There was a gasp and I felt a camera being placed in my hand. "I'm going to check out the other rooms. I'll be right back," said LaVern, as he left the room followed quickly by Everett. Chuck had returned and was standing in the hallway.

"Why didn't you tell me kids were involved?" I asked.

Doing his best to maintain eye contact, Chuck said, "I wasn't sure you would come. Burke was just coming from the Wood Lake Cemetery and I got him to pick up the bodies."

"How were they related?" I asked.

"The one I put in my truck when you first drove up was a brother. The sleeping one was their dad. I cuffed him to the bumper of your pickup," Chuck replied.

"Why did you cuff him to <u>my</u> pickup?" I asked.

"I thought you might be so upset you and LaVern would leave," he explained.

I couldn't hold it against Chuck. I remember asking him to clear out bodies prior to our investigations, especially if they were children. "Was anyone else in this room besides Burke?" I asked.

"No," Chuck replied, "I stayed with them until they were done."

"Got any ideas?"

"No, not really."

LaVern had returned to the bedroom. "Give me the camera," he requested.

I walked to the opposite side of the bed and stared at the silhouettes on the wall. "How old were they?"

"About three, five and eight," Chuck replied.

That's about right, I thought. The silhouettes were positioned in white on the wall in a kneeling position with the smallest to the largest, to the right of the shattered window. It was nearly impossible to believe that two individuals had extinguished this fire with a garden hose, but stranger things had happened over the years. *Everything had to be just right.*

As LaVern continued taking pictures he held up a piece of cardboard and asked, "Did you see this?"

A large hole was burned through the center of the material. "Put it back where you found it," I said. I walked around the bed to Chuck's side and we watched LaVern place the cardboard in a relatively clean position just under the edge of the bed. "What's that in the hole on the floor?" I asked.

"Part of a wick," LaVern said. "It was a candle."

A string of foam from the mattress hung like a fuse above the cardboard. Further up the fire had eaten a large hole into the mattress. "Do you think a candle started the fire?" Chuck asked.

"Looks like the candle burned up the mattress, and flames blocked the doorway. Fumes from the burning foam built up, ignited and blew out the window," LaVern offered.

"I suppose the kids were so scared, they just huddled against the wall," Chuck said. In a quiet voice he added, "Now I know what the brother meant when he said, 'I heard screaming and jumped out the window.'"

Once outside LaVern wound through the roll of film, unloaded the camera, and handed me the exposed rolls. "Did you see the hole in the wall in the bathroom?" he asked.

"The one above the bathtub?"

"Yeah, I could see the pasture outside."

Smiling despite the happenings of the last hour, I responded, "They fill the bathtub so the horses can get a drink."

"You're shitting me!" LaVern exclaimed.

"Why would I do something like that?"

CHAPTER 23

GOOD OLD 'BO'

It is important that a volunteer fire department consider a number of things when recruiting new personnel. Implementing guidelines for testing of prospective firemen is necessary for the well-being of everyone involved. Following the Garcia Rule, the need for a written set of testing requirements was evident. One morning in the early `80's the staff and I sat down with the local authority Curt Sinness, and developed a plan for testing firemen that required proving to Curt the need for each test. Items considered that morning included dragging hose, climbing ladders, carrying a fixed weight, coordination, and claustrophobia. Following a background check, the membership committee would meet with the applicant and discuss things such as family, job, and area of the community they lived in. The area of town a volunteer resided in was an important factor and proved to be beneficial on more than one occasion. When I first became Chief the greatest number of volunteers were from the west side, which made help immediately available when there were emergency calls to that side of town. This was the case one Monday in 1985 at 3:30 in the morning, when after receiving the alert from dispatch there were seven firemen on the scene of the emergency before the fire truck even arrived.

A call from the police department had indicated an officer on routine patrol had seen smoke coming from a one story home at 311-11th Street West. The officer said he had attempted to enter the home, but was driven back by heavy smoke conditions.

Driving toward the west side, I acknowledged a radio call from Police Officer Paulson indicating the home owner and his dog were out of the house and the responding pumper had just turned onto 11th Street West. Parking at the curb, I saw fire coming from the front of the house, and dark black smoke was rolling out the back door. Hose lines were stretched to both the front and back of the house, and Bill Eisenzimmer and Tim Kurtz were connecting the pumper's soft suction to a fire hydrant. What a *great bunch of men I've got on the west side*, I thought.

Just outside each doorway, two firemen wearing breathing apparatus were waiting for water. I watched as the hose stiffened with water pressure, and the teams tested their nozzles prior to entering the burning structure. Dispatch had paged an all-hands alarm, and both the snorkel and the back-up pumper were soon on the scene bringing additional personnel and equipment. Shortly after the snorkel arrived, Captain Hollevoet had his crew elevate the platform and illuminate the scene from above, giving me a better perspective as to what was going on. Watching the attack lines advance helped me gauge the two teams' progress into the structure.

Remembering what Officer Paulson had said about the owner being out of the house with his dog, I looked around in an attempt to locate them. "The owner and his dog are over by that tree," said Officer Paulson.

"Were you the officer that went in the house?"

"I tried, but the smoke was too thick," he replied.

"I wish you guys would wait for us. Don't get me wrong, I'm glad he got out and you didn't go in. You're not equipped for rescue."

"Maybe we should carry breathing apparatus in the police cars," he said.

"You've got enough to do maintaining traffic control," I replied, turning my attention back to the fire scene. *That's all we need; trying to figure out what happened to the officer driving the patrol car, and finding him after the fire is out.*

Two more hose lines and personnel had been added to each entrance for back-up to the entry teams, and smoke was beginning to diminish.

"Should we cut a hole in the roof?" my radio barked.

"No, just set up the fan," I replied.

Terry Straabe was walking around the yard without being dressed in his fire gear. Some firemen carried their gear in their vehicles, and others stored their bags on fire apparatus. Occasionally a fireman would borrow someone's gear when he didn't have his own, and when the owner did show up he would find his gear bag empty. Most of the time one person was responsible for this behavior. Dick Johnson was a good fireman. Although he had been given two sets of protective clothing, occasionally he appeared on the scene needing fire gear. Most of the time I let it go, because of his ability to respond to an emergency any hour of the day or night. But the real reason was that it was fun watching him when he was confronted by the owner of the gear he had 'BORROWED'.

"Have you seen Dickey?" It was Straabe with a perplexed look on his face.

"No, I've been looking for him myself," I replied.

"I'm goin' to kick his ass if he's got my gear on," Terry said.

"Wait until we get back to the station," I coached.

"If he makes that far," Terry replied.

I found Mike Veer and his dog Bo, sitting under a big elm tree at the rear of the property. As I headed in Mike's direction the shout of, "Chief," caught my attention. At the front of the house were two firemen carrying a recliner. I walked over to where they had set it on the ground and asked LaVern Bertsch, "What's with the recliner?"

LaVern removed his mask, showed me a piece of electrical cord, and said, "The fire looks like it started by this chair. See how brittle the cord is?"

The cord LaVern was showing me looked as if it had been exposed to the elements. It wasn't very heavy duty, and when he bent the cord back and forth, the insulation broke loose exposing bare electrical wires. "It sure looks like that cord has been around for awhile. Was it plugged in?"

"Yep," replied LaVern, "it even burned the carpet where it was laying."

"Did you see any smoke detectors?"

"Smoke was still too thick; I couldn't tell."

"Keep an eye on the chair; I'm going to talk to Mike Veer."

As I approached, Mike started to get up and I motioned for him to sit down. Joining him on the ground I asked, "What happened, smoke detector wake you up?"

"No, the dog did," Mike replied. "He was tugging on me and when I woke up the house was full of smoke. He kept tugging me and I crawled out of the house."

"Looks like he deserves a medal," I replied.

Mike reached for the big dog and gave him a hug. In return he received a sloppy wet loving kiss. "Bo deserves more than that," Mike said. *Mike doesn't realize how close he came to biting the bullet,* I thought, looking at the man hugging his benefactor.

"What do you think started the fire?" I asked.

"I haven't the foggiest idea," Mike said. "The only thing I can think of is the recliner in the front room."

"How does a recliner start a fire?"

"I don't know," he said. "I stored it in the barn out at the farm, and I haven't used it in three years. I hurt my back last week and the Doc told me to put heat on it. The recliner has a heater in it. Did the fire do a lot of damage?" Mike asked.

"I don't have a report yet, but flames were coming out the front window when I drove up. Can you think of anything else that might have caused the fire? Do you smoke?"

Mike looked pretty pathetic dressed in only a sweatshirt and pajama bottoms. I took off my fire coat and told him to sit on it and wrap his legs. "No, I don't smoke," he responded. Then suddenly Mike exclaimed, "What the hell!" I followed his gaze to the house where we saw a fireman coming through the back entrance. Normally no remarks would be made regarding firemen, but in this case I had to agree with Mike. A fireman dressed in oversized gear had come through the back door wearing a cowboy hat on top of his helmet. No sooner had Mike exclaimed 'what the hell' than the fireman, seeing us, jerked the cowboy hat from the top of his helmet. To the untrained eye his features were undetectable as he was wearing a mask attached to the air bottle on his back. I didn't need a poke with a sharp stick to know that Johnson had taken Straabe's gear again. At that moment Dick turned away and we could see the name Straabe glowing on the back of the helmet. "That's one of the firemen in Straabe's gear," I said.

"That wasn't funny," Mike mumbled.

Knowing what was in store for the baggily dressed fireman, I said, "Straabe will take care of him when he finds him."

The activity at the house had slowed as the volunteers brought the emergency under control. At the rear of the house was the sound of a gas powered fan Alvin had set up to push clean air through the house.

LaVern motioned for me to follow him, and we went through the front door of the home to begin our investigation. In the beam of my hand light I could see the destruction where the fire had curled paint and charred woodwork. To a lesser degree the fire moved down the hallway toward the north end of the house; this helped determine where the fire had originated. "There's what's left of a smoke detector," LaVern said.

Following his beam to the ceiling I could see what remained of a battery operated smoke detector. "See if you can find something to stand on," I ordered.

In a moment LaVern was back with a kitchen chair, and climbed it to remove the smoke detector. "Looks like the battery is gone," he said. Handing it down to me, I dug out my knife and peeled some of the melted plastic to reveal the space and connections where a nine volt battery belonged. The space was empty! *Another case of good luck*, I thought, remembering Bernadette Thoe's dog waking her up early one morning when there was a fire in the kitchen. *Lucky Mike had Bo.*

LaVern climbed down from the chair and was examining the floor below the smoke detector. "Pretty deep charring; the recliner was setting here."

"Check the outlet," I said.

Hanging from the outlet was a glob of plastic with two bare wires still attached to it. LaVern gave it a jerk and the glob pulled free from the wall. "Must have been a transformer. I'll have them bring the recliner back in," LaVern said.

Moments later the recliner was resting on the carpet where it had been when the fire started. "Fits perfectly," LaVern said. "Sure are a lot of wires in the back; you don't suppose the chair was heated?"

"Yes it was. Mike said he needed the heater for his back."

"I'm going after the camera." In moments LaVern returned to the living room and began taking pictures.

"I'm going out and talk to Mike," I said.

Mike and Bo hadn't moved from their position under the elm tree. "Say Mike, didn't you say the recliner was stored in the barn?"

"Yeah," Mike replied. "I took it out to the farm three or four years ago and stored it in the barn."

"Did you leave it plugged in after you used it last night?"

"Sure. Was there a problem with the chair?"

"From what LaVern and I could tell, the fire started in your recliner and spread up the wall."

"How could that happen?" he asked.

"Maybe mice got into it and ate through the heater wiring, or it just deteriorated from exposure to the weather. It wasn't meant to be outside. By the way, what happened to the battery in the smoke detector?" I asked.

Mike looked at me and then at the ground and said in a soft voice, "I took it out and put it in my radio."

This wouldn't be the last time I heard an excuse like this . . . some people will never learn.

CHAPTER 24

PERSHING BUILDING—

MULTIPLE CHALLENGES

The Pershing Building was a three story L-shaped brick structure constructed in 1916 to provide facilities for the education of school students. In 1936 a more modern structure was built and attached to the Pershing Building. Nineteen sixty-six saw the need for still more classrooms, and an area to the east of the '36 structure was chosen and a three story addition was added. The original Industrial Arts Shop was housed in a first floor area of the '36 wing. Increased enrollment eventually necessitated the remodeling of the shop into classrooms, and Industrial Arts classes were moved to the basement of the Pershing Building. A large overhead door was installed on the north end of the building.

Above the shop on the second level was the school cafeteria. The third floor contained ROTC classrooms and various storage rooms. The east-west portion of the 'T' contained classrooms and restroom facilities. A three story slide provided emergency escape from the upper floors, and a double door arrangement was constructed at ground level next to the slide. A separate door led into the gymnasium; from there you could access the newer classroom area. Prior to moving the Industrial Arts Shop to the Pershing Building basement, the electrical system was updated. In order to save dollars, a portion of the old electrical system was kept in service.

It was 5:00 p.m. on a Saturday evening in January 1988 when a fire was reported in the basement of the Pershing Building, 8th Street and Kelly Avenue, just five blocks east of the new fire hall. Bud Crowell and Dennis Olson responded with pumper 202 to the east entrance of the Pershing Building. Donning breathing apparatus and charging a hose line from the pumper tank discharge, they advanced into the smoky interior, leaving the pumper unattended.

Our volunteers were alerted, and because of the wintry conditions, the Devils Lake Rural Department and the Starkweather Fire Department were contacted for additional assistance. The men from Rural were asked to man our fire hall and standby in case of another emergency.

Quickly arriving at the scene was Don Nakken. A short, serious individual, his responsibility upon arrival was to take over the operation of pumper 202. Heavy, dark wood smoke rolled from the double doors nearly obscuring 202. Don climbed into the pumper cab and drove to a nearby hydrant, not realizing the attack line was still attached to the truck. Upon seeing the hose and realizing what had happened, Don radioed me with the information.

When Don disengaged the pump prior to driving away, the attack line to the interior went limp. Thinking the tank had emptied, Bud and Dennis began to retreat when the hose was jerked from their hands leaving them without a life line to the outside. Realizing the only way out of the basement was up the stairs they began feeling their way back out of the basement. Heat seemed to be coming from the west side of the stairway and the smoke made it impossible for them to see. In order to conserve breathing air, they communicated with their hands and feet, avoiding problems with verbal communications and possibly saving a little breathing air.

A search was begun to find the two men. Steve Chepulis, who had been a live-in at Rural radioed, "I'll get a team and go looking for them."

"217," Gayle radioed. "Could we give it a try through the overhead door?"

"Go ahead; if nothing else you'll vent the smoke," I replied.

As I was going to check on Gayle, Captain Ron Vetsch came through the doorway of the '36 wing. We discussed the construction between the two buildings and decided to place a two-and-a-half inch line in operation through the east entrance, and try to prevent fire from extending into the '36 structure. Turning to Jerome Hoffart, I said, "You can see over the gymnasium ceiling by crawling through the hatch in the announcer's booth. Set up the monitor in the gym, and don't let the fire get by you!" I warned Ron.

A commotion brought my attention to the doorway and I turned to see Steve giving members of the search team a 'High Five' as they exited the basement with Bud and Dennis between them. Relief surged through all of us.

Leaving that portion of the building in the hands of Jerome and Ron, I headed down the east side of the building to see how Gayle's entry team was doing. *Nice winter evening,* I thought as my boots crunched in the new fallen snow. "LEC—what's the weather report?" I radioed.

"Storm coming. Wind and snow, temperature is dropping to zero. The storm is in the Minnewaukan area now," replied LEC. *There goes the nice evening,* I thought.

Chris Soper came running toward me with a boat motor gas can in his hand. "Where are you going?" I asked, stopping him in his tracks.

"Tim needs gas for the generator." In the alley to the north of the fire, I noticed two more Scouts carrying metal cans. Chris turned and saw the Scouts approaching at a run with gas containers in their gloved hands. "Gotta go," he said. Turning he continued his run toward 203 with the two Scouts close behind. The Explorer Scouting program sponsored by the volunteers was only four years old, but proved invaluable when the little things needed doing.

Rounding the corner on the north end of the building, I noticed a crowd had gathered, and were watching Gayle and his team attempt to open the overhead door. As I climbed over a snow bank to get a better view from the street, I looked back in time to see the door give way. One of the firemen began pushing the door up with a pike pole. From inside the building came what can only be described as a moan; the dirty black smoke that had been coming out the doorway was sucked back into the building. The fireman using the pike pole threw it to the side and dove into a snow bank. Others followed suit; some dropped to their knees, and tipped their helmets toward the doorway. One look at the entrance team was the only indication I needed to warn me of what was to happen.

From behind me I heard, "Why did they do that?"

I was on the verge of answering the question, when out through the overhead door, just above the heads of the entrance team, came the biggest and meanest sheet of fire I had ever seen. "Duck!" I shouted, as the flames reached for the opposite side of the street, bringing screams of fear from the onlookers as they scurried for cover. "Oh, sweet Jesus," I heard one person exclaim, as he dove headfirst into a snow bank.

Following the burst of flame, two members of the entry team jogged to where 202 was connected to a hydrant and returned with a heavy two-and-a-half inch line. Realizing they needed help, two members of the

Starkweather Fire Department went to their assistance, and signaling Don to charge the line, they advanced toward the shop area. The crowd began returning, and the man who had been doing the commenting looked my way and asked, "How in the hell did they know what was coming?"

I smiled. "It's all about training."

Within moments the Snorkel crew indicated they could see fire glowing in an upstairs window. At the same time one of the Explorer Scouts rushed to where I was standing. "Doug Nelson told me Joe Green went upstairs to inventory the uniforms for ROTC, and nobody has seen him!" he breathlessly announced.

"204, can you get a search team through a third floor window on your side?"

"We'll give it a try," Bud replied. "What's up?"

"Might have someone trapped upstairs in the ROTC room."

On the west side of the building, two firemen climbed into the lowered snorkel basket with lengths of attack hose hanging from their shoulders. Guiding the basket to just outside a third floor window, Ray maneuvered the platform as Cliff reached out with an axe and broke out the glass. An attack hose was connected to a basket outlet, and the rescue team crawled into the building. Directly below the platform an extension ladder was being raised to the window and two firemen were readying themselves to back up the first team.

"217—219, the fire broke through the floor," Jerome radioed.

"Keep water on it, don't let it spread," I replied.

"Lyle Hoff is here," Jerome continued. "He wants to shut off the steam lines leading into the Pershing Building."

"Don't let him run around alone," I ordered.

"217—218, smoke is getting into the food supplies in the ramp," Gayle radioed.

"Are you able to gain access through the wall?" I asked.

"10-4, but all we can see is fire."

From inside the building I heard a rumble. "The roof area above the stairs just gave way," Jerome radioed.

"218—Plug the hole and get out of there!"

On the west side of the Pershing Building the fourth and last member of the entry team hoisted himself over the snorkel railing into the basket. As the basket and its occupants moved away from the building, smoke and flame came rolling through the window. "Chief, the Green youngster is safe; he's at home."

Officer Dallas Carlson was at my side. "Thanks, Dallas," I responded, with more relief than I thought possible. I radioed the firemen with the good news, and directed them to take a defensive stand. Horns sounded a steady tone for five seconds, alerting all the firemen to leave the building and work from the outside. *There's no sense jeopardizing any more personnel*, I thought.

"219—You and Ron keep an eye on the east end."

We had been on the scene for about an hour when Curt Fogel, Deputy Fire Marshal arrived. There had been a number of school fires in North Dakota during the past year, and investigation of causes was being supported by the Fire Marshal's office. Curt and his family had been having supper in Devils Lake when he heard about the fire. "I see you've taken a defensive stand," he said.

"We've had a couple of close calls," I replied.

"Do you want me to stay?"

Snow was falling, and the wind was increasing. "No. I'll call you."

Joe Belford had taken over command of the snorkel and was directing the bucket crew to change their fog nozzle to straight stream and wash down the wall between the Pershing Building and the `36 addition. "201, how does it look?"

"Okay so far," Ron replied.

As I returned to the east side of the building, I noticed a lone fireman spraying water on the fire through the outside entrance to the cafeteria area. Suddenly a brick fell, striking him on the helmet. The hose fell to the ground as he dropped to his knees. He shook his head and pulling himself up by the banister railing, stood and looked up to where the brick had dislodged. When he turned my way I realized Dick Johnson was the one who had taken a blow to the helmet. Waving to indicate he was all right, he stepped on the whipping hose, picked up the nozzle, and returned to spraying water through the doorway.

Dick had just moved back to the doorway when the sound of cracking timbers could be heard throughout the fire ground. Before I could shout, fire and sparks came from all the windows on the east side as the remainder of the roof caved in. Dick didn't hesitate leaving his perch on the door sill.

I hurried to the east entrance and was able to see some of the damage caused by the fire. I looked over the burning floor and tried to imagine where the fire had started. Realizing the amount of water we had placed on the fire, it seemed that something else had transpired. Being curious had been beneficial in our investigations. *It wasn't where I thought it would be*, I said to myself.

Ron came through the doorway leading to the gymnasium and joined me at the entrance into the Pershing Building, where I was watching Jerome's crew. "Did we stop it?" he asked.

"I think the fire had a pretty good head start before we got the call," I replied.

"What makes you think that?" he questioned.

Motioning toward the hole the hose team was spraying water into, I said, "That hole in the floor doesn't match the steps. How's it looking in the attic?"

"Good," Ron replied. "Never did see any smoke."

"Why don't you move the monitor to the north end and connect to the entry team's hose lines?" I suggested.

Most of the Pershing Building roof structure had separated from the '36 wing, but the fire was still far from being extinguished as the monitor was put into operation. Blowing snow increased, creating miserable conditions. The personnel in the snorkel basket were able to duck behind the basket covers, but other crews weren't so fortunate. They had to move to the opposite side of the building to get out of the wind and had to put up with the smoke. As one fireman said, "At least the wall is warm!" Ron had moved the monitor nozzle through the doorway of the shop area out of the wind. Not being able to reach the extreme end of the building with the present configuration, they made several attempts to change the tip size as water continued to flow through the nozzle. *Takes a lot of balls in this kind of weather*, I thought to myself.

Without a radio they were unable to communicate to Don Nakken at the pumper, the need to reduce the pressure. After a couple more tries they were successful, and with the smaller tip were able to reach to the opposite end of the Industrial Arts room.

It was almost 10:00 p.m. and after a walk-through of the '36 wing and the gymnasium, we found a hidden door from the stage area that led to the outside. Walt removed material and timbers securing the doorway and together we exited into the open area next to the snorkel. "Surprise!" Walt shouted as we came into Joe's line of vision.

"I never gave those doors any thought," Joe exclaimed. "They're painted just like the walls."

"You can keep an eye on both buildings tonight," I replied.

"Pretty convenient," Joe said.

The snorkel had been connected to a fire hydrant by a five inch supply line, and could handle extra hose lines with a careful operator. Joe had been Captain of the snorkel since the fire department had purchased it with Water Department monies in 1971, and understood the potential of the unit better than anyone, including Walter.

"I'll have the other hose lines reconnected to your unit. We'll take 201 and 202 back to the fire hall and thaw them out," I said. We had moved into the new fire hall in December, and this would be our first chance to try out the new hose rack and heated floor.

The following day, I called Curt Fogel and asked him to visit with me and the school board. Following a discussion with members of the board and the insurance carrier, it was decided to allow partial demolition of the Pershing Building in order to facilitate our investigation.

A crane was transported from Swingen Construction in Grand Forks to the site and removal of hanging floors and walls proceeded, with either Curt or me examining each clam shell load. As we got closer to the south end of the shop area, we both spent time examining each load of debris. It was getting dark when the crane operator asked to stop for the day. "How about another couple of buckets," Curt said, shining a light into the debris. "We're almost there."

One bucket led to two and then three, when I spotted a heat line pointing downward. "Look Curt, there's the heat line." Just below the heat line was a stainless steel sink pushed up against what remained of the south wall of the shop. To the east was a stairway which originally led to the upper floors. Curt gave a thumbs-up signal to the crane operator. Throttling down the crane motor so he could be understood and hear better, he stepped out onto the steel treads of the crane and shouted, "Did you find what you're lookin' for?"

"I think so," Curt replied. "Swing your crane in here for another bucket." Curt motioned to the operator as he moved the bucket into place for what might be the last time. Once the bucket came to rest, Curt and I loaded more debris, exposing the area around the sink. We kept an eye on the bucket as it was retracted and moved to the north. Instead of dumping the debris, Curt had the operator swing into an open area and set the clamshell on the ground.

I looked up toward the material remaining following the fire, and not seeing anything that might jeopardize my health, got down on my knees to look under the sink. Against the paneling behind a rear steel leg of the sink was a heavy, bare electrical cable. Further investigation indicated wear spots on the floor where the sink had been slid around. The cable led to a photo developer wired for 220 volts. The diagram that had been drawn for us by Lyle Hoff indicated a room behind the wall and under the landing of the first floor. "Look at the diagram," I said to Curt. "That's why I noticed a hole in the floor before fire came up the steps."

Curt looked at the diagram in my hand. He reached for the sink and pulled it from the wall. Behind the bare cable, a portion of the remodeled wall was burned through into the room under the landing. As Curt removed the bare wire for further investigation, he exclaimed, "Part of the copper was welded to the sink leg! It matches perfectly."

I called the station for a camera and more lights, and Curt told the crane operator to wrap it up.

As we waited for the camera, I followed Curt as he examined the room behind the remodeled wall. Daylight was almost non-existent when the lights and camera arrived. Determined to finish the investigation, we completed the drawing and took pictures. As we stood back from the remodeled wall on the opposite side from the sink, I could see how the fire progressed from the burn hole and up the wall into the ceiling area directly below the upper landing. "Bud and Dennis said the wall was hot when they crawled back up the basement steps," I said.

"By the looks of the burn and depth of charring, the fire had been perking for a while," Curt said.

"That looks like some of the old cable they chose not to remove," I said.

"There've been a number of school fires in North Dakota this year," Curt informed me, "and most of the time it's been because of corner cutting."

"Looks like Dennis and Bud are lucky the fire didn't come in from behind them," I said.

"Amen." Curt replied, "It was close."

Maybe Don's driving away with the truck was meant to be, I thought to myself.

[Author's note: cover picture is of the fire at the Pershing Building.]

CHAPTER 25

OVERWHELMING SADNESS

When six people lost their lives in the Colonial fire in 1977, civic leaders and fire department personnel were hoping that would be the worst loss-of-life fire that had ever happened in our fair city. However, in October of 1994, Devils Lake attained the dubious distinction of being the one community in North Dakota to have the most number of fatalities in a fire—an undesirable recognition.

The initial call from Darla Obenchain at 4:49 a.m. on October 8, 1994, stating there was a fire at 903-8th Avenue, brought paid fireman Denver 'Bud' Crowell and live-ins David Austin and Todd Erickson, to the scene. Upon arrival, an attack line was immediately advanced to the west side of the house.

From two blocks away, emergency lights from a police car were visible at the intersection of 8th Avenue and 9th Street. Heavy dark smoke rolled across the street to the north of the police car. To the west of the intersection, 201 had a hose stretched toward the burning structure.

"What's going on?" I asked an officer as I arrived on the scene.

"Neighbor told us there were six people living in the house. I don't think anyone got out."

I climbed from the cab of my pickup as 202 approached on 10th Street. Turning the corner at 8th Avenue, Gayle stopped at the hydrant. Across the street, Jay Wolsky was dressing in the fire gear he kept in his pickup. Moments later he donned a breathing apparatus from the side compartment of 202. *If anyone can get inside, he can,* I thought.

The remainder of the equipment and personnel arrived on the scene, and Mike Schultz advanced a two and half inch line to the front porch, where he began spraying water at the front room window. In moments that heavy stream pushed its way into the house and extinguished the majority of the fire.

"In moments, two attack lines were connected to Schultz's two-and-a-half inch line and were advanced inside the home to extinguish any remaining fire. On the north side of the house a ladder had been raised to the second story and firemen were already climbing in through the window. *Damn they're fast.*

I walked to the northeast corner of the house attempting to see where the fire traveled. Just to the right of the front door, the fire had broken through a small window opening and rolled up the wall to the porch roof and the side of the house. At the northeast corner I could see down the side of the house as I walked toward the alley. Two firemen were shining flashlights into a window opening at ground level, and glanced up when they heard crunching glass under my boots as I walked by. "Where's your gear?" Jerry Johnson asked.

Until that moment I hadn't paid much attention to being without the obligatory fire gear. "I guess I've got an ass-chewing coming," I replied.

Except for the sound of the gas operated fan and the occasional whoosh of water being sprayed on debris, the light from the bucket of the snorkel high above revealed an almost tranquil scene as the firemen went about their duties. Police Chief Bruce Kemmet came up beside me. "Did you find anyone in the house?"

"Jay and Roger just got inside; we should know soon."

"Our records show the Charbonneau family was living here," Bruce said.

We stood quietly for a few moments, our thoughts and imaginations fearing the worst, yet praying for a successful outcome. *Maybe no one was home,* I thought.

I wasn't surprised when Roger passed the word that he wanted to see me by the north bedroom window. "What have you got?" I asked.

Leaning out the window he said in a low voice, "We've got a couple of victims."

"Wrap them in blankets and pass them out the window." In moments, wrapped bodies were passed through the bedroom window and placed on a folded tarpaulin.

I found Chief Kemmet. "Better get the coroner," I said. "Keep the lookers from getting too close," I told the firemen. *One good thing about night time, there aren't a bunch of bystanders,* I thought.

"Chief," Jay called from the west end of the house.

I went down the north wall to the rear of the house where I met with

Jay. When not working an emergency Jay was overwhelming with his ability to make light of most moments. Over six feet tall and 240 pounds, he dominated those around him except for Tim Kurtz. His ability to perceive what was about to happen made him an excellent fireman, and whenever possible he passed his knowledge and experience on to those listening or following him into a burning structure.

"What have you got?" I asked.

"We found more victims upstairs."

"I understood there were six people living in the house."

In a low voice he said, "There are five upstairs."

The grimness of what Jay had seen showed in his sweat-covered face. "Has anyone gone downstairs?" I asked.

"Not that I know of; some of the new guys are having a hard time of it." Tears were streaming down Jay's cheeks and the stress of the situation was taking its toll.

"Stay here," I ordered. "I'll find someone else to go downstairs." A short time later the search team's report indicated two more bodies had been discovered in the basement.

Earl Reed, acting coroner, approached and motioning back to the tarp asked, "How come you moved the bodies?" Instead of remorse, the ambulance manager seemed to be taking his job a little too seriously. Rather than respond, I chose to keep my mouth shut in front of our audience. "Take pictures; I'll get some body bags," I said to Alvin. "Earl, you can go with Alvin. When you're done, we'll release the victims to the funeral home."

I had noticed Rodger Haugen and his helper backing a hearse and suburban into the yard at the rear of the house. Rodger came my way with an unusually grim look on his face. *He's got a helluva project ahead of him,* I thought.

"Could you explain what I need to do?" he asked.

"There are nine victims," I said. "I'm not sure of their size or ages, but we'll help you take them to the funeral home."

The sky was getting lighter, and looking at my watch I was surprised to see it read 7:10 a.m. Earl had left and Gilbertson's had transported the victims to the funeral home. Alvin and Jay were in the house investigating the cause of the fire.

"How's it looking in there?" I asked.

"We're just about wrapped up, but I want to come back later," Alvin replied.

"It looks like they were cooking on the stove," Jay remarked.

Most of the equipment had been put away and 201 had been moved to a position immediately behind the house. Next to the pumper was a galvanized garbage can. My curiosity piqued and I checked its contents. If the cause of the fire proved to be unattended cooking, alcohol consumption could have been a contributing factor as it was in at least 60 percent of such cases. Much to my relief I found only three empty beer cans. As I was replacing the lid, a car pulled up behind 201. I was about to run them out of the area when one of them said, "We left at 1:30. What happened?"

"We're still investigating," I said.

I questioned the individuals who indicated they had spent the evening with the Charbonneaus and left about 1:30 in the morning. They had gone to work on the early shift at Sioux Manufacturing when they heard about the fire and drove back to Devils Lake.

"Didn't they live on the west side? I haven't seen them all summer," I said.

"We helped them move in July."

I knew most of the family, and it was my responsibility to notify the relatives of the deceased. Thinking I'd have to go to Fort Totten, I was surprised when Kemmet said, "The parents live in a mobile home in Southview East." I borrowed some No Trespassing ribbon from a police officer and taped off the area. "Stay on the scene until we get back. Nobody gets close."

On 8th Avenue, members of the media were patiently waiting for any information I was willing to release. I recognized Eric Arndt, a reporter for KZZY Radio. Two others identified themselves as reporters for the Devils Lake Journal and WDAZ Television. Following a short news conference, Alvin, Jay and I drove back to the fire hall to discuss the information we had learned from the investigation. We were reviewing our findings when John Elstad, a Deputy Fire Marshal, came into the hall. I asked Al and Jay to go over our findings with him while I went to talk to the parents.

Knowing what I was about to do, the duty men looked away. *Probably think I might ask them to go with me.* I reviewed the fire in my mind and contemplated what I was going to say when I met with the family.

There were only a few cars on the street in front of the Charbonneau home when I drove up. Having lived in a trailer court when I first moved back to Devils Lake, I understood how difficult it could be to keep your lot presentable. Not the case for these owners. The home was newer and parked on a large, well-maintained lot on the south end of the trailer court. I stepped from the pickup and started up the walk to the mobile home when a young Catholic Priest and a woman came walking toward me. I could see she had been crying. The young Priest smiled and said, "Thank you for coming, the family is waiting for you." *I wondered how they knew I would be coming.*

Knocking on the door, I was greeted with, "Come in, Bill."

I stepped through the kitchen into a spacious living room, where relatives had gathered. Sitting on the couch were Charles and Theresa Charbonneau. I had known the two of them for over thirty years, but hadn't considered them to be the parents. *That's how they knew I'd be showing up, I* thought.

"Was Russell cooking on the stove?" Theresa asked.

"I'm not sure who was cooking, but it looks like the pot on the stove melted, and the heat set the cupboards on fire. The heat broke the kitchen window and the wind spread the fire throughout the kitchen."

"Did they suffer?" Charles asked.

"No, the furnace carried smoke through the house, and they died in their sleep."

We talked for over and hour about their children and grandchildren, and the tragic circumstances surrounding their deaths. It was more than anyone should have to endure. As I stood to leave, Theresa came and gave me a hug and Charlie shook my hand. "I hope it isn't too hard on the firemen," Theresa said. Charlie enclosed my hand in his massive grip and added, "Thanks for coming and visiting with us. Most people wouldn't care, but you're like your dad."

THE FUNERAL

The Tekawitha Center on the Devils Lake Sioux Reservation was filled to capacity for the funeral. A half-dozen star quilts hung from the metal walls behind the row of caskets. More quilts and bouquets of flowers covered each of the caskets, accompanied by framed pictures of each of the victims. Outside, hundreds of people stood in silence next to nine hearses waiting to carry their loved ones to the St. Jerome's Catholic Cemetery in rural Fort Totten.

Tears flowed freely among those in attendance as the names of the adults were read: Russell Charbonneau, 31; Richard Charbonneau Sr., 37; Carol Peltier Charbonneau, 27; Beverly Oglesby, 32 and April Mae Herald 21.

After a moment's hesitation Reverend Leute read the names of the children: Richard Charbonneau Jr., 12; Crystal Wasacase, 10; Kayla Grace Wasacase, 8, and Keith Charbonneau, 6.

The following calls in some way involved cooking and took place the week following the Charbonneau fire, which just happened to be Fire Prevention Week, 1994.

The Sunday following the Charbonneau fire, the duty man and the live-ins had just completed routine maintenance of the emergency equipment and were cleaning the apparatus floor when the Law Enforcement Center radioed: "Kitchen fire; 847 Kelly Avenue, everybody's out of the house!"

The location was just five blocks west from the disastrous 8th Avenue fire. This was a two-story house which had been converted into apartments with a separate entrance on each level. By the time I arrived smoke was coming from the open doorway of the upper level apartment, and firemen Dennis Olson and Jerome Hoffart were connecting the pumper to the corner hydrant. Arriving volunteers began advancing hoses; one line was positioned to advance through the smoke-filled doorway of the second floor, and the other was poised at the entrance of the ground floor apartment. Firemen had raised a ladder to the second story and were waiting for orders to break the window. Alvin removed a gas operated fan from 202 and placed it back from the doorway of the upper level apartment. Once the fan was started, creating a positive pressure situation, two firemen began advancing their attack line into the smoke-filled apartment.

Standing next to the pumper was an obviously distressed young lady, her fist pushed against her open mouth. As I shrugged on my fire coat, she turned and looked my way. "I was just talking to my mother and the pot melted."

"Are you all right?" I asked.

"I lost everything!" she replied.

"Give the firemen a chance; they're pretty good at what they're doing," I said, trying to reassure her. "What were you doing?"

"I was browning sugar when Mom called. We were talking on the phone and when I turned around the cabinets were on fire."

Another case of unattended cooking, I thought to myself. I put on my helmet and climbed the steps to the top floor apartment's entrance. I stepped around the fan and shined my flashlight into the interior where firemen were using the heat gun to check for extension of the fire. Under the debris on the stove I found the remains of an aluminum cooking pot, and next to it was a red hot heating coil. Examination of the control panel indicated two burners had been, and still were, turned on. It appeared that potholders and paper combustibles had been ignited by the unused burner which had apparently been turned on by accident. Heat lines extended to the north across the wall, and west toward the bedroom area. It was a mess.

The major structural damage was to the area above the stove where cabinets had burned away. In orderly fashion, firemen had cut away only as much sheetrock as necessary to look for fire extension. They had been taught not to damage any more than they had to in order to protect evidence. I climbed a kitchen chair to examine the charring on the 2x6's above the sheetrock. The guys had done a pretty good job; it would be easy to replace this ceiling, I observed.

I climbed down and followed the heat line down the hallway toward the bedroom. The door to the bathroom had been open during the fire and everything was covered in an oily black film. "220—turn off the fan," I radioed.

Once the rush of air halted I opened the bedroom door to a basically clean atmosphere. *Remarkable what a closed door can accomplish.* At the end of the hallway an open door revealed a broken window through which the fan had pushed smoke.

Late in the afternoon of October 10th I received a phone call from the Elks Club, saying "We've got a fire in the kitchen."

As the Elks Club had now moved to the eastern edge of town, I radioed the station: "Keep 201 back in the event there's another call." Turning into the tree bordered lane leading to the Elks Club, a low, multi-room structure, I could see black smoke coming from a ventilation stack on the kitchen roof. When 202 drove around to the back door of the kitchen to off-load hose before driving to the fire hydrant, I climbed from the cab of my pickup to direct oncoming firemen.

The ladder truck provided a safe way for firemen to get to the roof and begin opening up the area above the kitchen. As the roof was breached, an attack team entered through the back door into the kitchen. As the smoke fans increased the pressure inside the building, smoke rushed out through the hole in the roof and out the back door.

"We emptied 10 extinguishers into the duct, but it didn't help," said Harlan Eckholm, the kitchen manager.

"How did the fire start?"

"Grease was dripping from the duct above the grill, and caught fire."

"What happened to the filters?" I asked.

Harlan looked up toward the firemen on the roof and replied, "They weren't put back in place after they cleaned them Saturday night." *Another case of not paying attention,* I thought.

The fire was extinguished; 202 and the ladder truck were wrapping things up when a radio call informed me of a fire in a mobile home at Sunset Trailer Court. *That's at the opposite end of town! Glad I had a truck and crew stay back.*

Rather than drive through town, I decided to take the four-lane using my personal vehicle. Turning on lights and siren, I left the Elks Club and drove around town on Highway 2 to the Summers' crossing and came in on the back side of the trailer court. On my way down the highway I could look across the tracks toward the trailer court. Not seeing smoke, I slowed the pickup and turned off the flashing lights. Glancing in the rear view mirror, I could see a string of vehicles following me. *After the last few days, everybody is wondering what is going on,* I thought.

Crossing the tracks, I drove the miserable washboard road back east toward the trailer court. Pumper 201 had parked on 14th Street and stretched a hose to a mobile home 50 feet to the north. *Now that's the way to operate,* I thought.

Glancing around the exterior of the home I noticed electrical and gas meters were missing. Jay Wolsky came from inside the trailer and said, "Looks like someone was playing inside and built a bonfire."

Firemen were opening windows and a fan was operating at the front door, facilitating smoke removal. I climbed the steps and saw a cooking pot resting on what remained of the mobile home floor. Scattered around the room were pieces of brick. *Bet that scared the hell out of them when they exploded.*

A shout called me outside. At the bottom of the steps, two young boys waited near their father. It turned out that Dad had promised the boys a camping trip and the youngsters were in the abandoned mobile home practicing their cooking skills.

I noticed a bandage on the seven-year old's arm. "The fire blew up and cut me," he said.

Motioning the dad to step to the side out of hearing I asked the boys to sit with me on the ground. The bandage on the boy's arm made it easy to talk about the danger of fire. Eventually he uncovered the wound to show me the cut. Calling for a first aid kit, I cleaned and re-bandaged the wound.

After our conversation I shook hands with the boys and invited them to the fire hall to visit Sparky. They promised to be careful and assured me they would do as I asked. As they walked away with their father the youngest turned and waved. *I hope their dad doesn't give them too much grief,* I thought.

The fifth cooking-related incident of the week happened Wednesday evening, the 12th of October, when I received a radio message from the LEC indicating a fire at 503 1st Street. It was meeting night, and the fire hall was full of firemen. Hors d'oeuvres and beer had just been set out at the rear of the hall when I paged the call over the PA system. In moments the fire hall was empty, leaving the Fire Commissioner and me watching the last unit exit onto College Drive.

Bob Schumacher, a live-in who had been taking a shower, came running into dispatch pulling on his trousers with intentions of going out on a truck.

"You take the radio; Dick and I are going to the fire." A look of dismay crossed his face, but he sat down and started filling out the call sheet. A number of times before Dick became a City Commissioner he had ridden with me to emergencies, and no one paid attention to flashing lights. He put on his seat belt and held the wheel as I buckled mine in place. To our surprise, vehicles on both sides of the street pulled over as we drove past. "They must know you're driving," Dick said.

"They've never ridden with you," I replied.

Reminiscing, I said, "Remember the time we rode with Rich Hagel to investigate that fire outside of New Rockford; that had to be the fastest trip I ever made."

We passed the train depot on Railroad Avenue and I could see fire equipment positioned in the area of 503 1st Street. I parked in the Jerome Wholesale lot and we walked across the street to where we saw firemen coming out through the front door. As I approached, Jay Wolsky took off his mask and said, "Cooking pork chops in an aluminum skillet on the stove; he didn't turn off the heat. I turned off the power to the smoke detectors." This portion of the building had just been redone and turned into an apartment. The damage inside was limited to the stovetop where I could see the remains of a couple of pot holders and the skillet Jay had mentioned.

I heard one, and then two fans starting up and forcing outside air through the apartment. *The fire is out before they start ventilating, can't get much better than that,* I thought.

"Dad wants to see you," a voice said.

Turning, I shined my flashlight beam towards the voice and saw a young man covered in soot. "Where is he?"

"I took him to the car to keep him warm."

Outside at the rear of the apartment was a four-door Dodge with exhaust rising from the rear of the vehicle. I could see someone sitting in the passenger's seat. As I climbed into the driver's seat I recognized the man. He was related to the victims in the Charbonneau fire. "I'm sorry for your loss," I said.

"The fire scared me."

He was 76 years old, and had just returned from the funerals of nine relatives. *It had to be at the back of his mind,* I thought. "It's okay now," I said. "Jay turned off the smoke detectors."

The poor guy was visibly shaken and asked, "Do they squeal like stuck pigs?"

Smiling I replied, "Something like that; they keep you from dying in a fire."

"Did the kids have smoke detectors in their house?"

"The Housing Authority inspected the house in July before the family moved in and the detectors were operational. We never did find one. All I can say is they didn't suffer."

He stared out the window. "They were sure good kids."

CONSEQUENCES

Departments in communities twice our population and paid departments in larger cities had not been through what the Devils Lake Volunteer Fire Department had experienced during the previous six days. However, the young volunteers from the days of the <u>Arsonist Among Us</u> were now the veterans of many emergencies. They were getting tired, and in some cases their spouses jokingly threatened divorce. It seemed fire gear hardly had a chance to dry out before it was needed again. As a result, several volunteers and one of the department's paid personnel resigned from the fire service. Most of them still involve themselves in department activities, but have chosen not to be involved at emergencies.

The notoriety of the Charbonneau Fire and the number of cooking incidents that followed, were news topics on both local and national television networks. Consumer Products Safety Committee made numerous calls regarding the above incidents. A survey of other departments indicated problems in their jurisdictions with unattended cooking. The slogan for Fire Prevention Week in 1995 was changed to read *WATCH WHAT YOU HEAT.*

CHAPTER 26

FIRE IN THE AMBULANCE BAY

Mercy Hospital has always had a very efficient risk management program. Fire department personnel inspect the property at least once a year and are immediately available to Risk Management Officer Ray Frohlich when questions arise. Each year all hospital staff are required to attend workshops providing information on fire prevention as well as hands-on training relative to Life Safety. The hospital emergency plan is upgraded on a regular basis and is required reading by all personnel each year.

Over the years we've had numerous false alarms at the Hospital, and a couple of times we've responded to alarms which have amounted to smoke from unattended cooking situations on the fourth floor. This area is occupied by members of the Sisters of Mercy. On-call emergency room doctors also have accommodations there.

For many years, the sprinkler system was tested by fire department personnel and in the mid '90s the hospital staff took over the testing responsibility. I believed that the programs in place would prevent a minor incident from becoming a major problem. The biggest concern I'd had for years was the possibility of a fire in the ambulance bay. From time to time vehicles other than ambulances could be found parked in this bay, which was adjacent to the emergency room. Not once did I consider an ambulance being a problem due to their generally excellent maintenance record.

On October 2, 2001 at 4:20 p.m. the alarm board at the fire hall lit up indicating an emergency at Mercy Hospital. As Cory Meyer and Dennis Olson were responding in 201, a radio call from the LEC said the fire was in the ambulance bay. I stayed in dispatch and activated fire department pagers and sirens. *This should bring some help,* I thought. Through the window I saw Jay Wolsky and Lonnie Lacina swing in behind 201 as it drove east. Although the hospital was more than twelve blocks away, smoke was visible from the fire hall. In moments firemen began reporting to the hall, and Matt Herrick, one of the live-ins, came into the station and took over dispatch duties. I hurried outside and followed 201 to the scene of the emergency.

Fire department volunteers began responding—some to the scene, others to the fire hall for equipment and further orders, the flashing blue lights on their vehicles warning of their approach. Behind me 202 was coming into sight, followed by the 65-foot snorkel. I was approaching 4th Avenue in front of the Middle School when I saw the dirty black smoke turning gray. Glancing at my watch, I realized only seven minutes had gone by. *They're getting it under control,* I thought. Drivers must have sensed something extraordinary was happening, as they had pulled over as 201 passed and for the most part were still parked next to the curb as other fire equipment approached the scene.

At the intersection of 10th Avenue and 7th Street I looked toward the hospital and now could easily see the smoke coming from inside the ambulance bay. In my rear view mirror, I saw 202 closing the gap between us, and rather than go all the way to the hospital entrance from 7th Street I decided to approach the hospital by driving up the exit road to the front of the ambulance bay. Checking in my mirrors once again, I could see 202 following procedure and turning in behind me as 204 proceeded east to the hospital entrance. *If everything goes as preplanned the snorkel will be standing by in the hospital parking lot.*

Just in front of me 201 was parked by a hydrant between the clinic and hospital. Two hose lines were leading from 201 into the ambulance bay; one from the cross lay and the other from a rear one-and-a-half inch discharge. Volunteers were readying a heavy line for advancing to the east through the front entrance of the hospital. *Preplanning is working.* Although smoke continued to rush out through the large entrance to the ambulance bay, I caught a glimpse of the overhead door draped over the rear of what looked like a van.

As I climbed from my pickup, I heard the unmistakable sound of a tire exploding; suddenly the gray smoke returned to its former black color. I hurried to help Alvin remove a gas operated fan from its storage area at the rear of the pumper when an obviously shaken Lonnie Lacina staggered out from the ambulance bay. Dennis Olson had maneuvered the soft suction so he could connect to the hydrant and was opening the valve when the explosion occurred. He hesitated just long enough for me to notice, and returned to opening the valve, when Lonnie raised his hand to indicate he was okay. Alvin grabbed the fan and was hurrying toward the hospital entrance when he was joined by a volunteer from the backup team and together they disappeared though the entrance into the hospital. They hadn't been inside the hospital for more than a minute when the smoke volume increased and suddenly the black smoke turned gray and began dissipating. It was quiet as the firemen went about their duties, and in the background I could hear the sound of the 4-cycle motor on the fan. As the smoke cleared, I could see the stretched top of what looked like an ambulance.

The men on the scene began shuttling in and out of the ambulance bay replacing empty air tanks with full ones, taking a moment's rest, and gaining their composure before returning to their unpleasant duties. I was proud of the way the situation was being managed in the hands of Jay Wolsky, Cory Meyer and Lonnie Lacina. Knowing Alvin was in charge of ventilation inside gave me a sense of comfort as well.

I'm not sure how long I had been watching the activity, but the smoke was gone when Jay came out of the garage and motioned for me to come his way. A voice next to me said, "There's someone in the ambulance." I was unaware of anyone close by and was startled by the statement. The speaker was Dr. Anthony Rayer who was associated with the adjoining Lake Region Clinic. "She had a clinic appointment with me," he said, "and the ambulance was taking her back to the retirement home."

My stomach turned as I digested what Dr. Rayer had said, and now I knew why Jay waved for me to join him at the garage doorway. Jay was wiping sweat from his forehead when Dr. Rayer and I approached. I couldn't help but glance toward the rear of the ambulance: No one stood a chance in that mess.

"There's a body inside the ambulance," Jay said.

Fire had burned through the license plate holder and the windows were gone. There were numerous holes in the roof where fire had eaten through the fiberglass. I waited for Jay to compose himself, and then asked him to take pictures of the van but not the victim.

Alvin came through the hospital entrance wheeling the ventilation fan. "Should I help Jay?" he asked.

"Go ahead and work with him, but don't disturb anything."

"I noticed Sue Schwab standing by the hospital entrance," Alvin said. "Do you want her over here?"

On occasion Sue Schwab, a detective from the Police Department, would help and learn while assisting Jay and Alvin when they were doing a fire investigation as to cause and origin, but for some reason I chose not to include her at that moment. "No, not yet," I replied, there's a body in the ambulance, and I want you to look around inside first."

The glass panels in the rear doors had melted during the early stages of the fire and Dr. Rayer, Alvin and I were able to see through the openings into the interior of the ambulance. A soot-covered body lay on a gurney in the rear of the ambulance. Quickly averting his eyes Alvin muttered, "I'm going to get a blanket."

"It was Detective Schwab's mother. Do you think she suffered?" Dr. Rayer asked.

I was startled to learn the identity of the victim, and relieved that Detective Schwab was still outside. As I watched Jay take pictures, I did my best to avoid looking toward the victim. I examined the damage to the ambulance, and considering the speed with which everything had happened, responded, "No, she didn't suffer." Twice more that evening Dr. Rayer stood by me and asked if she had suffered. *The sooner we get this vehicle out of here*, I thought, *the better it will be for everyone involved.*

Not wanting any mess to be tracked from the ambulance bay to the emergency room, I walked through the hospital entrance down the hall to the emergency room where I met with the charge nurse, Annette Savaloja. She explained what had happened. "I heard a pop and noticed smoke coming in the corridor from the ambulance bay. The alarm hadn't gone off, so I pulled the manual alarm handle, and Sarah Brown called 911."

"What color was the smoke?" I asked. I was trying to determine where the smoke had originated; black smoke would indicate fiberglass was burning and brownish smoke is produced by burning wood.

"It was dirty black; and it tracked all over."

She saw me looking at the floor. "We got maintenance to clean it up; we didn't want to track it around."

After visiting with Annette and Sarah for a few more minutes, and assuring them they had done the right thing, I returned to the parking lot where I noticed Detective Schwab standing next to Dr. Rayer. I went to her side and offered my condolences. "What do you think happened?" she asked.

"I'm not sure; Alvin and Jay are in there looking it over. Would you mind if I contacted the funeral home?" I had been considering leaving the victim where she lay covered by the blanket. *No*, I thought, *that doesn't show much respect for the dead.*

"I'd appreciate that," Sue replied.

Once again Dr. Rayer asked, "How do you know she didn't suffer?"

"No oxygen Doctor, she just went to sleep."

Policy on a fire death is to immediately contact the Fire Marshal's office for an investigator. Switching to scramble on my portable, I called the Law Enforcement Center and was told Police Chief Kemmet had already called for an investigator, and Deputy Marshal Jerry McCarty would be on the scene within the hour. I'd known Jerry since he'd started with the Fire Marshal's office and knew he would do his best to come to a reasonable conclusion as to the cause of the fire. Because the situation involved an ambulance and hospital, we were requested not to disturb or remove any material goods from the area. I finished the conversation by asking the LEC to contact the funeral home. "Fire Marshal will be here in a little while," I called to Alvin and Jay.

Not more than fifteen minutes had gone by when a commotion drew my attention to the arrival of a hearse driven by Rodger Haugen, the mortician who had bought the Gilbertson Funeral Home following the death of LaVerne 'Digger' Gloger. A very outgoing individual, Rodger was the type of person that could put the grieved family at ease, and instill in them the confidence that they were the only ones that mattered at the moment. *Which is the way it should be.* Stepping from the hearse and looking around, he spotted Dr. Rayer, Sue and me standing off to the side. Without hesitation he came to where we were standing and offered his condolences to Sue. Dr. Rayer and I moved away and out of hearing while he visited with Sue. Following their talk, Rodger asked, "Could the firemen help me load the gurney into the hearse?"

"Gayle," I called, "come here a minute." Following a short discussion, Gayle had the hearse backed up to the ambulance, and a dozen firemen assisted in transferring the victim while at the same time shielding the proceedings from onlookers. *That's one thing about those guys: they know how to handle a situation with respect.*

As the hearse was driving away, Gayle closed the ambulance doors and looking at me asked, "Could I take a couple of guys and help Rodger at the funeral home?"

"Go ahead. When you're done go to the fire hall and supervise cleanup. I'll stay here and wait for McCarty."

Ray Frohlich, Risk Manager for the hospital, invited the firemen inside for supper. The Deputy Fire Marshal was due any minute, so Jay and I stayed outside awaiting his arrival. It was a hundred mile drive from McCarty's home in Grafton, but shortly after the men went in to eat, he arrived. Having Jerry's expertise assisting the investigation would be a meaningful experience. My own education had allowed me to become comfortable when teaching others. To further our abilities I had sent Jay and Alvin to various State and Federal classes, so we might keep abreast with the most recent developments. Insurance companies would send their own high priced investigators, who would usually give the scene a cursory look, fill out their worksheet from our records, shake my hand and send off a report to their head office.

As Jerry pulled on his coveralls, he questioned Jay and me on what had been done. I could feel Dr. Rayer's presence behind me and turning, inquired as to whether he had anything he wanted to ask Jerry.

"Do you think she suffered?" Doc Rayer asked.

Noticing the look and the slight shake of my head, Jerry said, "I haven't had time to look over the ambulance, but with what Bill has said, I don't think she even knew what happened."

'Butch' Zacher, the director of maintenance for the hospital, had provided us with portable flood lights. Although there was plenty of light outside, additional lighting was necessary in the garage as everything was black with soot and there was no power. Jay positioned the lights, and now that Alvin had returned, Jay went into the cafeteria to have a sandwich. Alvin and Jerry were just completing a walk-around of the ambulance when Jay came back, and together the three of them began examining the interior of the burned vehicle, taking notes and additional pictures. It was at least thirty minutes later when I noticed they had just about reached the rear of the ambulance. The spare ambulance had arrived and Jon Kraft, the paramedic who had been in back with the victim, stepped from the cab. I introduced him to Jerry and they began discussing what had transpired, while Jay and Alvin continued to the back of the ambulance and opened the doors.

At the rear of the ambulance, on the passenger's side, I could see what remained of a wooden storage box, and visible inside the container were the remains of a steel oxygen bottle. Closer examination revealed what appeared to be a tapering of the burn toward the floor of the ambulance. At the top of the tank was a regulator with holes melted in its cover, and directly above the regulator were holes in the fiberglass roof. Normal attachments such as nasal cannulas and suction devices were missing. It appeared oxygen had escaped from the regulator and facilitated burning other parts of the ambulance, including holes in the roof. I could imagine this must have been what the inside of Apollo I looked like after a switch spark ignited the oxygen-enriched atmosphere in the shuttle disaster in 1967.

It was after 8:00 p.m. when Jerry declared he was done, and asked me to take the oxygen tank to the fire hall and lock it up. "Did you find the ignition source?" I asked.

"No," Jerry replied, "but the driver said after he shut the back door he stepped around the ambulance and heard a pop, and fire appeared to be coming from the roof in the back corner above the oxygen tank."

"What about Jon Kraft?" I asked.

"He barely got out; he climbed over the seat and the driver helped him out through the passenger's side door. I noticed the sprinklers didn't operate," Jerry said.

"The valve inside the wall cavity was shut off," Alvin interjected.

"It wouldn't have helped. The driver said when he heard a pop; he looked up and saw fire coming from the rear of the ambulance toward him. He's had fire department training," Jerry continued, "and would have rescued the victim if there had been a chance. As it was, he got out just in time."

"A number of years ago there was a recall on certain oxygen regulators. I passed the information to Earl," I said, "but I don't know if he did anything about it."

"We'll let the insurance investigators decide what's to blame. They'll want to examine the ambulance and tank. Is there a place where the ambulance can be stored?" Jerry asked.

A phone call to Dan Heit brought him and Kevin from Cowboy's Towing to the scene about twenty minutes later. I introduced Jerry to Dan and Kevin and together they developed a plan for storing the ambulance. "Anything you want me to tell them?" Jerry asked.

"Take the shortest route," I said to Kevin, "we don't want to draw any attention."

After taking some more pictures of the oxygen tank and its wooden storage container, I helped Alvin load it into Jay's pickup for transporting to the fire hall. Once there it was secured in a locker and the key placed in the safe.

I hurried out to Dan's storage garages in hopes of meeting with him and Kevin before they parked the ambulance under wraps. Kevin hadn't arrived so Dan and I went over the procedure for safeguarding the ambulance. We had just changed the subject and were talking about the structural damage done at the hospital when Kevin rounded the corner of the shop towing the ambulance. "Did you have a problem?" I asked when he came to a stop.

"I had to change tires on the front end so I could tow it." *I should have thought of that when I called him.* "Sorry, I should have told you they were needed."

"No problem," Kevin replied, "I had a couple in the truck. The problem was jacking it up; I'm glad OSHA wasn't around!"

Dan quickly opened the garage door and Kevin backed the ambulance inside. "We're done contracting for the season, and if they want illumination, I won't have to run power to a storage garage."

Various investigators were allowed to examine the chassis for a couple of weeks and eventually a storage garage was provided to house the ambulance. The only key for this building was kept at the fire hall for over a year until everyone had examined the unit and it was then returned to Dan Heit. It was a burden we didn't need; we had to be on site each time it was examined. Investigators came to the hall and looked over the oxygen tank and regulator and eventually it, too, was taken off our hands and sent to Minneapolis where it was examined extensively. In March of 2003, depositions were taken and it appeared a civil suit was being orchestrated by lawyers retained by the Anderson family.

This particular incident caused a lot of stress on everyone in the department, especially those who had been involved in the Colonial and Charbonneau fires. Portions of department meetings were set aside at the volunteers' request to discuss the fatality. Having had others try to help us work through our discomfort following the Charbonneau fire had not worked as well as visiting among ourselves. Interaction during these sessions was quite emotional, but because they involved only firemen, the results were more successful.

WRAP-UP

Each of us in the fire service has moments that change our lives, sometimes forever. When my health deteriorated and I was no longer physically
able to be involved in the rigors of the profession, I had to learn what was

for me a difficult lesson—to delegate responsibility and do the job for which I had been hired.

It's been over two years since I retired from active service in the Devils Lake Fire Department. On my weekly trips to the fire hall, and bi-monthly attendance at meetings and drills, I still see many of the same men who served with me in the past. But it's gratifying to meet and get to know the new guys - younger men who are willing to step up and face the challenges that firefighting requires.

Better equipment, training, inspection, and construction all combine to make our community a safer place to live, but the spirit and enthusiasm with which these men face their responsibility is unfailing. I am proud of the small part I played in the history of this fine department.

The chapters of this book were meant to tie together and represent a great portion of my life. It is a historical account of the sometimes humorous, but mostly serious aspects of fire emergencies in the community where I lived and worked. Each chapter has a moral. Whether through laughter or tears, it is my hope that the reader will have found a lesson within these pages.

153277